W9-BNY-048

Topics in West African History

Second Edition

Adu Boahen
with J. F. Ade Ajayi and Michael Tidy

WINGATE UNIVERSITY LIBRARY

Addison Wesley Longman Limited
Edinburgh Gate, Harlow,
Essex CM20 2JE, England
and Associated Companies throughout the world.

© Longman Group Limited 1986

All rights reserved; no part of this publication
may be reproduced, stored in a retrieval system,
or transmitted in any form or by any means,
electronic, mechanical, photocopying, recording,
or otherwise, without the prior written
permission of the Publishers.

First published 1965
Second Edition 1986
Tenth impression 1997

ISBN 0 582 58504 X

Set in 10/11pt Linotron 202 Times Roman

Illustrations by Oxford Illustrators

Produced by Longman Singapore Publishers Pte Ltd
Printed in Singapore

Contents

List of Maps

Preface

Nobody has been more conscious of the need for a new edition of *Topics in West African History* than the author himself. Indeed, I feel I owe an apology to readers for not undertaking this new edition till now. For one thing, the original work grew out of circumstances that no longer apply. As indicated in the preface to the first edition, it was the product of a series of radio talks addressed to and therefore slanted in favour of a Ghanaian audience. Since the book, in spite of this limitation, has been so popular throughout West Africa, and even beyond, a new edition should have appeared long ago to redress this slant.

Secondly, since the publication of *Topics*, much new material has been published on West African history, such as articles that have appeared in the *Journal of African History*, books in the Ibadan History Series and the Legon History Series, various surveys, such as the five volume history of colonialism in Africa edited by Gann and Duignan, the two volume survey of West African history edited by Ajayi and Crowder, the recent monumental and ongoing eight volume general histories of Africa produced by Cambridge University Press and by UNESCO and the numerous specialist surveys dealing with subjects such as resistance to colonialism, the slave trade, chieftaincy, economic history, and the religions of Africa. This is in addition to the individual specialist works dealing with specific themes and specific countries. Many new historical anthologies of primary sources have appeared, such as Thomas Hodgkin's *Nigerian Perspectives* and above all the indispensable collection of Arabic sources dealing with the history of West Africa from the seventh to the fifteenth centuries by Hopkins and Levtzion. All these sources on the one hand have rendered some of the evidence adduced in *Topics* out of date, while on the other they have thrown fresh light on themes that were then quite obscure.

Thirdly, since *Topics* was published in 1966, only six years after the end of colonial rule, not much could be written on independent West Africa. Finally, *Topics* was published very much with the needs of secondary school students in mind and since a new West African history syllabus has just been introduced by WAEC a new edition has become imperative. As will be seen, some of the old topics have been dropped, others have been amalgamated and rewritten, while new topics have been added, including a completely new section dealing with West Africa since independence. In the light of the above it was felt that the book should be completely rewritten rather than simply revised. It remains a discussion of selected topics rather than a history of West Africa as a whole.

This new edition, like the first one, is essentially a work of synthesis rather than original research. Not only did I find this more difficult to write, but my indebtedness to those scholars whose brains I picked is even greater still. I could not have completed this task of rewriting during sabbatical leave between October 1981 and October 1982, but for the excellent and most congenial atmosphere provided by the Mary Trevelyan Hall overlooking Regent's Park in London where I lived. To the landlord, warden and staff of that Hall, I extend my deep gratitude and appreciation. The librarian and staff of the School of Oriental and African Studies and those of the Institute of Commonwealth Studies were also most helpful and deserve my thanks. Above all, but for the support, encouragement and subtle prodding of my publishers, this work could not have been completed during the time at my disposal. My University deserves a word of thanks for granting me sabbatical leave. I should also like to thank my fellow writers, especially Michael Tidy, for the stimulating discussions that we had together, for their criticisms and their extensive contributions.

Finally, as has been pointed out above, this edition was very much influenced by the new West African History syllabus of WAEC. I do sincerely hope that secondary students everywhere and the general reader will derive enlightenment and pleasure from this edition.

A. Adu Boahen,
University of Ghana,
Legon, August, 1984.

1 The Trans-Saharan trade

The history of West Africa, like that of most regions or countries in the world, is the result of internal and external factors. The internal or local factors, which are usually more fundamental and far more important, consist of the people or the inhabitants of the region and their geographical resources such as the land, vegetation, minerals, rainfall and climate. After all, history is primarily a study of what man has made of his intellectual and geographical resources. The foreign, or external factors consist of a whole variety of new forces – trade, religion, new tools or weapons, new means of transport or warfare, new technologies or different ways of making things and new people – that are brought or introduced into the area.

We will discuss the internal factors as we go along, but in these first two chapters let us look at two of the external factors that have had a very important impact on the history of West Africa, namely, the trans-Saharan trade and the coming of Islam.

Beginnings and development

The trans-Saharan trade or the caravan trade, that is, the trade that linked together North Africa, the Mediterranean world and Europe, the Sahara, the savanna and forest areas of West Africa, began, according to the latest evidence, in the third or fourth century. Its development gathered a great deal of momentum from the seventh century onwards and reached its peak and intensity between the fourteenth and sixteenth centuries, that is, between 1300 and 1600. It decreased relatively in volume during the seventeenth and eighteenth centuries especially in the western areas. But it appears to have picked up in volume especially in the central and eastern areas in the nineteenth century and the trans-Saharan trade did not come to an end on some of the routes till the twentieth century. How, then, do we account for the rise and development of this trade? How was it conducted and what commodities were involved in it, and, finally, what impact did it make or what effect did it have on the peoples and states of West Africa?

The rise and development of the trans-Saharan trade was more or less historically inevitable. In the first place, each of the regions involved in the trade produced certain commodities that could be sold or were urgently required in one or the other of the zones. These were the industrial goods of the Mediterranean world, Europe and North Africa; the salt, copper and dates of the Sahara, the ivory, gold, slaves and provisions of the savanna, and the gold and kola nuts of the forest areas. Particularly important in this context were the items of salt, iron, gold, and slaves. Salt and iron were in hot demand in the savanna and forest areas while gold and slaves were equally desired in the Sahara, Europe and the Mediterranean world. Indeed, as Levtzion has pointed out: 'Until the discovery of America, the Sudan was the principal source of gold both for the Muslim world and for Europe,' and that by the fourteenth century, 'two-thirds of the world's production of gold came from the Sudan to replenish the raw material needed for the European mints.'

The second important reason for the development of the trans-Saharan trade was the introduction of the camel into North Africa. After much heated scholarly debate, it seems to be generally agreed now that the camel was introduced into North Africa by the Romans during the first century AD, that is during the first hundred years of the Christian era. This was an animal tailor-made by nature for use in the desert since it can travel for days without food or water and can carry quite a load, while its flat feet can cope easily with the sands of the desert. It is not surprising, then, that the Berbers of the Sahara adopted it from the Romans and used it in their migrations southwards. They settled in the oases in the desert down to the southern fringes of the Sahara where they established trading relations with the Sudanese or black inhabitants between the second and fifth centuries. It was the subsequent spread of the use of the camel from the seventh century onwards that greatly quickened the pace of the development of the trans-Saharan trade in that and the following centuries.

The third reason for the development of the trans-Saharan trade was the conquest of the whole of North Africa by the Arabs from the Middle East between 641 and 708 AD. In the first place, this conquest undoubtedly increased the use of the camel in North Africa as well as the Sahara. Secondly, among the soldiers were not only religious zealots, as we shall see later, but also traders. Moreover, following the conquest, traders from the eastern parts of the Muslim world especially from Iraq migrated to North Africa and settled in the termini of the caravan routes from the Sudan. Later, some of them especially the Ibadites moved further inland and settled in such caravan centres as Ghadames, Ghat, Tadmekka and Awdaghost, all in the Sahara itself. These people combined trading with missionary activities, and it was they and their Berber converts in the Sahara who were to increase the volume of the trans-Saharan traffic and to open new routes especially between the eighth and the eleventh centuries.

The fourth reason for the development of the trans-Saharan trade was the political developments that took place in the western Sudan between the seventh and the sixteenth centuries. Those centuries saw the emergence of a number of kingdoms and empires such as Ghana, Kanem, Mali, Songhai, Borno and finally the Hausa states. The rulers of all these states contributed to or promoted the growth of the trans-Saharan trade in a number of ways. In the first place, they ensured the safety, security and provisioning of the in-coming Muslim traders. Secondly, even where local rulers did not embrace Islam until much later, (as was the case of Ghana,) they guaranteed absolute freedom of worship to the incoming Muslims, who were allowed to settle in their own quarters of the towns, the *zongo* or foreign quarters. They also ensured that justice was done to the foreign traders and that any official who tried to cheat or take advantage of them was punished. It is reported that a Massufa (Berber) trader who had been underpaid by an official at the Walata market was able to complain to the ruler, Mansa Sulayman of Mali who immediately summoned the official to the capital, ordered him to pay the full price and then dismissed him. Above all, the rulers ensured the security and maintenance of the trade routes; some of them dug wells on the routes, while others extended their control northward into the Sahara and established friendly relations with the rulers of the Barbary states and even with the Sultan of Turkey. Finally, the rulers took part in the trade themselves. All gold nuggets for instance were by law reserved for the kings of Ghana who obviously sold them into northern markets. In all these ways, then, the rulers secured and promoted the free flow of traffic across the Sahara.

A fifth important reason for the development of the caravan trade and for its growth, especially in the fifteenth and sixteenth centuries, was the contribution made by Islam. How Islam was introduced, how it spread and its impact in the political and social fields will be discussed later. Here we shall confine ourselves to the impact of Islam in the economic field and in particular on the development of the trans-Saharan trade from the seventh century. In the first place, some of the early great Islamic authorities issued the injunction that 'Trade to the territory of the enemy and to the land of the Sudan is reprehensible,' and by this they meant trade to the land of the infidel. Once the Sudan became Islamised, this order no longer applied. Secondly, these traders must also have felt much more at home in the Islamised courts and towns of these empires and kingdoms than before, especially since Islam encouraged the spread of Arabic as a lingua franca. Thirdly, Islamic dress habits followed the spread of Islam and this must have given a great boost both to the import trade in textiles and later to the local textile industries in which the Hausa soon became great experts. Fourthly, the introduction of Islam led to a great increase in Islamic learning and education in the Western Sudan, and this, in turn, greatly encouraged the trade in paper, books and manuscripts. Leo Africanus who visited the Western Sudan himself in 1510, was greatly struck by the brisk business being done by the bookshops in Timbuctu. To quote his words: 'Here is a great store of doctors, judges, priests and other learned men that are bountifully maintained at the king's cost and charges, and hitherto are brought diverse manuscripts or written books out of Barbary, which are sold for more money than any other merchandise.'

There is no doubt, however, that the greatest contribution which Islam made to the growth of the caravan trade was the pilgrimage or *hajj* that was demanded of its members. Many of the Sudanese rulers of the period took this obligation very seriously and went on the pilgrimage to Mecca thus drawing attention of the Muslim world to their states and further attracting traders and scholars.

The final, and undoubtedly one of the most important reasons for the growth of the caravan trade, especially from the fourteenth to the sixteenth centuries, was the extension of the trans-Saharan trade into the savanna and forest areas to the south, first by the Mande in general and the Dyula or Wangara in particular, and then by the Hausa. Following the fall of both Ghana and Mali in the twelfth and fourteenth centuries, the Mande migrated in large numbers, southwards into the gold and kola producing areas of modern Sierra Leone, Ivory Coast and Ghana. In these areas, which they probably reached in the thirteenth century, they pioneered the trade in gold and kola nuts, first into the area of the Niger bend or middle Niger, and then into Hausaland. It was for the effective conduct of this trade that the Mande founded first Begho in the northern fringes of the forest belt in the fourteenth century and later Bobo Dyulaso, Kong and Buna to act as the main trading and collecting centres for the forest products. Some of the Dyula also settled in the Mossi kingdoms where they became known as the Yarse. The Mande also migrated eastwards into Hausaland and Air, during the second half of the fourteenth century. Wherever they went the Mande developed the regional and trans-Saharan trade network. From the sixteenth century onwards the Hausa themselves took over or joined the trade with northern Ghana. It was the extension of the caravan trade into the gold and kola producing areas that further accounts for the tremendous increase in the volume and value of the trade, especially between the fourteenth and sixteenth centuries. This increase is borne out by the fact that the annual average volume of gold exported by the Akan northwards rose, according to Garrard, from 250 000 oz by 1400 to 500 000 oz by 1500 and 850 000 oz by 1600.

Decline in the seventeenth and eighteenth centuries

The trans-Saharan trade continued in the seventeenth and eighteenth centuries. However, by all accounts, there was a relative decline especially in the volume of trade in the western sector. This is borne out again by the figures provided by Garrard in his recent study which show that the annual volume of gold exported northwards dropped from 850 000 oz in 1600 to 500 000 oz in 1700 and to 400 000 oz by 1800. This should not surprise us. In the first place, the Sudan was marked by some instability following the conquest and overthrow of Songhai by the Moroccan forces in the 1590s. Thus, though the caravan trade did not cease as some historians used to think, recent research has confirmed that its volume decreased considerably along the western routes. It is true that some of the traders moved into Hausaland and Borno; but the power struggle in Hausaland and the outright decline of Borno during the seventeenth and eighteenth centuries could not have provided the stability and safety of the pre-sixteenth century period, trade, therefore, must have been reduced.

But an even more important reason for the relative overall decline was the increasing commercial activity of the Europeans on the coast of West Africa which began in the first half of the fifteenth century. From the seventeenth century onwards, far more gold was being exported by sea than by land, as Garrard's figures clearly show. Thus, while the total volume of Akan gold exported northwards had dropped to 500 000 oz by 1700, the gold exported southwards and by sea to Europe rose from only 550 000 oz by 1600 to 1500 000 oz by 1700.

In discussing this decline, however, it should be emphasised that the western sector of the trade, that is between the area west of the Niger bend and Morocco, suffered a greater decline than the Hausaland and Borno sectors. The volume of trans-Saharan trade rose again during the first half of the nineteenth century as the accounts of European explorers such as Denham, Clapperton and Barth clearly show. This was undoubtedly due to the impact of the Fulani *jihads* of that period.

It used to be thought that the trans-Saharan trade came to a complete halt in the 1860s and 1870s. However, recent research has shown conclusively that while the trade in the western zone sharply declined in the 1870s and had ceased completely by 1900, the traffic through and from Hausaland and Borno continued and even reached a boom period between the 1870s and 1890s. It was not until 1913 that partly because of the opening of the railway from Kano to Lagos in 1912 and the Italo-Turkish wars of the same year, the centuries-old traffic came to a complete halt.

The caravan routes

How then was this ancient traffic conducted? Let us first discuss the routes that were used. The trans-Saharan trade was carried on along seven principal routes all running from north to south with their sub-branches. These were (1) Fez-Marrakesh-Wadan-Audaghost-Takrur/Ghana; (2) Fez-Sijilmasa-Taghaza-Tichit-Walata-Jenne/Timbuctu-Mali; (3) Algiers-In Salah-Arawan-Timbuctu; (4) Qarawayn (Kairouan)-Wargla-Tadmekka-Gao; (5) Tripoli-Ghadames-Ghat-Takedda/Agades-Katsina/Kano; (6) Tripoli-Fezzan-Bilma-Kanem/Borno/Hausaland; and (7) Cyrenaica-Kufra-Wadai. Of all these routes the shortest and the one which remained in continuous use for the longest time was route 6, also known as the old Garamantian route. These were a few west-east routes, the most important being Timbuctu/Gao-Takedda-Agades-Bilma-Tibesti and Cairo, and the Timbuctu/Gao-Tadmekka-Ghat-Fezzan-Aujila-Cairo route.

From the savanna, further routes radiated southwards into the forest areas. The most important of these routes were the Jenne-Bobo Dyulasso-Kong-Begho-Kumasi route; the Katsina-Say-Fada N' Gurma-Sansannemango-Yendi-Salaga-Kumasi route; the Kano-Zaria-Birnin Yauri-Nikki-Djougou-Yendi-Salaga-Kumasi route; the Kano-Zaria-Old Oyo-Benin route; and finally Katsina-Kano-Bauchi-Wukari route.

It is important to note that the volume of traffic on these routes changed with the centuries depending very much on the political conditions in the Sudan and the security of the routes. From the eighth to the eleventh centuries, that is during the heyday of ancient Ghana, it appears that the most important were routes (1) to (3). Between the eleventh and fourteenth centuries when Mali and Kanem were the dominant powers, routes (2), (3) and (6) were the most active. From the fourteenth to the sixteenth centuries, the centuries of the Songhai and Borno empires, routes (2), (3), (4) and (6) became the leading routes while in the seventeenth and eighteenth centuries, the period of the Hausa states, routes (5) and (6) were easily the most important. Finally, in the nineteenth century, following the rise of the Sanusiyya and the kingdom of Wadai, routes (6) and especially (7) remained in active use; the latter was used by the final caravans in the twentieth century. It was also between the fourteenth and the sixteenth centuries that the southern routes radiating from Jenne in the west and Katsina in the east into the gold and kola producing countries came into prominence. The Gao-Ghat-Fezzan-Aujila-Cairo route became the principal route for the pilgrimage to Mecca.

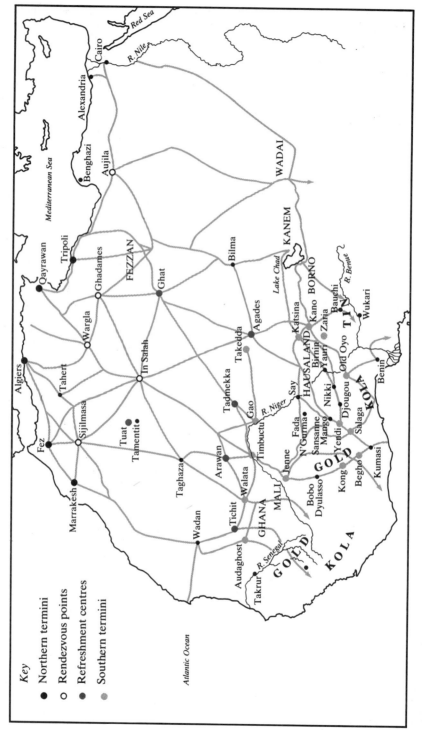

Trans-Saharan Trade Routes

Each of these routes had four main important points. These were the northern termini, the rendezvous or meeting-points, the refreshment centres or 'coaling' stations and the southern termini. These are all indicated on the map with special symbols. The northern termini contains the homes of some of the great merchants. The rendezvous or meeting-points were the centres where all the caravans assembled, where provisions and camels were bought, where camel drivers and guides could be hired and where some of the financiers lived. The 'coaling' stations were usually situated in the fertile oases where water and food could always be obtained and guides could be changed. At these centres, caravans remained for long periods, and goods from the north and south were exchanged. Some of the big traders and financiers lived or had their agents here.

The caravans, as a rule, left the Barbary states or North Africa between September and October, and departed from the Sudan at the beginning of the rainy season in April or May each year. The size of each caravan varied from one consisting of only five camels to one of 2000 camels. The caravans were led by professional guides who were usually Berbers, the indigenous peoples of the Sahara and who knew where the wells and the watering-points were. The whole journey, which lasted from seventy to ninety days depending on the size of the caravan, was an exceedingly dangerous one and whole caravans could perish if they lost their way. Other dangers were sandstorms, which could bury caravans alive, and shortage of water due to the unexpected drying up of wells.

What were the goods involved in the trans-Saharan trade? First, from Europe and the Muslim world came manufactured goods which were mainly textiles and garments, made from wool, and later also from silk, brocade, velvet or satin. In the nineteenth century bleached and unbleached calicoes together with metals such as brass, copper, silver, tin and lead were major items of trade. From the Barbary states or North Africa, horses were amongst the most important exports and remained in great demand throughout the centuries. These horses were used in warfare and were sold almost exclusively to the rulers of the trading states. Other exports from the Mediterranean world were books, writing paper, cowries (which became the main currency throughout the Western Sudan except Borno), tea, coffee, sugar, spices, jewellery, perfumes, bracelets, looking-glasses, needles, razors, snuff-boxes, scissors, knives, trinkets, carpets and beads.

The main exports from the Sahara were first and foremost salt, which remained the mainstay of the caravan trade to the south throughout all those centuries. It was used not only for cooking but also for the care of animals, the making of dyes and other industrial purposes. This salt was mined first at Awlil and then at Taghaza, Taodeni, Idjil and Bilma. It was mined in blocks and sent into the Sudan where each block was broken into small pieces before being exported as far south as the forest areas. Copper was the second leading Saharan export, mined mainly at Takedda, and it is believed by some authorities that it was exported as far south as Yorubaland and Benin. Other Saharan exports were tobacco and dates.

In exchange for all this, the Western Sudan or the savanna areas exported millet, sorghum, wheat and livestock into the Sahara, it also exported gum, shea butter, ivory, ostrich feathers, Kano cloth, gold from Bambuk and Bure (known in the Arabic records as Wangara,) and slaves, into the Sahara and the Barbary states. To the south, the Western Sudan exported the important commodity of natron, mainly from Borno, which was used in the making of soap, in dyeing and tanning, as animal feed and as salt. Other exports included manufactured goods such as cloth and dresses from Hausaland, Nupe and Timbuctu, and leather goods such as bags, cushions, sandals and shoes.

The forest and southern savanna areas in turn exported first and foremost gold from the Akan and Lobi goldfields, then kola nuts, ivory and slaves. While, as we have seen, the volume of gold declined from the seventeenth century, kola nuts remained the most important export from the forest area till the end of the traffic.

How were these goods exchanged? The medium of exchange or the sale of goods varied from place to place. The most common system of exchange which remained throughout the centuries was one of barter in the market places in the Sudan. Under this system a certain weight of gold was exchanged for salt, or a piece of Kano or European cloth or a number of kola nuts. In addition to barter, various types of currencies were used. The first to come into use not only in the Western and Central Sudan but also in the forest regions to the south as well as the Sahara were cowries. Later, French francs, Spanish and Austrian or Maria Theresa Thalers (dollars) were also used. In Borno, Wadai and Bagirmi where cowries were not accepted, strips of cotton of different sizes were used in small purchases while major exchanges involving ivory, slaves, horses, natron, were done by barter.

The impact of the trans-Saharan trade

Such then was the trans-Saharan trade. The final question, then, is what impact did this trade make or what effect did it have on the peoples and states of West Africa. Or, to put the question differently, what was the importance of the trans-Saharan trade in the history of West Africa? There is no doubt that it had far-reaching political, social and economic effects in West Africa. The first political effect was its contribution to the formation of states and kingdoms in West Africa. Even before the development of the trans-Saharan trade, a number of different communities, villages and even towns had already emerged. One of the things that the trans-Saharan trade did was to create in the rulers of these communities the desire to establish control over the trade routes that were emerging, as well as over the areas that could produce gold and other commodities such as salt or kola needed in the new trade. It was surely with a view to controlling the trade routes as well as the salt mines that, for instance, the rulers of Ghana, in 990 AD, conquered Awdaghost, while those of Mali and Songhai extended their conquests into the Sahara as far north as Taghaza and Takedda, the salt and copper producing areas, and those of both Kanem and Borno extended their control as far north as the Fezzan. In other words, the caravan trade greatly encouraged the formation of large kingdoms and empires.

Secondly, the trans-Saharan trade provided the means for undertaking the wars of conquest and expansion through the supply of effective means-of warfare, such as horses and metals suitable for the manufacture of arms such as spears, arrowheads, or axes. There is no doubt that it was the use of cavalry by the rulers of the Sahel and the savanna which enabled them to establish large kingdoms and empires.

The third political effect or impact of the caravan trade was to greatly increase the power of the rulers, first by ensuring a regular source of income through the custom duties that they were able to impose on imports and exports, and secondly, by enabling the rulers to gain control or monopoly over goods of great political importance, such as horses, and probably metals, imported into the country.

The caravan trade also brought about great improvements in the political administration of the kingdoms through the employment of the usually well-educated Muslim traders whom the trans-Saharan trade attracted into the Sudan as advisers, civil servants and ministers. As we shall see, even non-Muslim rulers such as those of Ghana, appointed some of the Muslim traders and scholars as secretaries and ministers.

The final political effect of the trans-Saharan trade was to bring the states and peoples of West Africa first to the attention of and then in touch with the Barbary states north of the Sahara in particular and the Muslim world in general. As early as the eighth century AD, before even the introduction of Islam, Ghana was already known in the courts of the Abbasid caliphs of Baghdad as the 'land of gold'.

No less important were the economic and social effects of the caravan trade in West Africa. Economically, the trade greatly promoted the exploitation of natural resources. Surely, the Western Sudan would not have become so famous throughout Europe and the Muslim world as a gold-producing area, nor would the salt mines of the Sahara have been so exploited but for the stimulus provided by the caravan trade. Also, by encouraging the export of foodstuffs and provisions into the Sahara, the caravan trade must have stimulated agriculture in the Sudan. Above all, the caravan trade greatly stimulated the development of the textile industry for which the Sudan in general and Timbuctu and Kano in particular became so famous from the fifteenth and sixteenth centuries onwards. It is indeed believed by some scholars that the technique of weaving cloth may have been imported into the Sudan from either Egypt or the Barbary states by the Muslim traders who came in from the north.

Socially, the trans-Saharan trade, promoted urbanisation, that is the development of small villages and settlements into large towns and cities. Such towns as Kumbi Saleh, Jenne, Timbuctu and Gao owed their foundation or rapid development to the trans-Saharan trade. Nowhere is this more true than in Hausaland, where there were only numerous fortified agricultural villages and small towns, until the increase in trade from the fifteenth century onwards when villages like Kano, Katsina, Gobir and Zaria began their rapid development into towns and cities. This happened because the caravan trade made them centres into which foreign traders as well as local merchants came to settle.

Secondly, not only was the development of the trans-Saharan trade assisted by Islam but the caravan trade itself also greatly accelerated the spread of that religion itself in the Western Sudan. It should always be borne in mind that in Islam there was no clear distinction between a trader and a teacher or evangelist, and that teachers, except a few clerics or holy men, were also traders, and vice versa. Consequently, the expansion of trade by the Muslim traders meant, at the same time, the expansion of Islamic influence. Similarly, through the books, writing paper, ink and other goods that the trade brought into West Africa, the spread of education and literacy was greatly promoted.

Finally, the caravan trade led to the emergence of at least two new social classes in West Africa. The first was a class of resident foreign merchants who were usually found living in their own quarters of the towns; the second was a class of local professional traders such as the Dyula or Wangara among the Mande and the Hausa. It is also worth noting that the trade improved the general standard of life as a result of the clothes and luxury items introduced into West Africa by the caravans.

In all these ways, then, it can be safely concluded that the trans-Saharan trade did have a very important impact on West Africa, and that its introduction and development should be taken as one of the major factors in West Africa's history.

2   Islam in West Africa

Introduction and spread of Islam

The spread of Islam into West Africa began with the Arab conquest and occupation of the whole of North Africa from Egypt to Morocco between 639 and 708 A.D. The Arabs were motivated both by religious zeal and economic gain: among the invaders were merchants and fanatical Muslims, and it was these two groups which began the slow spread of Islam into the interior parts of Africa. The first West Africans to be converted were the inhabitants of the Sahara, the Berbers, and it is generally agreed that by the second half of the tenth century, the Sahara had become *Dar al-Islam*, that is 'the country of Islam'.

From the Sahara, Islam spread into the Western Sudan from the closing decades of the tenth century first into the regions west of the Niger Bend, then into the Chad region and finally into Hausaland. According to some Arabic sources the first black ruler to embrace Islam was the king of Gao who had done so by 1009, while the first king of Mali to become Muslim was Barmandana, who was reigning by the middle of the eleventh century. The kings of Ghana, on the other hand, did not embrace Islam until about the beginning of the twelfth century. In the Chad region, it appears from the Arabic sources that Umme Jilmi, who became the king of Kanem in 1086, was the first Muslim king. Islam was first introduced into Hausaland from either Kanem or Air in the twelfth or thirteenth century, but it did not really take root there until during the second half of the fourteenth century. It was in the same century or probably a century earlier that Islam spread into the southern Savanna and the forest fringes of West Africa and had taken firm root in Dagomba and Gonja by the end of the sixteenth century.

It used to be thought that Islam stagnated or declined in the Western Sudan during the seventeenth and eighteenth centuries. However, recent research has shown rather that Islam was strengthened, especially in the rural areas of the Niger Bend, Futa Jallon and Futa Toro, and that it expanded further into Mossi and the forest areas as far south as Kumasi and gained further ground in Hausaland, Nupe and Yorubaland during those two centuries.

Reasons for the spread of Islam

By the end of the sixteenth century Islam has spread southwards right to the fringes of the forest belt. Christianity on the other hand, though an older religion, had been largely displaced from North Africa and made little impact on the coast of West Africa. How then do we account for this unrivalled spread of Islam in West Africa? The answer lies partly in the very nature of Islam: its acceptance of polygamy, its tolerance of traditional African religions, its simplicity of doctrine and mode of worship – all these elements made Islam easily adaptable to the African communities with which it came in contact. Indeed, as Levtzion has so neatly put it: 'The Islamisation of Africa was paralleled by the Africanisation of Islam.' The making and sale of charms and amulets, which were believed to offer protection against evil forces and generally ensure success in life, were important in winning over converts. To quote Levtzion again: 'It was the magical aspects of Islam that aided Muslims to win over the chief in competition with local priests.'

But the fact that Islam was more readily acceptable to Africans because of its very nature is not the only reason why it spread so relatively rapidly in the Western Sudan. Equally important were the very effective and varied means of spreading Islam; through the activities of traders, scholars, rulers and soldiers, in a peaceful or quietist manner as well as in a forceful or militant manner.

The earliest and certainly the most widespread means of propagating Islam was the trans-Saharan trade network. As we have already seen, trade really got going from the fifth or sixth century, while from the seventh century onwards Muslim traders from the Maghreb and the Sahara started settling first in some of the market centres in the Sahel and then in the savanna areas.

Al-Bakri, writing in 1067, says that the capital of ancient Ghana was already divided into two parts, about six miles apart, the Muslim traders' part which had as many as twelve mosques, and the king's part, which also had one mosque for the use of the king's Muslim visitors. There is no doubt that it was these resident Muslim traders who converted the rulers and the principal local townspeople to Islam. Indeed, the *Kano Chronicle* puts it quite clearly that in the reign of Yaji, the king of Kano from 1349 to 1385, 'The Wangarawa came from Mele bringing the Mohammedan religion'. As the caravan trade grew the process of Islamisation or conversion to Islam also gathered momentum.

The second way in which Islam spread into the Western Sudan was through the activities of Muslim clerics, marabouts and scholars or mallams. The arrival of such people and the conversion of rulers marked the second stage in the pattern of Islamisation in the Western Sudan. These clerics, or learned men founded their own religious centres which attracted students from all parts of the Western Sudan and who on the completion of their studies and training went back to their own homes to win converts. Many of them went on lecture or missionary tours to convert people, while others became advisers to Sudanese kings on how to become effective rulers. Some clerics devoted a great deal of their time to writing books and instructions on all aspects of Islam for the education and conversion of people or for the purification and strengthening of Islam. One of the very first of a long line of such clerics was Abd Allah ibn Yasin who was invited by Yahya ibn Ibrahim, the head of the Sanhaja Confederation based at Awdaghost, to accompany him on his return from his pilgrimage to Mecca in 1048. Ibn Yasin established a *Zawiya* or college and founded the Almoravid movement whose considerable contribution to the spread of Islam in the Sahara and Western Sudan will be discussed later. Ibn Khadija al-Kumi, a Muslim missionary, and Abu Ishag al-Sahili, a poet, scholar and architect, were both invited by Mansa

Musa to accompany him on his return from his celebrated pilgrimage in 1324–5. Both of them settled in Mali where they taught Islam. Al-Sahili also built the great mosque of Timbuctu as well as a magnificent palace for Mansa Musa in Niani, the capital of Mali. The great Mande scholar, Abd Rahman Zaite (now identified as Abd al-Rahman Jakhite), settled in Kano on the invitation of Rumfa, the king of Kano. Not only did he build the Friday mosque but also he is believed to have introduced the practice of nightly Koran recital and other devotional exercises.

One of the greatest clerics and missionaries of the Western Sudan was al-Hajj Salim Suware, the Soninke scholar who lived during the second half of the twelfth and the first half of the thirteenth centuries. He founded the important *Zawiya* at Diakha-Bambukhu which attracted students from all over the Western Sudan, whom he trained and sent out as missionaries. In his teaching, he rejected the use of force as an instrument of religious or political change and emphasised the peaceful aspects of the *jihad* to convert people to Islam. Salim Suware went on extensive missionary tours throughout the region of Upper Niger and the Senegambia during which he established mosques, upgraded existing ones, gathered students for his centre and preached to both Muslims and non-Muslims.

Even more successful was the work of a fanatical but brilliant Berber scholar, Abd al-Rahman al-Maghili. In 1477–78 he established his *zawiya* in Tuat and from there went on a missionary tour of the Western Sudan which lasted from 1492 to 1503. During this tour, he visited Aîr, Takedda, Kano, Katsina and Gao, and preached to both rulers and commoners. In Aîr, he is said to have built a mosque and held classes in the Quranic sciences in Takedda. He stayed in Kano for some time where he was well received by Rumfa, on whose request al-Maghili wrote his now famous treatise or book on statecraft for rulers entitled *The Obligation of Princes*, probably in 1491–92. According to the *Kano Chronicle*, by the time al-Maghili left Kano, Islam had become universal in the state. He also visited and stayed in Gao where he arrived in 1492 and became advisor to the then ruler, the great Askia Mohammed (1493–1528) for whom he wrote a whole series of answers to the questionnaires prepared by Askia which are still available. He returned to Tuat in 1503 and died there in 1504 or 1505. Al-Maghili also introduced the Qadiriyya brother-hood into the Sahara and Western Sudan and he is still remembered as a reformer, a great authority on Islamic jurisprudence and a holy man. Al-Maghili certainly did a lot to purify and spread Islam during the second half of the fifteenth century and as a recent scholar has concluded: 'No African scholar earned as great a reputation or had so far-reaching an impact on both North and West Africa as al-Maghili.'

Important too was the role played at this time by a Berber clerical family, the Kunta. Their contribution to the spread of Islam really began under the leadership of Sheikh Sidi Umar-Shaykh (1460–1552/3) who, it is interesting to note, was a contemporary and disciple of al-Maghili. He united the various feuding groups of the family and spread Islam and the Qadiriyya order among the Berbers of the southern Sahara. But the greatest contribution made by this family was during the leadership of Sidi Mukhtar al-Kunti (1729–1811). He first established a *zawiya* in Azawad where he taught the Islamic sciences with an emphasis on mysticism. He believed that he was the reformer (the *mujaddid*) called upon by Allah to renew and spread

Islam not only in West Africa but throughout the Muslim world. Among his many treatises on mysticism was a book in which he outlined his own form of the Qadiri doctrines or principles; and this book is still used as a major reference in many parts of West Africa. He established *zawiyas* in different parts of the Sahara and the Western Sudan in which he trained his followers and sent them out to spread and strengthen Islam. Because of the activities of his pupils and disciples, the influence of Sidi al-Mukhtar spread throughout the Sahara and the Western Sudan during the second half of the eighteenth century.

The third way in which Islam gained ground was through the activities of the individual rulers in the Western Sudan. We have already noted how they encouraged the trans-Saharan trade and extended hospitality to both traders and visiting clerics; but perhaps one of the most important ways in which they encouraged acceptance of Islam was through their own conversion. With a Muslim king or ruler it rapidly became a matter of prestige among the aristocracy also to convert to Islam. Many rulers made considerable efforts to encourage Muslim institutions such as Islamic tax and legal systems, or the provision of facilities such as mosques; through the appointment of Muslim officials such as *qadis* or judges, *awla* or butchers who observe the Islamic code and *imams* to lead prayers; or by celebrating Muslim festival and ordering every town under their control to observe the ritual prayers. According to the Kano Chronicle, the king of Kano did many of these things soon after the arrival of Abd Rahman Zaite. Above all, the pilgrimages that many of the rulers undertook, had a considerable spiritual effect, increasing their determination both to strengthen and purify Islam and to spread it even further.

The final way in which Islam was introduced and spread in West Africa in general and the Western Sudan in particular was the militant *jihad* or the waging of a holy war against infidels or luke-warm Muslims. This militant or forceful method usually marked the third and final stage of the process of Islamisation and reached its climax with the nineteenth century *jihads* in the Western Sudan. The first *jihad* in the Western Sudan of which we have accounts was that waged by the head of the Sanhaja Confederation, Tarsina, against the Sudanese people in 1023 soon after his return from the pilgrimage to Mecca during which he was killed. The second is that of the king of Takrur, War-Djabi, before his death in 1040. The third and the best known of these early jihads was the one declared by the Almoravid movement founded among the Sanhaja Berbers to the north of ancient Ghana between 1048 and 1054 by the scholar, Abdallah ibn Yasin. Between 1056 and 1070, the Almoravids conquered the whole area between ancient Ghana and Sijilmasa. By 1087 the Almoravid empire stretched from the Senegal in the south across the Mediterranean to Spain in the north.

There is no doubt that the Almoravid *jihad* purified and strengthened Islam in the Sahara and the Senegambia regions. It also led to the conversion of the rulers of Ghana to Islam. Furthermore, the Almoravid conquests in the south set in motion waves of migration into the southern part of the Western Sudan of the Soninke people who helped to spread the trans-Saharan trade and Islam. Thus, if by the end of the eleventh century, Islam had become firmly established in the Sahel and the northern savanna areas, it was due in no small measure to the activities of the Almoravids.

From the eleventh right through to the nineteenth century, there were periodic *jihad* movements. As we shall see later, many of the rulers of the empires of Mali, Songhai, Kanem and Borno declared *jihads*. In the seventeenth century at least two *jihads* were launched, the first by Nasr al-Din in southern Mauretania in 1673 and the second by Malik Dauda Sy in the 1690s which resulted in the establishment of the imamate of Bundu in the Senegambia region. In the eighteenth century, *jihads* were declared by Boubo Malik Sy in Futa Jallon in 1726 and by Sulaiman Ba in Futa Toro in 1776 resulting in the establishment of the Muslim states or imamates of Futa Jallon and Futa Toro and the spread and strengthening of Islam in those areas.

The impact of Islam

The final topic to be discussed in this chapter is the impact that Islam made on the people and states of Western Sudan or on the history of the Western Sudan. It should first be pointed out that unlike Christianity, Islam is not just a religion or a mass of doctrines or beliefs and rituals, but rather a complete way of life or civilisation. It has its own system of writing, laws, taxation, education and warfare; it also had its own social regulations about eating, drinking, marriage, divorce, and inheritance besides the five 'pillars of the faith', the obligatory duties of praying, fasting, giving alms, undertaking the pilgrimage and confessing the faith.

Politically, since Islam cut across family, clan and ethnic ties and loyalties and emphasised unity and brotherhood, it enabled rulers to build larger kingdoms and empires embracing different peoples and linguistic groups. It also provided them with a commonly accepted basis of authority in place of African traditional religions which differed from place to place. As we shall see, many of the rulers of Western Sudan, such as Mansa Musa of Mali, Askia Mohammed of Songhai and Idris Alooma of Borno did attempt to use Islam in these ways, to generate a feeling of unity and as a basis of their authority.

Secondly, most of the Muslim rulers of Western Sudan adopted the Muslim systems of justice and taxation. Thus, Islam promoted a more efficient administration in some of the states of Western Sudan since it enabled the rulers to employ educated Muslims as secretaries, administrators, judges and diplomats and also to correspond with provincial rulers and administrators. It is significant that even non-Muslim rulers such as those of ancient Ghana before the eleventh century employed some Muslims in their administration. Furthermore, the holy wars, which some rulers waged helped to extend the frontiers of their states.

The pilgrimage or *hajj* which Muslims, and especially Muslim rulers, were expected to undertake if they were able to do so contributed in many ways to the growth and strength of some of the states. The *hajj* enabled the pilgrim to acquire first the highly coveted title of Al-hajj, or Hajj, and even more important the *baraka*, that is, the spiritual power which a pilgrim acquired by touching the Black Stone of the Ka'ba or Great Temple in Mecca and visiting the tomb of the Prophet at Medina. This power was of great importance especially for the rulers since it greatly increased their reputation and religious standing among their subjects. Indeed, it is because of the acquisition of this power that the *hajj* was and is still so popular among Muslims, especially Muslim rulers.

Secondly, the *hajj* brought pilgrims into contact with the technology and scholarship at the centre of the Muslim world, which were often adopted and introduced when the pilgrims returned home. For instance, as will be seen later, Idris Alooma of Borno brought back from his pilgrimage a group of musketeers and Turkish military instructors and created a musketeer corps in his army which enabled him to extend the frontiers of his state with relative ease. The *hajj* also enabled rulers to meet and invite some of the leading theologians, architects, judges and other experts of the Muslim world. At the same time it also enabled the pilgrim rulers to establish diplomatic relations with other Muslim rulers abroad as Mansa Musa and Idris Alooma did with those of Egypt and Tunis respectively. Finally the *hajj* undoubtedly gave great publicity to the states of the rulers who undertook them.

In all these ways, then, Islam did have a decisive positive and far-reaching impact on the Western Sudan. But in some respects, Islam had a negative effect. In the first place, it challenged traditional African religion, weakening the basis on which some of the Sudanese states such as Kanem and ancient Ghana rested, contributing to their downfall. Secondly, it often divided the ruling group into Muslim and non-Muslim factions, conflict between which further weakened some of the states such as Songhai. Thirdly, the *jihad* not only caused periodic outbreaks of instability and chaos in the Western Sudan but also precipitated the downfall of some states – the Hausa states, for example, as will be discussed later.

Socially, Islam introduced literacy as well as Muslim education into the Western Sudan, and with these factors emerged an educated class, some of whose members, as we have seen already, were employed by the rulers of the Sudanese states. Literacy also made possible the preservation of the history and the oral traditions of some of the states in books. Examples of such books are the *Tarikh al Fattash* and the *Tarikh as-Sudan* written in Timbuctu in the sixteenth and seventeenth centuries. Literacy also enabled people in the Western Sudan to gain access to the invaluable Islamic literature, sciences and philosophy which broadened their knowledge, improved their statecraft and widened their horizons. Furthermore, as its schools and educational centres tended to be situated in towns, Islam contributed to urbanisation, that is to the growth of large towns and cities, in the Western Sudan. Such towns as Jenne, Timbuctu, Gao, Kano and Katsina were as much creations of the Islamisation of the Western Sudan as they were of the trans-Saharan trade.

In concluding this chapter on the spread of Islam, however, it should be emphasised that although its impact on state formation and development was considerable, it remained, even as late as the end of the eighteenth century, very much the religion and culture of the rulers, the administrators, the foreign merchants and the town dwellers; indeed, as a recent authority has pointed out, Islam 'made little impact on the way of life and beliefs of the farmers, fishermen and the people in the rural areas in general'.

3 Ancient Ghana

On the attainment of independence in 1957, the Gold Coast was renamed Ghana after an empire that rose and fell between about 500 AD and 1250 in the region between the bend of the Niger and the middle reaches of the Senegal and Gambia rivers. Ghana was, of course, not the only state that emerged in that region. There were also the states of Takrur, Mali, Songhai to the west, and the Hausa states of Kano, Katsina, Zaria, Gobir and the Chadic states of Kanem and Borno to the east.

The rise of Ghana

In the case of Ghana, the first important reason for its rise, and this is true of all the savannah states, was the early growth of settled population in that area. Mainly because of the desiccation of the area of the Sahara, which started about 5 000 BC and reached its peak by 1000 BC, the inhabitants migrated north and south into the Maghreb and the savanna belts respectively.

The growth of population in the savanna must have been further accelerated by the independent neolithic revolution, that is, the change from gathering to the cultivation of food crops. Many historians and archaeologists are now coming round to the view that there was an independent revolution in agriculture or the cultivation of certain crops by the Mande people in the areas between the Niger Bend and the upper reaches of the Senegal and the Gambia rivers by 1000 BC and that from there that knowledge spread westwards and southwards.

Another factor which must have further increased the rate of population growth was the use of iron. Whether there was also an independent invention of the use of iron in the Western Sudan or whether it was introduced from either the Maghreb or Meroe in modern Sudan or both is a matter of dispute among scholars. Whatever the case may be, it is certain that iron tools were being used in the Sahara and savanna areas by about 500 BC and this must have greatly facilitated agricultural activities.

It seems obvious then, that as a result of all these factors, there was a more rapid growth and a far greater concentration of population in the savanna belt by, say, the beginning of the first century AD, than anywhere else in West Africa. Moreover, this population must have been greater in the Sahel region which was by then certainly more fertile and more habitable then than it is now, and more in the Niger-Senegal area than elsewhere. The populations were Mande-speaking, and, as recent archaeological excavations in the Tichit-Walata and Jenne areas have shown, they were organised first

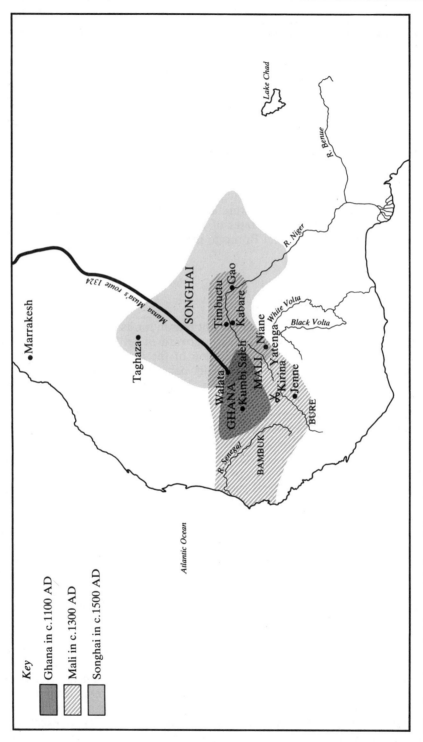

The Empires of Ghana, Mali and Songhai

into settlements by 1000 BC, then into villages by 600 BC and then into chieftaincies with administrative capitals; some of these villages or settlements had developed into large urban centres such as Old Jenne between 400 and 900 AD. The most northern of these people were the Soninke and it was they who founded the empire of Ghana, and not any white invaders as it used to be thought.

The second important reason for the emergence of ancient Ghana was economic, and this was the development first of local and regional trade and secondly the trans-Saharan trade. Inter-regional trade between the inhabitants of the Sahara and those of Sahel and the rest of the savanna must have started very early on, probably from about 500 BC onwards. This consisted of an exchange of salt and copper of the Sahara for the gold, slaves, rice, dried fish and other staples of the savanna. Excavations at Old Jenne have produced iron objects dated to 250 BC–50 AD. Since there are no sources of iron in the whole of the inland delta region, the iron at Old Jenne must have been imported from the nearest source of abundant iron in the Benedugu area, near San to the west. Similarly, copper ornaments were found dated to 400–900 AD and the closest sources of copper ore are in the Sahara at Akjoujt, Nioro and in Aîr. This clearly shows first that there was an inter-regional trade between the Sahara and Jenne-Jeno by 500 AD, and that the Niger was being used as a commercial highway by as early as that date. Evidence from the Jenne excavations has suggested that the early foundation of Jenne-Jeno in 250 BC and its rapid development into a large urban centre between 400 and 900 AD must have been due to its dual position as a trade and rich agricultural centre. This early development of inter-regional trade must also have further accelerated the evolution of more and more chiefdoms.

There is no doubt, however, that the caravan or trans-Sahara trade contributed most significantly to the conversion or development of some of these chiefdoms into very large kingdoms and empires. The general ways in which the trans-Saharan trade contributed to this process have already been discussed in Chapter One.

However, the Soninke chiefdom of Ghana had one specific advantage over all the others, particularly with regard to the fruits of the trans-Saharan trade caravans: namely, its strategic position. Geographically, the Soninke chiefdom emerged in the very area of the meeting point between the Sahara and the savanna, thus enabling it to play the crucial role of middleman in the developing trade between the Maghreb and the Sahara to the north and the savanna areas to the south. That Ghana played this role is clearly borne out by this extract from the book written by Yaqut as early as between 1212 and 1229:

'Ghana is a great town to the south of the Maghrib, adjacent to the land of the Sudan [i.e. of the Blacks]. Merchants meet in Ghana and from there one enters the arid wastes towards the land of Gold. Were it not for Ghana, this journey would be impossible, because the land of Gold is in a place isolated from the west in the land of the Sudan. From Ghana the merchants take provisions on the way to the land of Gold . . . '

It played a leading and decisive role to present a united force against the nomads and to achieve a wider and more effective control over trade. Since

Ghana was not only the northernmost of all the Sahelian states but also the main controller of the trade in gold, it must have felt the pressure earlier and more than the other states such as Takrur or Kanem. It is not surprising, then, that it was the first to grow into a large defensive empire.

Unfortunately, owing to the lack of evidence, we do not know exactly how the conversion of the small Soninke chiefdom into the empire of Ghana was accomplished. However, it is reasonable to assume that this conversion must have been done mainly through military conquests under the leadership of some great, but unknown kings. By the end of the tenth century Ghana had developed into a large empire. What, then, was it like at the peak of its power by the middle of the eleventh century?

The government of Ghana

First, what was the area of Ghana at the peak of its power? It appears from two Arabic sources – al-Bakri (1067) and al-Idrisi (1154) – that the empire extended as far as the Senegal river which marked it from the independent kingdom of Takrur to the west, as far as the Niger to the east, as far as the boundaries of the gold-producing region of Bambuk to the south while it included the Berber trading centre of Awdaghost to the north.

For what was ancient Ghana best known to the outside world? It was best known for its wealth in gold. On this all the early Arab writers of the eighth to tenth centuries agree. Al-Bakri and al-Idrisi also confirm this view; al-Bakri states that gold was so plentiful that even the dogs which guarded the king while he sat in state wore collars of gold and silver. Al-Idrisi, writing in 1154, was also convinced that the king had in his possession 'a nugget of pure gold weighing 30 lb of absolutely natural formation'. It appears from these accounts, however, that a great deal of this gold was not mined in Ghana itself, but in the region of Bambuk and Bure to the south.

That the ordinary Ghanaians were quite well off, mainly as a result of the caravan trade, is clear from their high standard of living which surprised the Arabic writers. According to al-Bakri, while only the king and heir apparent could wear sewn clothes, all the other people wore robes of cotton, silk or brocade 'according to their means'. Al-Idrisi also wrote nearly a hundred years later: 'The clothing [of the Ghanaians] consists of robes, loin-cloths and mantles, everybody dressing himself according to his means.'

How was the empire governed? In the first place it seems that at the peak of its power Ghana consisted of two parts: metropolitan Ghana and provincial Ghana. The former was the nucleus and the latter consisted of the states that had been conquered and annexed. At the head of the entire empire was the king whose title according to al-Bakri was 'Ghana' though according to the *Tarikhs* of Timbuctu it was 'Kaya-Magha' or 'Tunkka', a Soninke word meaning king or sovereign. He was regarded as divine by his people and when they approached him, they would 'fall on their knees and sprinkle dust on their heads for this is their way of greeting him'.

In administering the empire, the king was assisted by a council of ministers and the governor of the capital city. According to al-Bakri, the king's interpreter, the official in charge of the treasury, and a majority of his ministers, were all Muslim. A detailed description of the capital city, Kumbi Saleh or Ghana, from which the king administered the empire, is given by al-Bakri:

'The city of Ghana consists of two towns situated on a plain. One of these towns, which is inhabited by Muslims, is large and possesses twelve mosques in one of which they assemble for the Friday prayer. There are salaried imams and muezzins as well as jurists and scholars. In the environs are wells of sweet water, from which they drink and with which they grow vegetables. The king's town is six miles distant from this one and bears the name of al-Ghaba [the forest]. Between these two towns there are continuous habitations. The houses of the inhabitants are of stone and acacia wood. The king has a palace and a number of domed dwellings all surounded with an enclosure like a city wall. In the king's town, and not far from his court of justice, is a mosque where the Muslims who arrive at his court pray.'

Provincial administration was left in the hands of the kings of the conquered states. It appears that in order to ensure their continued allegiance, the kings of Ghana insisted on the son of each vassal king being sent to the sovereign court. Al-Bakri informs us that when the king of Ghana sat in state, he was flanked not only by his ministers but also by 'the sons of the vassal kings of his country, wearing splendid garments and their hair plaited with gold'. For the defence of the kingdom, the kings of Ghana could call upon an army of 200 000 of whom 40 000 were archers. According to al-Idrisi, their weapons were mostly bows and arrows but they also use 'maces which they make of ebony with much cunning and craft'.

The administration of justice in ancient Ghana was also the responsibility of the king. According to al-Idrisi, the king went out every day on his horse and commanded everyone who had suffered injustice or misfortune to come before him and stay till the wrong was remedied. Trial by wood was also practised in ancient Ghana. 'When a man is accused of denying a debt or having shed blood or some other crime,' writes al-Bakri, 'the official in charge takes a thin piece of wood, which is sour and bitter to taste, and pours upon it some water, which he then gives to the defendant to drink. If the man vomits his innocence is recognised and he is congratulated. If he does not vomit and the drink remains in his stomach the accusation is accepted as justified.'

To meet the cost of administration, the Soninke rulers of Ghana had definite sources of income. In the first place, according to al-Bakri, 'the nuggets [of gold] found in all the mines of his country are reserved for the king, only the gold dust being left for the people.' The reason for this was that 'but for this the people would accumulate gold until it lost its value'. Vassal kings also paid annual tribute. But the bulk of the state's income must have come from customs duties. According to al-Bakri: 'On every donkey-load of salt when it is brought into the country their king levies one golden dinar, and two dinars when it is sent out. From a load of copper the king's due is five mithqals, and from a load of other goods ten mithqals.' Considering the briskness of the caravan trade at the height of Ghana's power, the income from these duties must have been very considerable.

The culture of Ghana

Some aspects of the culture of ancient Ghana should be discussed here since they are surprisingly similar to those of the forest peoples of West Africa in general and those of the Akan of modern Ghana in particular. (The custom, for example, of reserving all gold nuggets for the king is also observed among the Akan.) Most of the Arabic writers were amazed at the fact that the system of inheritance, at least of the King's office, was matrilineal, and not patrilineal as in their own states; Tunka Manna, King at the time that al-Bakri wrote, was said to be the nephew of his predecessor, King Basi. Al-Bakri recorded: 'This is their custom and habit . . . that the kingdom is inherited only by the son of the king's sister.' The reason given for this is, interestingly enough, the very reason given by some Akan of modern Ghana for the same system of inheritance. To quote the words of the Arabic scholar written nearly a thousand years ago: 'The king has no doubt that his successor is a son of his sister while he is not certain that his son is in fact his own, and he does not rely on the genuineness of this relationship.'

Not only does the system of inheritance in ancient Ghana remind one of the present-day Akan practice, but so also do the king's palace, the court etiquette, the use of drums, the burial of the king and the system of worship. The king lived in a palace which consisted of a number of domed dwellings surrounded by an enclosure like a city wall. When he sat in state, he adorned himself, 'like a woman [wearing necklaces] round his neck and [bracelets] on his forearms and he puts on a high cap decorated with gold and wrapped in a turban of fine cotton. Behind the king,' the description goes on, 'stand ten pages holding shields and swords decorated with gold.' It is interesting to note that audience was announced by the beating of a drum. Another author also states that a drum, covered with skin and making 'an awesome sound' when beaten, was used to assemble the people.

The way in which the kings of ancient Ghana were buried also has a familiar ring:

> When their king dies, they construct over the place where his tomb will be an enormous dome of *saj* or [teak] wood. Then they bring him on a bed covered with a few carpets and cushions and place him beside the dome. At his side they place his ornaments, his weapons and the vessels from which he used to eat and drink, filled with various kinds of food and beverages. They place there too the men who used to serve his meals. They close the door of the dome and cover it with mats and furnishings. Then the people assemble who heap earth upon it until it becomes like a big hillock and dig a ditch around it until the mound can be reached at only one place.

Equally familiar and interesting is the religion of the Soninke of Ghana. Like most of the forest and savanna peoples of West Africa, the ancient Ghanaians worshipped many gods. It appears that the state had its own gods served by priests who lived in one sector of the king's town. As al-Bakri puts it:

> Around the king's town are domed buildings and groves and thickets where the sorcerers of these people, men in charge of their religious cults,

live. In them too are their idols and the tombs of their kings. These woods are guarded and none may enter them and know what is there.

This bears very close resemblance to the Nanampow of the Fante or the stool-rooms of the Akan. The ancient Ghanaians also believed in ancestor worship and therefore made sacrifices 'to their dead and made offerings of intoxicating drinks'. They also believed in magic and witchcraft. 'In all the countries especially in Ghana,' wrote al-Umari (d.1399), 'magic was much employed. They are for ever litigating before their king because of saying such a one has killed my brother or son or daughter or sister by sorcery. The killer is sentenced to punishment by retaliation and the sorcerer is put to death.' In spite of their attachment to their traditional religion, it is obvious from al-Bakri's accounts that the kings of Ghana allowed freedom of religion and worship to the Muslims, and even went so far as to provide a mosque in their own part of the city for those Muslims who came to visit or do business with them.

Thus with a civil service, a strong monarchy, a cabinet, an army, an effective system of administering justice and a regular source of income, Ghana certainly presented, in the words of Davidson, 'the familiar picture of a centralised government which has discovered the art and exercise of taxation, another witness of stability and statehood'. Equally fascinating is the fact that many aspects of ancient Ghana's culture are virtually identical with those of the Akan of modern Ghana and so even if the Akan did not migrate from ancient Ghana, they can certainly claim to look upon her as their cultural ancestor.

The fall of Ghana

In spite of its splendour, opulence and wealth, evident by the middle of the eleventh century, the empire of Ghana had collapsed by the middle of the thirteenth. What then brought about its fall? The answers can be found in the weakness of the structure of the empire, the introduction of Islam into the Western Sudan, the impact of the activities of the Almoravids, and finally the defeat and conquest of Ghana, first by the Susu kings and then by those of Mali.

The first reason for the fall of Ghana was the weakness of its structure. The empire had no political, ethnic or cultural unity; it was made up of many states and peoples, and the kings of Ghana failed to weld them into a true nation-state. Different peoples such as the Soninke, the Susu, the Serer, the Berber and the Tukulor each with its own distinctive culture and language owed allegiance to the kings of Ghana. States which were conquered such as Takrur, Silla, Diara and Kaniaga were left under their own traditional rulers and were only expected to pay annual tributes and contribute contingents or levies to the kings of Ghana's army in times of war. As these conquered states and peoples were always anxious to regain their independence, the survival of the empire came to depend on the military strength of the central government of Ghana. It follows, therefore, that when that military power became weakened, the empire was bound to break up into its component parts. This was exactly what happened from the second half of the eleventh century onwards, owing first to the introduction of Islam into the Sahara and the Western Sudan, and secondly to the activities of the Almoravids.

By the middle of the eleventh century, though the rulers of Ghana themselves and a majority of their subjects had not embraced Islam, some of the rulers of the vassal states such as those of Silla, Diara and Takrur had. Some of the enterprising Soninke traders had also become Muslim. Thus, in addition to the division of Ghana into metropolitan Ghana and provincial Ghana, it was further divided into Muslim and non-Muslim vassal states, which further weakened the structure of the empire.

Another factor was the activities of the Almoravids, whose rise and development was mentioned in Chapter 2. The exact nature of Almoravid involvement in the collapse of the Ghana empire is one of bitter controversy among modern scholars, many of whom now contend that the Almoravids did not overrun the empire and capture its capital Kumbi Saleh but that they maintained an interdependent relationship with Ghana which was by no means always hostile.

However, even taking such arguments into account, we do know that in 1054 the Almoravids conquered Awdaghost in the north of Ghana's empire; this conquest alone must surely have weakened metropolitan control, encouraging other vassal states such as Takrur, Silla and Diara to break away.

Equally seriously, the activities of the Almoravids must have had a disastrous effect on Ghana's role in the trans-Saharan trade and on the revenue that both the rulers and many of their subjects derived from it. It used to be thought that the activities of the Almoravids caused a decline in the trans-Saharan trade, but recent research has shown that far from ruining the trade, the Almoravids rather increased it. However, because of the Almoravid capture of both Awdaghost and Sijilmasa the Almoravids and the Berbers rather than the Ghanaians must have been the main beneficiaries of the prosperous trans-Saharan trade. At the same time, because of the disturbances on the traditional Marrakesh-Wadan-Awdaghost route, trade shifted eastwards into the Sijilmasa-Taghaza-Walata route into the rapidly developing commercial centres first of Walata, and then Timbuctu, Mali, Gao and Jenne, and so beyond the control of the rulers of Ghana. Awdaghost, the great Ghanaian commercial centre, was replaced by Walata in importance, and by the time of al-Idrisi in 1154 it had become 'a small town in the desert with little water. Its population is not numerous and there is no large trade.' All this meant then that Ghana lost a great deal of the revenue that it derived from the trans-Saharan trade which could not but have had disastrous effects on its economy and military power.

However, perhaps the most immediate reason for the collapse of the empire were the defeats inflicted on Ghana first by the Susu rulers and then by those of Mali. In 1203, Sumanguru Kante, king of Susu – formerly a vassal state – conquered and reduced Ghana in turn to a tributary state. But the Susu empire itself had only a brief spell of life. In 1235, Sumanguru was killed by the ruler of Mali, another rising empire and five years later the capital city Ghana was razed to the ground by the Mali army.

Thus, divided by Islam, weakened politically and economically by the Almoravids, defeated first by the Susu and then by Mali, the ancient Empire of Ghana disappeared from the stage of imperial history. Its place had, by the middle of the thirteenth century, been taken by Mali whose evolution and development we will next consider.

24

4   The rise and fall of Mali

Mali seems to have started life as a small Mandingo or Malinke chiefdom called Kangaba by some historians. Its capital was the town of Jeriba situated near the junction of the river Sankarani and the Niger – not far from the modern town of Bamako. The evolution of this little principality from a group of independent families living in small villages, probably similar to those of the Tichit-Walata tradition, appears to have been completed by the tenth century. Let us first look at some of the reasons for its transformation into the centre of the Mali empire.

If you look at the map of the Western Sudan, you will see that Kangaba occupied an even more advantageous position geographically than ancient Ghana. It was situated right within the savanna belt and it controlled particularly the very fertile plains of the Sankarani river, a tributary of the Niger. This good position meant that the Malinke people of Kangaba could make their living and derive as much wealth from agriculture and fishing as from trade. Indeed, they became great farmers, cultivating millet, rice and sorghum which they exported to the people of the Sahel and the desert. The kings of Mali not only had their own farms, where slaves produced food for the royal household but they also obtained a profit on agriculture generally through taxation. Even more important, Kangaba was just on the edge of the gold-producing regions of Bure and Bambuk and its rulers soon succeeded in conquering these districts. Thus, while ancient Ghana never actually controlled the gold-producing regions, Mali had control over them right from the beginning of its rise, and the kings of Mali made good use of this advantage. Thirdly, because of their position, the Malinke of Kangaba became the greatest beneficiaries when the Akan and Lobi gold-fields to the south were opened by the Dyula in the thirteenth and fourteenth centuries. It is not surprising, then, that Mali was to become so fabulously rich by the middle of the early decades of the fourteenth century.

Without the trans-Saharan trade, however, the Malinke could not have made full use of these favourable natural resources. By the end of the twelfth century, the caravan trade had already been established and the Mandingo empire-builders must have enjoyed all the benefits that trade generated, and in view of their superior resources, made considerably more profit than the Soninke of Ghana ever did. A further benefit was the diversion of the trade traffic as a result of Almoravid activity (see Chapter 3), since the new, preferred routes terminated in Mali.

With all these advantages, it is not surprising that by the middle of the fourteenth century, four towns in Mali – Niani the capital, Jenne, Timbuctu and Gao, had become the main commercial centres of the Western Sudan. In 1353, Ibn Khaldun, the famous historian, met the King of Takedda, the copper-producing region, who told him that there passed through his city in that year a caravan of 12 000 loaded camels on its way to Mali. It was the same Ibn Khaldun who wrote that the capital of Mali was 'an extensive place, well-watered, cultivated and populated. It has brisk markets, and is now a stopping place for trading caravans from the Maghrib, Ifriqiya and Egypt. Wares are brought here from every country.'

Another important factor that contributed to the rise of Mali was the introduction of Islam. Unlike Ghana, Mali really started and ended as an Islamic or Muslim state. In its rise to power, therefore, Mali undoubtedly benefited from the new statecraft, the new system of administering justice and the literacy introduced into the Sudan by Islam. According to al-Umari, the kings of Mali had scribes and chancelleries and maintained correspondence with external powers obviously in Arabic, and if non-Muslim Ghana used educated Muslims as civil servants and ministers, it is obvious that Muslim Mali would have done so to an even greater degree. Finally, as we shall soon see, the royal pilgrimages had the effect of strengthening Mali as a Muslim state and as a centre for the propagation of Islam into Hausaland and areas to the south.

However, there is no doubt that the most important factors for the rise of Mali were political. First of all, the weakening of the Soninke of Ghana created a political vacuum which was only briefly filled by the Susu empire of Sumanguru Kante. The weakening of the Soninke also meant that the Malinke of Mali did not encounter any really strong resistance or opposition in their drive to control the commercially important Sahelian areas.

But even more important were the political conditions among the Malinke themselves. Mainly as a result of the trans-Saharan trade and, as the excavations of ancient Jenne have clearly shown, by the eleventh century, the Mandingo had formed a number of chiefdoms in the area to the south of the Soninke under various noble Malinke clans. Among them were Kiri ruled by the Traore, Do or Dodougon by the Konate, Sibi by the Kamara and finally Kangaba by the Keita. More important still, cutting across these political divisions, were the various hunters' associations among the Malinke. These associations were armed groups which could therefore be easily organised into a strong military force. Indeed, some of the earlier rulers of Kangaba used the hunters' associations in such a way that by the end of the twelfth century Kangaba had already become dominant among the other Malinke chiefdoms. This meant that any future ambitious ruler of Kangaba had the military basis for developing a large kingdom or empire.

The possibility of doing this was greatly enhanced by two other political factors, namely, the conquest and subjugation of the Malinke chiefdoms by Sumanguru Kante, the king of Susu and the emergence, first of Sundiata as king of Kangaba, and then two of his successors, Mansa Musa and Mansa Sulayman. After overthrowing ancient Ghana, Sumanguru Kante turned his attention to the Malinke chiefdoms, which he had conquered by the end of the third decade of the thirteenth century. His rule over the Malinke also turned out to be very tyrannical and oppressive. He is said to have imposed heavy taxes on the people and one report says that he deprived the Mandingo of 'their most beautiful women as well as their food and gold'. All of them therefore longed to regain their independence and were ready to revolt if a leader could be found.

The reign of Sundiata (1234–55)

A leader was indeed found in the person of Sundiata, or Mari Jata as he is known in oral sources. Tradition varies as to the reasons Sundiata left his home at the court in Niani and entered into exile; it may have been as a direct result of Sumanguru's invasion, or as an earlier reaction to rivalries within the royal family. Similarly we cannot be sure whether from his exile Sundiata personally resolved to exploit the favourable political conditions and convert the chiefdom of Kangaba into an empire, or whether as in some versions of the oral traditions of Mali, it was the hunters' associations of the Mandingo which planned the war of liberation against Sumanguru and invited Sundiata to lead it. Whatever the reason might have been, Sundiata returned to his state at the head of a strong army including a cavalry wing; with the assistance of the Malinke chiefs who hailed him as a saviour, he inflicted one defeat after another on the Susu and finally seized the throne of Kangaba.

According to Niane's transcription of the Sundiata' epic, after these initial victories, Sundiata assembled all the Malinke chiefs at Sibi at which unity against Sumanguru was confirmed. It was as the head of the army of this Malinke nation that he defeated and killed Sumanguru at the famous battle of Kirina in 1235. This battle assured the independence of the Malinke people. Again, following Niane's account, Sundiata convened another meeting at Kaba or Kangaba at which the Malinke chiefs recognised him as their sovereign ruler and swore the oath of allegiance to him; each of them then accepted his own chiefdom from Sundiata. After this great meeting, Sundiata moved to Niani which was then in ruins, but which he soon developed into the capital, first of the new united Malinke kingdom and then of the Mali empire.

Having thus created an independent and united Malinke kingdom, Sundiata embarked on a career of conquest. From Kirina, he pressed on and occupied what was left of ancient Ghana in 1240. Next, he turned south west to the gold-producing region of Bambuk which he conquered and continued westwards to defeat the king of the Jolof. By the end of his reign, Sundiata had extended the frontiers of the small chiefdom of Kangaba to include Ghana and the Western Sahel in the north, Upper Senegal and Gambia in the west, and the gold-producing regions of Bambuk and Bure in the south, and the middle Niger in the east.

Sundiata was not just a conqueror, but also an able administrator. He is said to have divided his empire into provinces and to have placed one of his generals in charge of each of them. He died in 1255 after having effectively established the empire of Mali.

Mansa Musa (1312–1337)

Between 1255 when Sundiata died and 1312 when Mansa Musa became king, there was a period of instability: continuity of rule within the royal family was broken and there were no less than seven accessions to the throne of Mali. So both the royal office and the central government of the empire must have been greatly weakened at the time of the accession of Mansa Munsa. The very fact that he was able to remain on the throne for twenty-five good years and he was smoothly succeeded first by his son Mansa Maghan, who reigned for four years, and then by his brother Mansa Sulayman, who reigned for twenty years (1341–1360) shows that Mansa Musa did succeed in establishing continuity and stability as well as respect for the institution of monarchy. This, surely, must be reckoned as his first political achievement.

His second political achievement was to maintain, strengthen and extend the empire that he inherited. It used to be thought that Mansa Musa extended the frontiers of the empire by conquering Walata, Timbuctu, Takedda and Gao. Recent research has shown conclusively that all these areas except the last were part of the empire before his accession to office, having been conquered either by Mansa Uli (1255–1270), the immediate successor of Sundiata, or by Sakura or by both of them. There is no doubt, however, that the control of the kings over these peripheral regions of the empire had become greatly weakened as a result of the instability at the centre.

What Mansa Musa did then was to use his army which was said to be 100 000 strong, (of which 10 000 were horsemen) to tighten the grip of the central government on the provinces to ensure peace and order and to reconquer those states such as Gao that had broken away during the period of instability. Mansa Musa is also reported by the contemporary writer al-Umari to have said that he had conquered twenty-four cities 'each with its surrounding districts and villages and estates'. If Mansa Musa was correct and was not merely boasting, then he must also have extended the frontiers of the empire most probably in the eastern and southern areas. Mansa Musa therefore not only strengthened the empire but brought it to its widest territorial extent.

His third political achievement was that he improved upon the administrative machinery of the empire. There were at least fourteen provinces in the south including the province of Mali, the chief province in which the king's capital Niani was situated. Most of the provinces, according to al-Umari, were ruled by governors or emirs (dya-mana-tigi) who were usually famous generals. Others, such as the Berber provinces, were governed by their own sheikhs. Some of the important commercial centres also had governors or farbas of their own. All these provincial administrators were responsible to the Mansa or King, and they were all well paid. Some were given fiefs while other received as much as 1 500 mithqals of gold every year, as well as horses and clothes.

With a view to obtaining more devoted service, Mansa Musa also instituted national honours, the highest being the National Honour of the Trousers. 'Whenever a hero adds to the list of his exploits,' Al-Dukhari, (who had lived in Niani during the reign of Mansa Musa and his successor), told Al-Umari, 'the king gives him a pair of wide trousers, and the greater the number of a knight's exploits, the bigger the size of his trousers. These trousers are characterised by narrowness in the leg and ampleness in the seat.'

Besides all this, Mansa Musa is said to have regularly invited and dealt with any complaints and appeals against oppression by the governors. His impartiality and great sense of justice were remembered and admired long after his death.

The other notable political achievement of Mansa Musa was the friendly relations he established with other African states especially with Morocco and

Egypt. Ibn Khaldun recorded that there were diplomatic relations and exchanges of gifts between Mansa Musa and the contemporary King of Morocco, Sultan Abu al-Hasan, and 'that high-ranking statesmen of the two kingdoms were exchanged as ambassadors'. Mansa Musa's successors maintained these contacts and exchanged gifts.

The empire of Mali enjoyed not only stability and good government under Mansa Musa but also commercial prosperity. As both the salt-producing regions and the gold districts came under its control, Mali naturally attracted traders from the north as well as from the south. Furthermore, the king's team of efficient governors and his strong army were able to maintain order even among the turbulent Berber of the south-western regions of the Sahara, so that traders and travellers could travel to and fro with ease and a sense of security. Thus, commerce became very brisk and traders from as far away as Egypt and Morocco could be found in the commercial towns of Mali, such as Timbuctu, Gao, and Niani the imperial capital.

Important as trade was, it must have been limited to a small percentage of the Malinke, most of whom were mainly engaged in agriculture, fishing and cattle-breeding. There were also castes or groups of people who specialised as blacksmiths, weavers and carvers. As specialists, agriculturalists and traders, the people of Mali became wealthy and enjoyed a high standard of living. They lived in good houses – their kings in palaces and the ordinary people in mud houses. Al-Umari has written an interesting description of the style of building in ancient Mali, and this sounds strikingly and fascinatingly similar to the indigenous style still in vogue on the west coast:

'Building is by means of clay, like the walls of the gardens of Damascus. They build up clay to the height of two-thirds of a cubit and then leave it till it dries. Then a like amount is added again and so on till the end. Their roofs are built of timber and reeds mostly in the form of circular domes or camel backs like vaults. The floors are earth mixed with sand.'

One of the reasons why Mansa Musa became so famous was his work in the religious field. Contemporary sources confirm that he was a very pious man and a great lover of virtue. Indeed, he is reported to have told the Egyptian tourist officer who took him round Cairo during his famous pilgrimage (1324–25) that he would hand over his throne to his son and return to Mecca to live near the sanctuary. Only death prevented him from fulfilling this wish. It is not surprising then that he devoted a great deal of his time to purifying, strengthening and spreading Islam in Mali.

The pilgrimage of Mansa Musa

About no other activity of Mansa Musa has so much been written as his pilgrimage to Mecca which lasted from 1324 to 1325. This pilgrimage, was undertaken on a scale unheard of before. Before setting off, Mansa Musa ordered provisions from all over the empire. According to al-Umari, he left Mali with the fantastic amount of 100 camel-loads of gold (Ibn Khaldun puts the figure at 80). Five hundred slaves were also said to have gone before the king, each carrying a gold staff weighing 4 lb. He also took with him thousands of his subjects including slaves to carry his personal effects, soldiers to protect the entire caravan and officials and dignitaries, as well as his senior wife who was attended by 500 slaves and maids.

Mansa Musa and his entourage and caravan left Niani, proceeded along the Niger to Mema and thence through Taghaza to Tuat and eastwards to Cairo which they entered in July 1324. They remained there for three months and then left for Mecca in September 1324. After staying there for about four months, Mansa Musa returned to Cairo, and then through Ghadames and Timbuctu to Niani. Though he took so much gold with him, Mansa Musa was so generous in Cairo and Mecca to rulers, officials, dignitaries and so on and he made so many purchases of his own that he ran out of money. Consequently, he had to borrow money at fantastic rates of interest before he could return home. Al-Umari, who visited Cairo twelve years later, wrote that Mansa Musa 'left no emir or holder of a royal office without a gift of a load of gold. He and his company gave out so much gold that they depressed its value in Egypt and caused its price to fall.'

However, the more interesting aspect of this rather extravagant pilgrimage was the effect that it had on Mansa Musa himself and on his state. First and foremost, the *hajj* definitely gave a great deal of publicity to Mali; the empire appeared for the first time on a European map, the 'Mappa Mundi' or 'Map of the World' drawn by Angelino Dulcert in 1339, (that is, only two years after the death of Mansa Musa) and on later maps too, it appeared in greater detail. Secondly, trade between Mali and Egypt increased. According to Ibn Khaldun, Egyptian traders frequented Mali after the pilgrimage; Mansa Musa and his entourage bought all sorts of goods while in Cairo and it is exceedingly likely that these commercial relationships with Egypt continued after Mansa Musa returned home.

Mansa Musa himself returned to Mali filled with a renewed determination to purify and strengthen Islam, to promote education and to introduce some of the new things that he had seen on his journey; to this end he brought with him religious scholars, missionaries and technical experts such as the Spanish scholar, poet, and architect called Abu Ishag al-Sahili, an Ismaili missionary al-Muammar, whom he met in Ghadames on his return journey and four sharifs of the Prophet's group (the *Quraysh*) from Mecca 'so that the people there would be blessed by their looking at them, and the country would be blessed by their footprints.'

He began his reforms by ordering that the five pillars of Islam should be strictly observed. To facilitate worship he commissioned the Muslim architect, al-Sahili, to build a number of mosques. The greatest of these was the Friday mosque at Timbuctu where al-Sahili settled and died in October 1346. It was probably Mansa Musa who ruled that the imams of that mosque should always be Sudanese, that is blacks. Al-Sahili also built a palace for Mansa Musa which was described by one of Ibn Khaldun's informers as 'a square building with a dome plastered over and covered with coloured patterns' so that it turned out to be the most elegant of buildings. It is generally admitted that al-Sahili's style of building influenced architecture in the Western Sudan. Mansa Musa also promoted Islamic learning by sending Malinke students to study in Fez, a practice which was continued by some of his successors. He also laid the foundation of what Timbuctu later became, the commercial and educational centre of the Western Sudan, not only by having the Friday mosque built there but also by attracting scholars.

Mansa Musa's achievements

So, despite the unprecedented extravagance of his pilgrimage, which must have caused unnecessary hardship in his own country, Mansa Musa is primarily remembered as a great ruler who succeeded in establishing peace and order in Mali, in promoting trade and commerce, in purifying and strengthening Islam and giving his state a decidedly Islamic atmosphere and outlook, and finally, in making the name of Mali known both in Europe and throughout the Muslim world. At the time of his death, the empire of Mali stretched from Takrur and the Gambia in the west to Gao and Tadmekka in the east and from the Sahel and Walata in the north to the Upper Niger in the south. His years were, indeed, the golden age of Mali. It is not surprising that after his death in 1337, his name was remembered and cherished for many centuries.

Mali after Mansa Musa

His immediate successor was Mansa Maghan who had a brief and uneventful reign from 1337 to 1341. Then Mansa Sulayman, Mansa Musa's brother, became king and he reigned till 1359. Fortunately for posterity, Ibn Battuta, the celebrated Arabic scholar and one of the greatest travellers of history, was sent by Abu Inan, Sultan of Morocco, to Mali in 1352–3, and he has left an eye-witness account of the empire. It is absolutely clear from his account as well as those of al-Umari, that Mansa Sulayman was another extremely competent, devout ruler and a worthy successor of Mansa Musa.

Ibn Battuta was also struck by the order and racial tolerance that prevailed in Mali, and the care with which the people observed prayers in the empire:

> The Negroes [that is the people of Mali] are seldom unjust, and have a greater abhorrence of injustice than any other people. Their Sultan shows no mercy to any one guilty of the least act of it. There is complete security in their country. Neither traveller nor inhabitant in it has anything to fear from robbers or men of violence.

Surely, this could be said of only very few contemporary European or Middle Eastern states in the middle of the fourteenth century.

The fall of Mali

During the latter half of the fourteenth century, the decline of the empire set in. This and its eventual collapse can be traced internally to the inordinate ambition, frivolity and incompetence of the ruling dynasty and the court of Mali, and externally to the attacks of the Mossi and Tuareg from the south and north respectively, and the rise of Songhai to the east.

The history of the kings of Mali from the end of the reign of Mansa Sulayman to the end of the fourteenth century was nothing but a record of assassinations, insurrections and coups d'état. Sulayman was succeeded by his son Qasa but the son of Magha I who had succeeded Mansa Musa, called Mari Djata, organised a rebellion against him. This led to a civil war which lasted nine months in which Qasa was killed. Mari Djata then became king and managed to remain on the throne for fourteen years. He was, however, a very extravagant, wicked and corrupt ruler who emptied the state treasury and, as Ibn Khaldun put it, 'nearly pulled down the structure of government'. He died of sleeping sickness in 1373 and was succeeded by his son, Mansa Musa II (1373–1387). Though he had the best of intentions, he was a very weak ruler and power was seized by one of his ministers who is said to have placed him under house arrest. In short, within the period of thirty years from 1360 to 1390, as many as seven rulers sat on the throne, three of whom were killed after a reign of a year or less each, clear evidence of instability, anarchy and weakness at the centre.

As one would expect, some of the vassal states such as the Soninke states of Diara, Diafunu and Meme, the Songhai state of Gao and the Wolof and Toro states, took advantage of the weakened power of Mali and broke away. Clearly, then, just as the Almoravid defeat of Ghana in 1076 signalled the disintegration of Ghana, so the struggle for power among the members of the ruling family and the courtiers heralded the disintegration of Mali.

Had Mali been left alone, perhaps yet another Sundiata or Mansa Musa or Sulayman would have emerged and rebuilt the fortunes of the state. But in the following century, Mali was attacked not by one but three different powers. During the first half of the fifteenth century, it was attacked from the north by the Tuareg and from the south by the Mossi. By 1433, Arawan and Timbuctu and other parts of the Sahel had been captured by the Tuareg, led by their famous king Akillu Akamalwal. At the same time, the Mossi raided the south-eastern districts of Mali, sacked Timbuctu and forced the representative of Mali there to escape; they also raided the Middle Niger and the Lake Debo area in 1430. In 1477, they attacked Masina and from there besieged Walata in 1480, where they were defeated in 1483 and driven back to their country by Sunni Ali. By the middle of the fifteenth century, Mali had lost virtually all its northern and Sahelian vassal states and with that lost its control over the trans-Saharan trade which further accelerated its decline. The final blow was, however, delivered by the new star that arose to the east of Mali. That new star was Songhai, and its rise and achievements are the subject of the next chapter.

5   The Songhai empire

The empire of Songhai, which replaced Mali during the second half of the fifteenth century, grew out of the kingdom of Gao or al Kawkaw founded by the Dia dynasty with Kukiya as its capital. This kingdom was founded by the Songhai at about the same time as the Soninke kingdom of Ghana, that is between 500 and 700 AD, probably in the seventh century. Writing in 947, the scholar al-Masudi refers to al-Kawkaw 'as the greatest of all the kingdoms of the as-Sudan' and adds that many kingdoms were dependent on Al-Kawkaw.

That al-Kawkaw should have emerged about the same time as Ghana should not surprise us, since both of them were essentially the products of the trans-Saharan trade in which both were involved at the same time. Besides the trans-Saharan trade, another factor accounting for its early formation was that al-Kawkaw, unlike Ghana but rather like Mali, arose in the fertile Sudan savanna area. The river on whose bank both Kukiya and the later capital, Gao, were situated also afforded excellent opportunities for fishing, and the Songhai made full use of these natural resources. By the time they entered the stage of history, they were already divided into three specialised professional groups: the Sorko, who were the fishermen and were mobile and warlike, the Gow or Gabibi, who were hunters and the Do who concentrated on agriculture, cattle-rearing and hunting. Thirdly, it has also been seen that a ruler of Gao was probably the first Sudanese or black ruler to embrace Islam. In its early development, therefore, al-Kawkaw must have greatly benefitted from all the new ideas and advantages that Islam introduced into the Western Sudan.

However, while its contemporary state, Ghana, had developed into a large empire by the middle of the eleventh century, Gao or al-Kawkaw was still a relatively small, homogeneous kingdom confined to the valley of the Niger around its two main towns of Gao and Kukiya. After the fall of the Soninke empire of Ghana in the thirteenth century, Gao still did not rise to prominence, but as we saw in the previous chapter, became a tributary state of Mali; it was not until the last quarter of the fourteenth century that Gao completely regained her independence.

The fascinating questions raised in the case of Songhai, then, are not, as in the case of Ghana and Mali, why an empire arose but rather why it did not rise to greatness until towards the end of the fifteenth century, and, secondly, why it also followed its predecessors into obscurity exactly a hundred years later.

The first obvious answer to the first question relating to the delay of Songhai's rise to greatness is the geographical position of the nucleus of the empire. As is evident from the map of the Western Sudan, though the Songhai of Kukiya lived in the Sudan savanna and therefore enjoyed all the advantages that the Malinke enjoyed, they were much further away from the gold-producing areas of Bambuk and Bure than both the Soninke of Ghana and the Malinke of Mali, and much further south of the meeting-point of the Sahara. Indeed, it was not until the extension of the trans-Saharan trade into Hausaland in the fourteenth and fifteenth centuries that Songhai became the focus of the trade routes from both the north-west and the north-east. Until the fifteenth century, then, the motivation for expansion could not have been as great among the Songhai as it was among the Soninke and the Malinke to the west and the Kanuri to the east.

Secondly, there was lack of continuity and stability at the centre in Songhai. Unlike Mali, and more notably the later Kanem-Borno states, Songhai had as many as three different dynasties. Such fundamental changes of the basis of power and authority could not but delay the process of political evolution or development.

Thirdly, it is clear from the available evidence that all the rulers of the second dynasty, the Sunni dynasty, were attached to their traditional religion more than to Islam, and paid far more attention to their idols, priests and diviners than to the Koran and the mallams. Indeed, they became known as magician-kings, and as Levtzion has pointed out: 'even after they had lost temporal power, the Sohantyr, descendants of Sunni Ali, retained their prestige as powerful magicians.' Sunni Ali himself, though generous to the Muslims, did not hesitate to punish or persecute them if they stood in his way. Throughout his reign, the traditional Songhai religion remained the basis of his authority, and it was only because Islam was gaining ground in the western part of his kingdom that Sunni Ali had to keep up an outward Muslim appearance by saying prayers, fasting and so on.

Thus, during the period of the Sunni rulers, Islam never became the religion of the state and could not therefore provide the stimulus or the state-building devices that it did for say Mali or Takrur, or, as we shall see later, for Kanem. It was not until the time of the third dynasty, the Askia dynasty, that Islam became the basis of the state religion and of royal authority, with consequences to be discussed later.

But probably the most important reason for the relatively late emergence of the Songhai empire was that the necessary political prerequisites or suitable conditions were lacking. As has already been indicated, from the eleventh until the fifteenth century, the Songhai were on the defensive; so preoccupied were they with remaining independent, first from the Soninke, then the Susu, and finally the Mandingo, that they were unable to embark on any wars of expansion. They regained their independence from Mali towards the end of the thirteenth century, thanks to the ability and bravery of two princes, Ali Kolen and his brother Salman (or Sulayman) Mari; according to al-Sadi's account, they escaped from the court of Mali, where they were being held as royal hostages, freed Gao from its vassal status, and founded the Sunni dynasty. But this period of independence was short-lived; probably by the beginning of the fourteenth century Mali was once again in control. Certainly this was the case when Ibn Battuta visited the Western Sudan in 1353. It was not until about twenty years later that the Songhai were able to finally overthrow the yoke of Mali and regain their independence.

However, it was not until the second half of the fifteenth century and the early decades of the sixteenth that they were able to convert their kingdom into the empire of Songhai. Why did they achieve what they had been unable to do all these five centuries? There are two main answers: the political conditions were suitable, and leaders with the necessary drive, ability and ambition emerged in the persons of Sunni Ali and Askia Mohammed.

As we have seen, though the Mali empire had collapsed by the end of the fourteenth century, up to the middle of the following century, no state had emerged to fill the vacuum created by Mali's collapse. Furthermore, in view of the raids of the Mossi up and down the Western Sudan and the oppression and extortions of the Tuareg rulers of Timbuctu and the other sahelian states, the people of the area must have been looking for a deliverer. Indeed, it was the people of Timbuctu who, feeling the Tuareg rule particularly unbearable, extended an invitation to the then Songhai ruler, Sunni Ali, to come to their rescue soon after he became king.

The reign of Sunni Ali (1464–1492)

Fortunately, like Sundiata in Mali, Sunni Ali who mounted the throne in 1464, had the courage, tact, shrewdness and ability to turn the political situation to his advantage and also to that of Gao. Having consolidated his position at home and built a strong army consisting of cavalry and infantry wings, and above all a very powerful fleet of ships manned by Sorko fishermen for use on the Niger, he embarked on a career of conquest. He first turned his attention northwards and using the invitation of the people of Timbuctu as an excuse, he marched on that town in 1469 and captured it without any difficulty. From there he invaded Azawad, north-east of Timbuctu in 1470. These two invasions ensured the security of the north-western regions.

From there, he turned south-westwards and attacked Jenne which was then a very prosperous commercial town as well as a great Muslim educational centre. He took that town in 1473, after a siege said by tradition to have lasted seven years, seven months and seven days. From Jenne, Sunni Ali attacked Mali itself, and annexed at least its province of Kata. In 1483, he succeeded in driving the Mossi out of the Walata-Baghana areas and chased them into their own country. He launched other expeditions westwards into Masina against the Fulbe. He then turned south-westwards and conquered the regions south of Timbuctu as far as the northern borders of Yatenga and attempted to subdue the Mossi. In November, 1492, Sunni Ali was returning from one of his campaigns in that region when he died in rather mysterious circumstances.

In extending the frontiers of his kingdom, Sunni Ali realised the need for an effective system of government. He divided his conquests into provinces. Over some of these provinces, he appointed new governors, but in districts where the rulers readily submitted, he left them in control provided they paid an annual tribute. He also appointed a commander-in-chief, or rather chief naval officer, called the *hi-koy*, for his fleet. For the administration of the turbulent Hombori region, that is the region to the south of Timbuctu and north of the Mossi kingdom, he created a special governor called the *tondifari*, a Songhai term meaning a governor of the mountains.

Sunni Ali was ruthless to anybody who tried to defy his authority. Thus, he is said to have murdered most of the clerics and scholars of Timbuctu, because, according to the *Tarikh as-Sudan*, Sunni Ali claimed that 'they were close friends of the Tuareg and that it was on this account he hated them.' On the other hand, he treated the scholars of Jenne who readily submitted, with marked generosity. Sunni Ali was said to have been particularly hostile to the Fulani. One chronicle relates that 'he hated no enemy more bitterly than the Fulbe [i.e. the Fulani], he could not see one, whether learned or ignorant, man or woman, without wanting to kill him. He admitted no Fulbe into the administration or judiciary. He so decimated the Sangara tribe [a Fulani group] that the remnant which survived could have been gathered under the shade of one tree.' This was most probably because of the fact that not only were the Fulani conducting raids but they would not acknowledge the jurisdiction of the empire into which they were steadily infiltrating. Furthermore, they dominated the vital Niger waterway between Timbuctu and Jenne.

Within a period of twenty-eight years, Sunni Ali converted the little kingdom of Gao into the huge empire of Songhai stretching from the Niger in the east to Jenne in the west, and from Timbuctu in the north to Hombori in the south. However, the Muslim Sudanese chroniclers were, not surprisingly, hostile in their tributes to Sunni Ali. One of them called him 'an impious monarch and horrible tyrant'; a second described him as 'a great oppressor and destroyer of towns, with a hard and unjust heart', and a third as, 'a sanguinary despot who slaughtered so many thousands of people that God alone knows their number; he was cruel to the pious and wise, he humiliated them and put them to death'. Such chronicles perhaps overlooked the fact that Sunni Ali laid the solid foundation on which his immediate successor, Mohammed Askia, was able to build a Muslim State.

At least one chronicler favoured Sunni Ali. 'He surpassed all the kings, his predecessors, in numbers and valour of his soldiery,' he wrote, 'his conquests were many and his renown extended from the rising to the setting of the sun. If it is the will of God, he will be long spoken of.' Sunni Ali was certainly long spoken of by the Sudanese scholars but, alas, not in complimentary terms. It is to be hoped that modern African scholars will be more generous to him for he was a clever politician, a brave soldier and an able administrator.

Askia Mohammed the Great

Sunni Ali died before he could complete the consolidation of his conquests and the establishment of an effective system of administration for his empire. Furthermore, his wars had greatly interrupted commerce, and Islam also suffered because of the treatment he gave to some of the devout Muslims and scholars. His successor, Mohammed Askia, then, had to complete his administrative work, pacify Timbuctu and exploit its strategic situation, strengthen and purify Islam, and revive trade and commerce dislocated by Ali's wars. Above all, he had to consolidate himself and his family on the throne. Mohammed Askia was not a member of the royal family of Songhai but rather one of Sunni Ali's senior commanders, who had come to the throne as a result of a coup d'état; he had organised this with the assistance of the pro-Muslim faction at the court against his master's son and successor, Abu Bakr Dao in April 1493. In his coup d'état, his closest ally was Mansa Kura chief of Bara, south-west of Timbuctu, while Sunni Dao was supported by the Dendi-Fari, the commander of the eastern part of Songhai. Thus the revolt could be interpreted as the revolt of the Islamised part of the empire west of Timbuctu against the eastern part of Songhai proper.

As one would expect, the first problem that Askia Mohammed tackled was that of strengthening his position on the throne and ensuring that his children, or family, would continue to rule in Songhai. First of all, he either killed or expelled from the empire the surviving members of the previous two dynasties, the Dia or Za and the Sunni dynasties. Mohammed Askia was so successful in this that the dynasty which he founded and which became known as the Askia dynasty, continued to rule in Songhai till the fall of the empire.

Next he tried to win the support and allegiance of the people. Mohammed naturally saw Islam as the alternative power base to traditional religions and did all he could to use it to win the allegiance and respect of the Songhai people and the scholars, to unify his kingdom and develop Timbuctu as a rival to Kukiya, the Traditional religious centre of the Songhai. Hence, immediately after his accession to the throne, he started courting the friendship of the mallams and devout Muslims whom his predecessor had persecuted. He showered gifts on them, especially those of Walata and Timbuctu, and appointed many of them as his advisers and courtiers.

More notably as if to remove any doubts about the change in royal attitude to Islam and the Muslims, he went on the pilgrimage to Mecca in October or November 1496, that is only three years after staging the coup, and returned in August 1498. The very fact he was able to leave for the pilgrimage and to stay away for two years shows quite clearly that he had firmly established his control over the state prior to his departure.

This pilgrimage was probably deliberately organised on a scale that surpassed that of Mansa Musa. Askia Mohammed was said to have been accompanied by 1000 infantry and 500 horsemen carrying 300 500 mithqals of gold. He spent this huge amount on alms, presents and on a hostel which he bought in Cairo for the use of Sudanese pilgrims.

The first and most important effect of this *hajj* was that it provided him and his dynasty with the very respect and legitimacy that he so urgently needed. He brought back not only the usual highly coveted title of *al-hajj* but he also acquired the even more valued *baraka*; he also acquired the unique title of Caliph of the Blacks (*Khalifatu biladi al-Takrur*) and its insignia, namely a green gown, a green cap, a white turban and an Arabian sword which became the insignia or emblems of the throne of Songhai from then on. Levtzion has pointed out the significance of the title: 'as a caliph, he became the acknowledged head of the community of believers in the Western Sudan, including the scholars of Timbuctu.' Furthermore, the *hajj* enabled Askia Mohammed to establish direct contact with some of the leading scholars of the day and to take advice from them. The best known of these was the distinguished scholar Jalal al-Din al-Suyuti whom he met in Cairo. The Songhai court also began to attract some of these scholars, notable among whom was, as we have seen already, Mohammed al-Maghili.

Finally, as was the case with Mana Musa before him, the *hajj* had a considerable effect an Askia Mohammed himself, and thus as the objectives of his government; it is significant that one of the very first things he did on his return home was to declare a *jihad* against the Mossi of Yatenga. To encourage the purification of Islam, he attacked illiteracy among the mallams, saw to it that the ritual prayers and other duties such as fasting and alms-giving were observed, and insisted that women should go about veiled, making his own family set the example. He also ensured that his officials imposed no illegal taxes, he appointed the first *qadi* of Jenne and established courts in other towns. All the chroniclers agree that Islam was greatly strengthened and purified during his reign. To quote one of them, 'He eliminated all the innovations, forbidden practices and bloodshedding characteristics of the Shi [i.e. Sunni Ali] and established Islam upon sure foundations.'

Equally memorable and successful was his encouragement of higher education. Scholars and professors, attracted by the peace and order of the empire as well as the generosity of Mohammed Askia, flocked into Timbuctu which became, during his reign, not only a commercial but also a great educational metropolis. The university, in the mosque of Sankore, produced many distinguished scholars; among them were the two great historians Mahmoud Kati and Abderahman As-Sadi on whose history books, the *Tarikh al-Fattash* and *Tarikh as-Sudan* we have been relying for the reconstruction of the history of Songhai. Mahmoud Kati himself had this to say of the intellectual life of his town, Timbuctu:

> In those days Timbuctu did not have its equal . . . from the province of Mali to the extreme limits of the region of the Maghrib for the solidity of its institutions, its political liberties, the purity of its morals, the security of persons, its consideration and compassion towards foreigners, its courtesy towards students and men of learning and the financial assistance which it provided for the latter; the scholars of this period were the most respected among the believers for their generosity, force of character and their discretion.

Leo Africanus's eyewitness account of the intellectual life of the city corroborates Mahmoud Kati's. 'Here are great stores of doctors, judges, priests and other learned men that are bountifully maintained at the king's cost and charges,' he wrote, 'and hither are brought divers manuscripts or written books out of Barbary, which are sold for more money than any other merchandise.'

It should be pointed out, however, that Mohammed Askia's work in the religious field was more effective in the western parts of the empire, and especially in Timbuctu, than in the eastern parts or the Songhai nucleus around Gao and Kukiya. Here traditional religion remained strong while in Gao itself, some non-Muslim practices and the traditional protocol were maintained. For instance, in Gao, people continued to throw themselves down before the Askia and cover their heads with dust.

Under the stimulus of the *hajj* and in pursuit of his personal and dynastic interests, Askia Mohammed also endeavoured to consolidate and expand the conquests of Sunni Ali and thereby completed the rise of the Songhai empire.

He began by creating a full-time professional army whose cavalry and infantry wings he greatly strengthened. The first people he attacked were the Mossi to the south; like his predecessors, he failed to defeat them, but he was able to strengthen the hold of Songhai on the southern regions. From the south, he turned eastwards and conquered the important commercial centre of Aîr in 1499–1500 and imposed an annual tribute on its rulers. He invaded Aîr again in 1516, and, to tighten his control over the area, left a Songhai garrison there and, most probably, an administrator too.

In the north, Askia Mohammed also consolidated Ali's conquests and extended Songhai's territories by conquering Baghana, the core of the ancient Ghana empire, and Taghaza, the important and lucrative caravan and salt-producing centre. The conquest of Taghaza made Songhai the first Sudanic state in the western area to extend that far north into the Sahara. Further conquerts to the west meant that, before the end of his reign, Askia Mohammed was able to convert the state that he inherited from Sunni Ali into the largest empire ever known in the Western Sudan, extending from Taghaza in the Sahara to the borders of the Mossi kingdoms in the south and from Aîr in the north-east to the Futa Toro in the region of the Senegambia in the south-west.

Mohammed Askia was also an excellent and shrewd administrator. According to Hunwick, in this area Askia Mohammed did not implement Islamic models but merely improved upon or expanded the existing traditional system. He divided his empire into provinces; each of these provinces was governed by a governor or *koi* or *fari*, who particularly in the western, Islamised provinces was very often a relative of Askia himself. He also appointed governors for the main towns of Timbuctu, Jenne, Masina and Taghaza, each entitled *mundyo*, as well as harbour-masters and customs officials for the ports of Gao and Kabara. He grouped the provinces into regions each under a regional commissioner or viceroy, who was again a relative – usually a brother or son. The ruler of the eastern province was the *dendi-fari* while that of the western province was *gurman-fari* or *kurmina-fari* with his seat at Tindirnia. Each was advised by a council of ministers. Thus, the *kurmina-fari* was advised by a council consisting of the *balama*, the commander of the Songhai forces in the west, the *binga-farma* and the *bana-farma*, all of whom were royal princes.

At the centre, Askia Mohammed established a council of ministers to assist him in all aspects of government. Most of these central posts were filled with people who were either from his own family, or who had married into it, and he could depose any of them at any time. This was also true of the military chiefs included in the council.

To meet the cost of an administrative machinery of this magnitude and complexity as well as a standing army, Mohammed Askia had reliable sources of income. The most important of these sources were the royal estates established throughout the empire and worked by slaves under the supervision of estate managers. Each had to produce a fixed quantity of a particular commodity per year; some had to produce corn, or rice, and others bales of dried fish, for example. He also had certain groups of slaves who were craftsmen and had to produce a fixed number of, say, boats, spears, or arrows per year. For example, the Dyam Tene and Dyam Wali peoples had to supply the king with 100 spears and 100 arrows per family per year. All these provisions and equipment were used to maintain the army and the surplus was sold. Other sources of income consisted of tribute from vassal states, regular contributions from the generals who obtained their revenue from taxes on peasants and farmers, and, above all, customs duties.

To ensure maximum income from tolls and customs duties, Mohammed Askia and his civil servants did everything to promote trade and commerce. He made the routes safe by rigidly controlling the troublesome Tuareg. Furthermore, he unified the system of weights and measures throughout the empire, and appointed inspectors for all the important markets. His creation of a professional standing army also made it possible for the civilians to participate fully in commercial activities. The result of these measures was that trade boomed.

The commercial activities of Songhai were centred on its three main cities. These were Jenne, the centre for the internal commerce, Timbuctu, which controlled commercial relations with the west and north-west, and Gao, which served the regions to the east and north-east like Kano, Tripoli and Egypt. These towns also became important centres of industry. There were as many as twenty-six *tindi* or tailors' shops in Timbuctu alone, each of which had between fifty and a hundred apprentices.

Leo Africanus has left us eyewitness accounts of both Timbuctu and Gao. Of Timbuctu, he wrote: 'here are many shops of artificers and merchants and especially of such as weave linen and cotton cloth. And thither do the Barbary merchants bring cloth of Europe. The inhabitants and especially the strangers there residing are exceedingly rich, in so much that the king is now married both his daughters unto two rich merchants.' He also described Gao as a town full of 'exceedingly rich merchants and hither continually resort great store of Negroes which buy cloth brought out of Barbary and Europe. It is wonder to see what plenty merchandise is daily brought thither, and how costly and sumptuous all things be'.

The main exports of Songhai remained the traditional ones of gold, ivory and slaves, while her leading imports were salt from Taghaza, and horses from North Africa. The medium of exchange was the usual cowries, though Leo Africanus noticed that gold coins without any stamp or superscription were in circulation in Timbuctu.

It should be obvious from the above that Askia Mohammed succeeded in completing the establishment of the empire of Songhai and in strengthening and spreading Islam, in promoting learning and education, and in promoting the peace and trade of the empire. He certainly deserves the title of 'the Great'. But alas, by the end of the sixteenth century this great empire had completely collapsed, for reasons we shall next discover.

The fall of Songhai

In the first edition of this book, the present writer came to the conclusion that the fall of Songhai was 'essentially due to external rather than to internal factors, that is, to the Moroccan invasion at the end of the sixteenth century, and not to her internal decline.' From the new evidence now available, this conclusion needs some revision. It seems obvious now that the fall of

Songhai, rather like that of Mali, was due as much to internal as to external factors, that is, as much to the internal decline of the empire as to the Moroccan invasion at the turn of the sixteenth century.

The first principal reason for the fall of the empire was the lack of an effective rule of succession to the throne, which led to periodic outbreaks of revolts, plots, depositions, assassinations and murders. It appears that every child of an Askia could succeed him. In Songhai, however, it appears that from the time of Askia the Great, the *kurmina-fari* was recognised as second to the Askia in the Songhai hierarchy, and should by convention succeed. Unfortunately, as the regional commissioner of the western province based at Tindirnia far to the south-west of Timbuctu, the *Kurmina-fari* was almost always out of Gao on the death of the reigning Askia; so before he could reach Gao the other princes and court dignitaries had chosen an alternative successor. Thus, only two *kurmina-fari* ever became Askia while three others merely led their armies to Gao in an unsuccessful bid to seize the throne. On the other hand, four *fari-mondyo*, who were always the senior princes in Gao, became Askia.

The second reason was the inordinate ambition of many of the children of Askia Mohammed and his brothers. Some of them even deposed their famous father who was then blind and very old in 1528. But Askia Mohammed's son and successor, Musa, the *fari-mondyo*, was assassinated only three years later to be succeeded by Askia's nephew Askia Bankouri or Bankan who was in turn deposed with the help of the viceroy of Dendi province in 1537. He was replaced by Ismail, another son of Askia Mohammed, who unfortunately died in 1539.

The period 1539 to 1587 was one of stability and saw the rule of only two people, both sons of Askia Mohammed, namely, Askia Ishaq I who reigned from 1539 to 1549 and Askia Daud from 1549 to 1582. Daud was a particularly efficient and brilliant ruler and was able to restore Songhai to the earlier peak of its power and prosperity. However, as soon as Daud died, the usual power struggles resumed. Daud's son and successor, al-Hajj, was deposed after four years in 1586 by his own brothers, to be succeeded by one of them, Mohammed Bani, who died in 1588.

The third internal weakness was of course the division of the empire into the Muslim west and the traditional and non-Muslim east, or Songhai proper. It may be recalled that Askia Mohammed staged his coup with the help of the western provinces. During his rule, those provinces became even more Islamised while the eastern part or nuclear Songhai remained under the control of the non-Muslim traditional aristocracy. Even the administration of the two areas was different; while all the important offices of governor and viceroy in the western area were filled by royal princes or brothers and cousins of Askias or local rulers married invariably to the daughters of either the Askias or the *kurmina-fari*, those of the traditional eastern areas were filled by and large as in the pre-Askia days by former slaves or non-royal dignitaries including even the very important offices of *dendi-fari* and the *hi-koi* – the commanders of the eastern region and the fleet respectively. The eastern part of the empire ruled by non-royals, always remained loyal to the reigning Askia, but the western part, regardless of its Islamic ties, was open to the personal ambitions of the royals who ruled it, namely the sons and brothers of the Askia.

This division and the internal weakness of the empire came to a climax during the civil war which broke out in 1588. On the death of Askia Bani after only a two-year reign the officers of the court at Gao selected Ishaq, a son of Askia Daud, as Askia, while the army of the western province, led by its commander and most of the chiefs of the province as well as the scholars and merchants of Timbuctu, proclaimed Sadiq, the *kurmina-fari* and another son of the same Askia Daud as their Askia. The inevitable civil war between the two sides took place in April 1588 and ended in a total defeat of the western forces. Askia Ishaq II then went on to depose all the chiefs of the western province and appointed new ones.

The civil war of 1588 hastened the fall of the empire in three main ways. In the first place, the Songhai army was greatly weakened as thousands of soldiers – more than half its total strength – together with most of the leaders of the western part of the empire, were killed. Ishaq II's victory therefore was a typical example of a pyrrhic victory, that is one in which the victors lose more than the losers. Secondly, the civil war hardened the division of the empire into east and west with the latter very much weakened and obviously full of a spirit of revenge and uncooperation. Thirdly, and the most serious effect of all, the civil war actually precipitated the final invasion of the empire.

For several years now, Sultan al-Mansur of Morocco had been planning an invasion, not only of Songhai but the whole of the Western Sudan, with a view to getting control of the trade routes and the sources of the gold supplies flowing northwards, and establishing a large African empire. As early as 1583, therefore, he had planted a spy at Gao who returned to Morocco in April 1589 with a full account of the bitter civil war and its consequences. The spy was accompanied by a brother of Ishaq II who is alleged to have appealed to al-Mansur to assist him to overthrow his brother. All this must have convinced al-Mansur that the time was opportune for an invasion of Songhai, for in October 1590, he gave the order to his army to march across the desert to Songhai.

Remembering the failure of two earlier expeditions in 1584, al-Mansur took no chances in 1590. The army consisted of 4 000 men carefully selected for their discipline and courage, and 600 engineers. Only 1 500 were Moroccans; the rest were all hardened Andalusian or renegade mercenary soldiers from Spain, Portugal and Turkey. Their commander was Judar Pasha, a young Spanish eunuch in the employment of the Sultan.

The invading force left Morocco on 16 October 1590, successfully crossed the desert at some cost, and reached the Niger at Bamba, half-way between Timbuctu and Gao, in February 1591. Askia Ishaq II hurriedly raised an army, composed, according to al-Saadi, of 18 000 cavalry and 9 700 infantry and courageously marched to meet the invaders. At the battle of Tondibi, thirty-five miles from Gao on 13 March 1591, the relatively large army of Ishaq was completely defeated and routed. The Moroccans pressed on and seized Gao without a blow and then marched north-westwards and occupied Timbuctu. This great town was thoroughly sacked in 1593 when the inhabitants revolted against the oppressive demands and taxes of the Moroccans. Many of the scholars and their families were sent in chains to Marrakesh, among them Ahmed Baba, the famous scholar and writer.

Why was the Songhai army so easily defeated? The first reason was the divided and weakened state of the Songhai army as a result of the devastating civil war of 1588 only three years before the battle of Tondibi. In contrast, the Moroccan army was a well-trained and well-disciplined army full of hardened professional fighters. However, the most important reason was the superior technology of the Moroccan army. Of the 4 000 soldiers, 2 000 were each armed with an arquebus (an early type of portable gun supported on a three-legged stand), 500 were mounted gunmen and there were in addition 70 European musketeers. Their baggage included 31 000 pounds of gun-powder and a similar weight of lead carried by 800 camels. The Songhai army, on the other hand, was armed simply with bows and arrows, spears, swords and clubs. Assuming that even half the number of the Moroccans perished en route-and according to Mahmoud Kati, the Moroccan army was only 1 000 strong at the battle of Tondibi-armed as it was with guns and muskets, it could easily rout any force armed as the Songhai army was. Indeed, so shocked and terrified were the Songhai by the noise and the smoke made by the guns which they had never heard or seen before that they simply fled in all directions and later gave the name 'Ruma' (meaning shooter) to the Moroccan soldiers, a name by which the descendants of the soldiers in the region of Timbuctu are known to this day.

However, it should be pointed out that when it had recovered from the first shock and panic, the Songhai army bravely put up some resistance. It deposed the demoralised Ishaq II and enthroned Askia Kagho, who bravely took the field and, using guerilla tactics, harassed the Moroccans. Indeed, so troublesome did he become that the Moroccans resorted to treachery to get rid of him. They summoned him to what was described as peace talks and then murdered him and his followers in cold blood. But this did not end the resistance of the Songhai. Askia Nuh succeeded his elder brother and kept the guerilla struggle going in the regions of Dendi and Borgu. He inflicted a number of defeats on the Moroccans, in one of which their commander was killed. In 1595, Askia Nuh was deposed and after three short reigns Harun Dankatiya emerged as Askia. He intensified the resistance against the Moroccans and between 1604 and 1617 even assumed the offensive. But by that date the great Songhai empire had completely disintegrated. The section of the empire from Jenne to Gao had been brought under the domination of the Moroccans and the great Songhai empire had become a province of the empire of al-Mansur, the Sultan of Morocco, while the remaining part in the area of Dendi had broken up into independent chieftaincies.

6 The nineteenth-century jihads

The history of the Western Sudan during the first half of the nineteenth century was dominated by three Islamic revolutions or *jihads* (holy wars). These revolutions broke out in Hausaland in 1804, in Masina in 1818 and in the Futa Jallon area in 1851 under the leadership of Usuman dan Fodio, Seku Ahmadu or Ahmad Lobbo and al-Hajj Umar Tall respectively. These revolutions broke out for three main reasons. The first was the religious conditions in the world of Islam in general and in the Western Sudan in particular by the beginning of the nineteenth century. The second was the political and social conditions in the Western Sudan about the same time, and the third lay in the individual activities of the various leaders.

After its rapid expansion in the period up to the end of the sixteenth century, Islam was put on the defensive throughout the world as a result of the growth of European power and Christianity overseas. The eighteenth century saw a determined effort to revive Islam beginning with the rise of the fundamentalist Wahhabi movement in Arabia. One consequence of this was the revival of the old Islamic orders or brotherhoods such as the Khalwatiyya and the Qadiriyya, and, the rise of a new one, the Tijaniyya.

Moreover, there was a widespread belief throughout the Muslim world that a *Mahdi* or saviour would be coming during the thirteenth Islamic century which was from November 1785 to November 1882. This belief raised a general air of expectation among Muslims throughout the world and made them more ready than otherwise to accept anyone who could convince them that he was either the *Mahdi* or his forerunner. It was the spread of these revivalist activities and these expectations of a *Mahdi* in the late eighteenth century that contributed to the outbreak of the *jihads* in question.

There is no doubt that the state of Islam in the Western Sudan by the end of the eighteenth century called for some revival and purification. In the first place, in spite of the spread of Islam in the Western Sudan, there were still whole areas such as the Mossi country, Borgu, Nupe and Adamawa which had not been touched by Islam. Even in the Muslim states, Islam was still largely a religion of the towns, the ruling group and the rich merchants. In large parts of the rural areas farmers and herdsmen were resistant to conversion, and it was to these people that the jihadists particularly appealed. Furthermore, though most of the ruling dynasties especially the Hausa states of the Western Sudan were Muslim, Islam sat very lightly on them, and all sorts of un-Islamic and unorthodox practices such as illegal taxation, enslavement of Muslims and unlawful seizure of property were going on. Among the Hausa, goddesses such as Uwandowa (goddess of hunting) and Uworgona (of agriculture) were still being worshipped, while belief in black magic was widespread. Indeed, Islam in Western Sudan in general and in Hausaland in particular, was in a state in which Islamic and indigenous

African religious customs and practices were existing side by side or in a mixed form. Thirdly, though learning and education did not die out in the Western Sudan in the eighteenth century, it is nevertheless true that the tradition of scholarship had declined. Some of the mallams could not even read the Arabic language, the language of the Koran.

This situation would probably have remained unchanged but for two factors, namely, the revival of the Qadiriyya in the Western Sudan during the second half of the eighteenth century, and the introduction of the Tjaniyya in the nineteenth century. The Qadiriyya had been introduced to the area in fifteenth century by the Kunta. At the start of the eighteenth century, however, it was in decline until under the leadership of Sidi al-Mukhtar al-Kunti (1729–1811) it underwent a revival. The ideas and books of the Qadiri leader greatly influenced the jihadists of the nineteenth century. Furthermore, his active teaching, writing and preaching gave a great stimulus to Islam, renewed interest in mystical studies and generated intellectual and ideological excitement. His revival of the Qadiriyya also strengthened the belief in the coming of a Mahdi and aroused great expectations in the Western Sudan.

The other factor which contributed to the outbreak of the *jihads*, especially that of al-Hajj Umar Tall, was the introduction of the Tijaniyya. This order, which was founded in Fez in North Africa in the late eighteenth century by Sidi Ahmed al-Tijani (1737–1815), was even more militant and insisted on an even stricter observance of the details of Islamic principles than did the Qadiriyya. It also taught that salvation came not through study and intellectual activity, as the Qadiriyya insisted, but through action, strict observance of the moral code of Islam and a vigorous pursuit of the spread of the faith. Since it emphasised action rather than study, and insisted that all members of the order were equal and that there was no elite, the new order appealed more to the ordinary people than the Qadiriyya, and, as such, had more potential as a mass movement.

However, the religious situation alone cannot explain the outbreak of the successive nineteenth-century *jihads*. The political and social conditions made that outbreak more or less inevitable. Politically, by as late as the beginning of the nineteenth century no single large centralised state or empire had emerged in either the area west of the Niger Bend or in Hausaland and it was obvious that sooner or later this political vacuum had to be filled.

Even more positive were the social conditions in the Western Sudan. One of the fascinating things about the Islamic revolutions that occurred both in the eighteenth century and in the early decades of the nineteenth, was that they were nearly all led by Fulani people who belonged to one single clan, namely, the Torodbe or Toronkawa clan. Why the Fulani in general and the Torodbe in particular should play such a decisive role should not surprise us. The Fulani originated in the area of the Senegambia and began to spread slowly eastwards. They entered Hausaland in two groups, the cattle Fulani, *Fulanin Bororo*, and the *Fulanin gida* or town Fulani in the fifteenth century. Their eastward migration continued and by the eighteenth century, they had reached the Benue-Adamawa regions. The cattle Fulani were still living in the rural areas, while the *Fulanin gida* lived in the towns, some were at the courts of the rulers employed as civil servants, tutors and diplomats, while others were engaged in commerce and in industry. By the eighteenth century, a third group had emerged, the Torodbe or Toronkawa clan. This clan was made up of those who had become specialist in Islamic learning and religion, education, law and administration. Most of them did not live in the town or enjoy the patronage of the kings, but had founded their own settlements or religious centres in the rural areas where they earned their living as writers and teachers. From there, they went to preach among the rural folk, especially the pastoralists and the peasant farmers. By the beginning of the nineteenth century, such communities led by members of the Torodbe clan were found throughout the Western Sudan, all preaching reform and criticising the rulers for their un-Islamic activities. More fanatical in their religious beliefs and practice, better educated and not without contempt for those people among whom they lived and served, the Fulani posed a serious question in the Western Sudan. This question was how long the Fulani in general and the Torodbe in particular were going to remain in this subordinate position taking orders from their lukewarm Muslim and illiterate or totally non-Muslim kings.

It was not the Fulani alone who were restless. Many of the rulers of the Western Sudanese states, especially the Hausa and Bambara kings, were certainly tyrannical, and neglected to administer justice impartially or in accordance with Islamic law. The ordinary people, whether Hausa, Songhai or Bambara, were therefore also feeling rebellious. Above all, the slaves who formed a very large percentage of the population of Hausaland in particular were all feeling very oppressed and were also ready to revolt. It is to these oppressed and disgruntled classes that, as we shall see, the leaders of the *jihad* particularly appealed.

With these prevailing conditions, all that was needed was a spark to set things ablaze; this was provided by the appearance of men filled with the religious zeal and the reformist ideas of the day and with the ability to provide the necessary ideology, leadership, and organisation. Such men did appear during the first half of the nineteenth century in the persons of Usuman dan Fodio, Seku Ahmadu or Ahmad Lobbo and al-Hajj Umar Tall and it was the activities of each one of them that precipitated each of the revolts and determined its nature.

The Sokoto jihad

The first of these nineteenth-century revolutionary leaders was Usuman dan Fodio. Born at Maralta in Gobir to an old scholarly family of the Toronkawa in December 1754, he studied under various scholars including Alfa Nuhu who initiated him into the Qadiriyya order and Jibril b. Umar, of Agadez who belonged to the Wahhabiyya order. At the early age of twenty, he started his career as a *shehu*, the Hausa word for *Sheikh* meaning teacher, writer and preacher, at Degel. From there he went on missionary tours throughout Hausaland, and especially to the rural areas of Zamfara, Kebbi and Daura. In his preaching and in his numerous writings, Usuman dan Fodio attacked all the unorthodox practices that were going on, condemned corrupt and unjust governments and illegal taxes, advocated education for women, and insisted on complete acceptance of the spiritual and moral values of Islam. It is

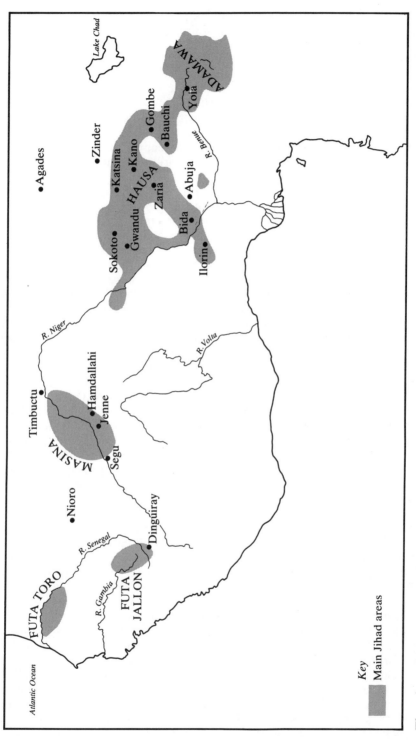

The nineteenth-century *Jihad* movements

important to note that he wrote both in prose and verse and not only in Arabic but also in Fulani and Hausa with a view to reaching the ordinary people who could not understand Arabic. All this won him a very large following, some of whom believed that he was the Mahdi. However, according to Hiskett he himself claimed rather to be the *mujaddid* – 'the Renewer' sent by God to prepare the way for the coming of the Mahdi. He appears to have won the support of Sultan Bawa of Gobir with whom he signed an agreement. Under this agreement Muslims were granted freedom of religion, exemption from unIslamic taxes, the release of Muslim prisoners from jail, and freedom for the Muslim men to wear turbans and the women to wear veils, both of which became the hallmark of members of the *shehu*'s community or followers.

However, after Bawa's death in 1790 and that of his successor in 1794–5, the next king, Nafata, was alarmed by the growing size of dan Fodio's following and under pressure from the aristocratic group, began to take measures against them. He ordered that nobody but dan Fodio was to preach, that there were to be no more conversions to Islam and that those who were not born Muslim were to return to their former religions.

Nafata died shortly after this (1802) but his successor, Yunfa, was even more determined to check the growing power of dan Fodio. According to some sources, Yunfa invited dan Fodio to his court and there attempted to murder him, but failed. Yunfa then went on to attack and capture some of Usuman's followers led by Abdul Salame in December 1803, and when Usuman caused the captives to be released at Degel and repeatedly refused to hand them over, Yunfa threatened to attack Degel itself. This threat led to the flight (*hijra*) of dan Fodio and his followers from Degel to Gudu on 21 February 1804, a date still honoured in northern Nigeria. At Dugu, he raised the standard of revolt by attacking the nearby towns of Gobir, and then having been proclaimed *Amir al-muminin*, Commander of the Believers, he proclaimed a *jihad* or holy war against the rulers of the Hausa states. Various Fulani rose up in rebellion in the other states and came to ask for flags from *Shehu* Usuman. Within a decade, all the Hausa *bokwoi* or principal states had been conquered and in the next two decades Nupe, parts of the Oyo empire (Ilorin) and Borno (Katagum and Gombe) were added to the Fulani empire with its new capital of Sokoto.

This revolt raises two questions. The first is why the Hausa states were so easily defeated. The answer to this is that, firstly, all the Hausa states were in a state of decline by the beginning of the nineteenth century mainly because of the internecine wars that had raged between them throughout the eighteenth century, leaving behind an atmosphere of mutual mistrust and animosity among the rulers. Secondly, while the Hausa kings could not count on each other, they could not count on all their subjects either. Many of these people had been alienated by the very high taxation, arbitrary imprisonment, injustice and the oppressive rule of their kings and they therefore looked to Usuman as a deliverer and rushed to support him.

One of the most important reasons for dan Fodio's success and the rulers' defeat, however, was undoubtedly the wholehearted support that the former received from his own kith and kin, namely the Fulani. Of the fourteen generals who rushed to Usuman for a flag and led the revolt in their respective states, thirteen were Fulani. Most of these flag-bearers were also of the Torodbe clan or were well educated. Secondly, the overwhelming majority of Usuman's army consisted of the Fulani pastoralists. A recent authority has estimated this majority as high as eighty per cent. Though they had their own grievances, particularly over the cattle-tax or *jangali*, the fact that so many of them joined Usuman's side may have been due to their identity with a general Fulani cause. Indeed, it is because of this overwhelming support given to Usuman by the Fulani and because of the fact that leadership was concentrated in the hands of the Fulani that this revolt has been considered by some scholars to some extent as a Fulani national revolt.

The fourth and certainly another important reason was the zeal and determination with which Usuman was able to infuse his followers by his preaching, coupled with the military ability of Abdullahi and Bello, his brother and son respectively. It is interesting to note that the Fulani failed to conquer Borno, where they encountered a leader in the person of al-Kanemi, who was able to provide the same sort of inspiration and leadership.

Usuman's jihad had far-reaching consequences both inside and outside Hausaland. Politically, it led to the establishment of a single Fulani empire in place of the many competing states in Hausaland. A second major consequence was that the most important political offices in Hausaland were now opened to scholars whereas before they had been occupied solely by the nobility. Most of the emirs of the new states within the empire, for example, were well-educated Muslim scholars. Outside Hausaland, as will be seen below, it contributed directly to the outbreak of the *jihads* of Seku Ahmadu and al-Hajj Umar in the regions west of the Niger bend. In Borno, it brought about the end of the old Sefawa dynasty and the emergence of a new dynasty, the Kanemi dynasty, founded by the son of al-Kanemi, which has been ruling Borno to this day. Finally, in Yorubaland, the *jihad*, as we shall see, contributed to the collapse of the Oyo empire and the conversion of the northern part into the Ilorin emirate.

The second consequence was economic. The establishment of a uniform system of government in place of the many competing ones meant a considerable reduction in the internecine wars that had characterised the history of the Hausa states in the eighteenth century. Peace and order reigned in most parts of the Fulani empire especially between the 1820s and 1850s and this greatly stimulated agricultural and industrial activities. Trade therefore boomed, as is borne out by the accounts of the European explorers who visited Hausaland during that period. With the partial destruction of Katsina during the wars, Kano took its place as the leading industrial and commercial metropolis of Hausaland.

From a social point of view the revolution brought about a great revival and spread of Islam which in turn meant a great stimulus to education, learning and the Qadiriyya order in Hausaland. Areas like Bauchi and Adamawa became converted for the first time. Furthermore, at least the first generation of emirs led by Mohammed Bello were sincere devotees who established true Islamic judicial, political and social institutions. Usuman, his brother Abdullahi and his son Bello were all very great scholars and wrote a large number of books mainly as textbooks for the guidance of their officials and followers. Their literary activities touched off a veritable renaissance in Hausaland. If today, Islam is a force to reckon with in Nigeria – and indeed in the Sudanese states of Senegal, Mali, Niger and even Guinea – it was because of the revolutionary Islamic movements of the late eighteenth and nineteenth centuries in general, and that of Usuman dan Fodio in particular.

The Masina jihad

Seku Ahmadu was born in 1775 of Fulani parents and studied under many scholars, including Usuman dan Fodio. He became as determined as his teacher to contribute to the revival and purification of Islam in accordance with the tenets of the Qadiriyya order, to which he belonged. Like Usuman dan Fodio, he claimed to be a *mujaddid*. As Hiskett has recently pointed out: 'in common with other West African jihadists before and after him, [Ahmadu] was affected by the climate of messianic expectancy in the Islamic world of the eighteenth and nineteenth centuries, and was able to exploit it.'

He began teaching and preaching near Jenne as early as 1797. He accused the Fulani clan leaders of unIslamic practices, such as drinking alcohol and idol worship, and he promised the oppressed a new and just society based solely on the rule of Islamic law. His activities and his growing following antagonised the Fulani clan and other leaders who appealed to their Bambara overlords to attack him. Seku Ahmadu therefore, like dan Fodio, performed the *hijra*, in 1818 and according to the latest authorities he sent envoys to the *shehu* to declare his allegiance to him and to ask for a flag. However, before the return of these envoys, Seku Ahmadu declared his *jihad* in 1818 and defeated the Bambara rulers at the decisive battle of Moukouma in March 1818. He then went on to conquer and annex Segu, Kaarta, the Songhai and Tuareg principalities and finally, in 1828, Timbuctu. He converted all these conquered states into the new empire of Masina for which he built a new capital, Hamdallahi, in 1821. He kept this empire intact till his death in 1844. Seku Ahmadu was so successful because of the support he was initially given, first and foremost by virtually all the Fulani, then the other oppressed classes, such as the slaves, and finally the Qadiri Kunta family of Azawad and Timbuctu.

The system of administration devised by Seku Ahmadu for his new state was even more closely based on Islamic law (the *sharia*) than that of Usuman dan Fodio. At the head of the empire he took for himself the title of *Amir al-Muminin* and ruled with the assistance of a Council of Forty. Members of this Council included many noted scholars or clerics, mostly Fulani, who were all expected to live in the capital city as an ideal Islamic community. The Council was responsible for the religious and moral matters of the state, taxation, civil appointments and the army. Seku Ahmadu then divided his empire into five provinces, over each of which he appointed an emir who was either a well-educated member of his family or a close associate. These emirs were responsible to the Council. In each province, a hierarchical structure on strict Islamic lines down to the village level was established. Particularly important in this set-up were the judges, who were expected to administer justice in strict accordance with Islamic laws.

All aspects of life in the empire were rigidly organised and controlled in accordance with the tenets of the Quran and the *sharia* as interpreted by the Qadiriyya. To promote Islam and religious worship, mosques were built and free education with examinations for the young was provided by the state.

Funds were also provided by the government for the support of widows, orphans, the aged, pilgrims and people who could not pay their debts. Alcoholic drinks and smoking were prohibited as well as music, dancing and the importation of dyed cloth to ensure a modest and austere style of living. A censor or inspector of public morals was appointed to promote the honesty and morality of the people, to see that no one had more than four wives, and to inspect weights and measures, which were standardised throughout the state. Again, to facilitate the provision of religious and educational services as well as administration and taxation, the nomadic mode of living was discouraged and the Fulani and other nomads were settled in specially-built quarters in existing towns or villages or in completely new towns.

In accordance with the Islamic obligation of the holy war and the spreading of the peace of Islam, Seku Ahmadu and his officials paid a great deal of attention to the army and military matters. A standing force of horsemen was maintained with horses and weapons provided by the state. In addition, every adult male – whether slave or free – was liable for service in a seasonal force. Under the command of the military leaders most of whom were appointed from within Seku Ahmadu's family the army was responsible for the defence of towns and cattle grazing in the surrounding countryside.

The economy of the state continued to be based on cattle-rearing, the only change being that the nomads were replaced by special herdsmen, employed to move the cattle to and fro in accordance with the seasons. There were also other castes such as smiths, leatherworkers, weavers and *griots*. These professionals had serfs or slaves who worked for five days on their masters' land and the remaining days of the week on their own land. Under this system, chattel slaves were transformed into serfs with some definite rights. Many people also carried on farming and exported food, especially grains, to Timbuctu. Fishing was done by the Somono and Bozo who were also, like the pastoralists, forced to settle down and subjected to the usual taxes.

Unlike the Hausa states, Masina produced no industrial goods for export, apart from the Kassa blankets woven from the wool of the Masina sheep and a few Segu cloths. The state, therefore, remained on the whole rather poor. It could not afford to buy firearms which partly accounts, as we shall see later, for its overthrow in the 1860s.

Seku Ahmadu's achievement then was to create a genuine Muslim state which unified a number of smaller Bambara, Arma and Songhai kingdoms and principalities in the single highly centralised Fulani theocratic empire of Masina. This state ruled by the learned *ulema* strengthened Islam in the region and encouraged scholarship and lasted until the 1860s.

The jihad of al-Hajj Umar

The circumstances out of which this *jihad* arose paralleled those of the earlier holy wars: a state of mixed Islam in Futa Toro with the neighbouring twin Bambara kingdoms of Segu and Kaarta remaining largely non-Mulism; revivalist activities within the Muslim world; and an oppressed and restless population generally. However, there were basic differences between the attitudes and activities of al-Hajj Umar and those of the earlier jihadists.

Of the three jihadists, al-Hajj Umar was the only one who actually went on the pilgrimage to Mecca. He returned to the Western Sudan filled with the reformist ideas of the day and therefore with an even greater inspiration and determination for the purification and spread of Islam. Unlike the first two jihadists who belonged to the Qadiriyya, he belonged to the Tijaniyya and it was he who was mainly responsible for its wide diffusion in the Western Sudan. Furthermore, he waged his *jihad* not only against Western Sudanese rulers but also against the French who had then begun their imperialist drive in the region of the Senegambia. Fourthly, he used more modern methods – a professional army, guns and the building of modern forts as soon as a town was captured – than the earlier leaders. Finally, unlike the first two jihadists, he was not a Fulani but a Tukulor though by this time the two groups had become almost fused together and were speaking the same language.

Al-Hajj Umar was born in Futa Toro in 1794 and his father was a Tukulor scholar. He was initiated into the Tijaniyya by his teacher Abd al-Karim b. al-Naqil before he set off on the pilgrimage in about 1825. In Mecca, he is said to have so impressed the Tijani authorities that he was appointed the *Khalifa* or leader of the Tijaniyya for the Sudan in 1831. After finishing studies in Cairo, he spent some years in Borno and Sokoto before finally leaving for Futa Jallon in 1838. Here he established a religious and a military training centre. In his book *Rimah* he attacked evil and illegal practices and condemned 'mixed Islam'. He also appealed to the masses and assured them of favoured treatment on the Day of Judgement as members of the Tijaniyya. His teaching was well, received by the ordinary people who were alienated by the elitism of the Qadiriyya. As one would expect, al-Hajj Umar's fame as a scholar, teacher and mystic attracted a very large following who regarded him as a *mujaddid*. This following, together with the growing desertion of the old order for the new one, alarmed both the old scholars and the rulers who expelled him from Futa Jallon.

Like Usuman dan Fodio and Seku Ahmadu before him, al-Hajj Umar Tall performed the *hijra* in 1851 to Dinguiray near the borders of Futa Jallon where he established an armed camp and raised a full-army made up of his disciples and students attracted from all over West Africa and mainly from the lower classes. He gave them good training and armed them with guns and powder bought from the coastal towns with money earned from the trade that he had established earlier. His army also had an auxiliary cavalry corps. Finally, he developed a corps of gunsmiths who could service and repair the guns and even manufacture such arms themselves.

Having thus carefully prepared himself, he infused his soldiers with religious fervour, and on the added strength of a vision, he declared the *jihad* against all infidels in the Sudan in 1852. He first conquered Tamba and a number of other states in the Senegambia, then took Bambuk and Khasso in 1854, and Kaarta between 1855 and 1857. He then turned against the French who had begun their imperial drive up the Senegal and attacked their fort at Medina in 1857 and another post at Matam in 1859. When in the same year the French counter-attacked and captured his fort at Guémou, he turned his attention eastwards and attacked the Bambara state of Segu, which he captured in 1861. In the following year, on the grounds that the Muslim state of Masina had refused to join him in his *jihad* and had assisted Segu, al-Hajj Umar attacked and conquered Masina. This victory brought the Tukulor empire to its widest territorial extent. Umar himself was killed in February 1863 in a rebellion in Masina led by the Qadiri leaders who were opposed to his imposition of the Tijaniyya. The empire, however, lasted under his eldest son, Ahmadu, until 1893 when it was overthrown by the French.

The nature and consequences of al-Hajj Umar's *jihad* are interesting and rather complicated. Firstly it was not simply the outcome of militant or reforming Islam against mixed or lukewarm Islam; in Masina and Jenne, it was also at least a clash of two militant forms of Sufi brotherhoods, the Qadiriyya and the Tijaniyya. Secondly, unlike the former *jihads* which were in effect a series of civil wars or rebellions by local Muslim *ulamas* against their own rulers, the *jihad* of al-Hajj Umar was really an invasion of independent states by an outside army. Thirdly, even though some of the generals were Hausa and Kanuri, since the leadership of the army was Tukulor and since most of the soldiers were also Tukulor, and finally since in this empire it was the military and not the intellectuals that held the prestigious and powerful positions, there is a great deal of justification for calling this revolt one of Tukulor imperialism, that is the desire of the Tukulor to impose their rule over the Bambara, Malinke, Fulani and the other peoples in that area.

The consequences of al-Hajj Umar's *jihad* have been profound. Politically it resulted in the creation of the Tukulor empire; although Umar died before he created an effective administrative machinery, his empire lasted till its overthrow by the French in 1893. Secondly, his resistance checked the tide of French imperialism in the Senegambia at least for some years. Socially, Islam was strengthened and its frontiers were further extended. Above all, the Tijaniyya gained ground from the Qadiriyya. Today, the Tijaniyya is the dominant order in West Africa and there is no doubt that this is partly if not mainly, due to the *jihad* and writings of al-Hajj Umar Tall. The Tijani emphasis on faith and action rather than on intellectual exercise and studies made it more acceptable to the ordinary people.

The nineteenth century Islamic movements were of great importance in the history of the Western Sudan. They led first and foremost to the revival, purification and the spread of Islam. They brought about the strengthening and diffusion of both the Qadiriyya and the Tijaniyya with the latter gaining wider grounds than the former, thanks mainly to the activities of al-Hajj Umar. They brought about fundamental political changes in which empires replaced petty states and kingdoms and power was given to a new governing class. They also strengthened both Fulani and Tukulor nationalism. The *jihads* also changed Western Sudanic society, elevated the status of the slaves and peasants, and forced some nomadic people to become settlers. Above all, the *jihads* also greatly expanded Islamic literacy, especially in the Hausa and Fulani-speaking areas, caused a wider spread of Muslim literacy and the setting up of many new centres of Islamic education, especially in the southern areas of the Western Sudan. If Islamic education became very strong and prevented the spread of western style education into the Western Sudan until only recently, it was because of these *jihads* and their emphasis on Islamic literacy and education. The *jihads* also contributed to the development of many new towns, such as Sokoto and Hamdallahi. Thus, Western Sudanese society by the 1860s was fundamentally different in many respects from what it was at the beginning of that century.

The states and kingdoms of the southern savanna, the forest and the Guinea coast

---

7 The rise and fall of the Asante empire

In section I, we dealt with the history of the states and empires which arose in the savanna belt from the mouths of the Gambia and the Senegal to the Nile. The process of state formation was not confined to this area: the southern savanna, the forest and coastal regions to the south all witnessed similar development. In this section, we shall look at the history of some of the states the emerged in these regions.

There is no doubt that one of the most famous of these states was the empire of Asante. By the middle of the eighteenth century, that empire was dominating virtually the whole of modern Ghana, together with parts of modern Ivory Coast and Togo. This empire remained powerful for over a hundred years but it disintegrated in the 1870s and was finally conquered by the British in 1900. What then led to the rise and fall of this great empire?

The rise of the Asante empire

There are two main categories of reasons for the rise of the Asante empire – the remote and the immediate. The remote causes, or if you like the stimulants, were, first, the rise of many states in the area of modern Kumasi; secondly, the very harsh and unpopular rule of Denkyira, and thirdly the rise of the Atlantic trade. The immediate causes, or the precipitants, were the very strong ties between the various Oyoko clan groups of people who were the last to arrive in the area, and secondly, the diplomatic skill, the martial ardour and statecraft displayed by the first three Oyoko rulers of Asante, namely, Obiri Yeboa, Osei Tutu and Opoku Ware.

The Asante, the founders of the Asante Empire, were part of the Akan people who constitute about fifty per cent of the population of modern Ghana. The cradle of the Akan has been located in the Adansi-Amansie area where they developed their peculiar matrilineal system of inheritance of kingly office and their matrilineal clan groups into which they are all divided. From their cradle, the Akan migrated in different clan groups into the area of modern Asante from about 500 AD onwards. By the middle of the seventeenth century, these earlier immigrants had founded a number of states all within about thirty miles radius of present-day Kumasi. These included Mampon, Afigyaase and Seniagya founded by the Bretuo clan groups, Abooso, Baman, Makom and Agona by the Asense clan groups; and Asokore, Otikrom, Sekyre and Kwaaman by Ekoona clan groups. The last group of states to emerge in the area were Dwaben, Kokofu, Nsuta, Bekwai and Kumasi, all founded by Oyoko clan groups which had migrated from Asumenya-Asantemanso in the Amansie area in the middle of the seventeenth century.

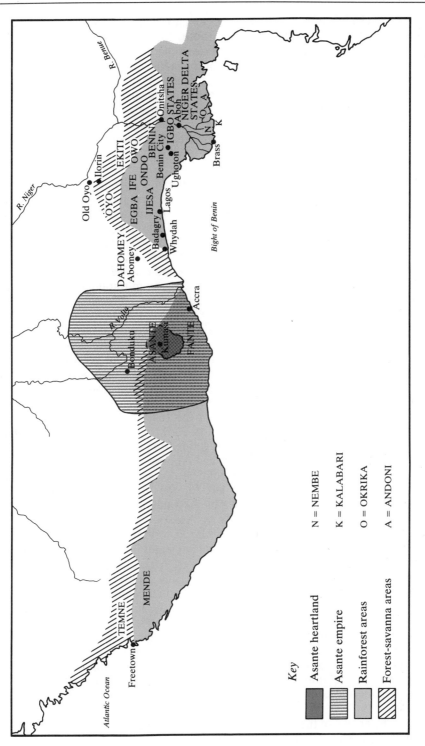

Key

Asante heartland

Asante empire

Rainforest areas

Forest-savanna areas

N = NEMBE

K = KALABARI

O = OKRIKA

A = ANDONI

The establishment of over twenty small states within such a limited area was undoubtedly because the trade routes to and from Mandeland to the north-west and Hausaland to the north-east met for the first time precisely in that region and from there further routes radiated southwards to the coast. That these routes should converge on this area is not surprising since it was the source of the two main products exported northwards, namely, gold and kola nuts. Obviously this region could not but attract these migrants from the south, land-hungry and poor as they were. Since it was these very states that were to form the core of the Asante Empire, their foundation is an important factor in the development of Asante as a whole.

The second important factor was the common hatred that all the pre-Asante states had for the oppressive rule of the Denkyira. According to various traditions, all these states were conquered and subjected to a very tyrannical rule. Local tradition is borne out by European sources. Bosman, an impartial and contemporary European observer, wrote: 'Denkyira, elevated by its great richness and power, became so arrogant that it looked on all other Negroes with a contemptible eye, esteeming them no more than slaves': What made the situation even more unbearable was the fact that the Denkyira prevented the people of these states from trading directly with the Europeans on the coast. For political and commercial reasons therefore, not only the states to the north but those to the south too, like Assin and Wassa, were all ready to revolt if only they could find somebody to raise the standard.

The third stimulant was the rise of the Atlantic trade, that is the trade between Europe and the Americas on the one hand and West Africa on the other. All the peoples of the interior became increasingly anxious to trade directly with the Europeans on the coast as the Atlantic trade grew in volume and profitability, particularly with the rise of the demand for slaves for the sugar plantations in the Americas from the 1640s onwards. But the coastal states and peoples persistently refused to allow those of the interior to come to the coast. They rather bought their goods from them at the inland markets such as Manso and Fosu in the west and Abonse in the east. When peaceful negotiations failed, conquest and political domination of the coastal states were the only other alternatives left for the inland peoples. This partly explains the occupation of the coast by Akwamu and Akyem in the east and Denkyira in the west and ultimately by Asante.

The rise of the Atlantic trade also contributed to the emergence of Asante in particular and all the other inland states in general by means of the guns and gunpowder it introduced into West Africa from 1650 onwards. The possessors of these new weapons certainly enjoyed an overwhelming advantage over those who did not have them in offensive as well as defensive wars. It is rather an interesting paradox that the first people to obtain these weapons, namely, the coastal peoples, failed to establish any great empires. But this was simply because of the active intervention of the rival European trading powers in their internal affairs. The Europeans were convinced that the emergence of a single strong empire on the coast would be detrimental to their commercial interests, and therefore did everything to prevent it, mainly by ensuring the continued independent existence of all the states along the coast.

The arrival of the Oyoko people was, however, the immediate reason for the rise of the Asante empire. The Oyoko clan groups were able to accomplish what the earlier groups could not do. Firstly they were a much more closely-knit group. When they left Asantemanso, like the earlier groups they founded a number of states. But there the similarity ends because unlike the founders of the earlier states, those of the Oyoko states believed that they came from a single lineage or family. The kings of Dwaben, Bekwai and Kumasi regarded and still regard themselves as brothers and they all looked upon the king of Kokofu as their uncle. Hence, instead of competing among themselves as the other states were doing, the Oyoko states co-operated closely and, as all of them were concentrated within an area of twenty miles radius from Kumasi, the nucleus or the core of an empire was thus created.

The growth of this nucleus into the empire of Asante under the rule of the Kumasi lineage of the Oyoko clan was the result of the work of the first three rulers of Kumasi, namely Obiri Yeboa, Osei Tutu and Opoku Ware. It appears that the branch of the Oyoko which moved into the Tafo area founded its own town, Kumasi, in the state of Kwaaman, and later, either through marriage, diplomacy or war, succeeded in establishing its domination over the Ekɔɔna and the other clan states in that region. This branch was led by Obiri Yeboa, who appears to have been a very shrewd ruler, for he won over some of the former rulers permanently by admitting them into the Oyoko clan. This move not only strengthened his own position and that of his lineage as the head of the new state, but it also considerably increased his following numerically. When he had thus established his position and increased his following, Obiri Yeboa embarked upon wars of expansion by attacking those states in the neighbourhood which had refused to recognise his regime. He was not very successful in this, for all traditional accounts agree that he was killed probably in the 1670s in a war against the Domaa who were then occupying the region of Suntreso, now a suburb of Kumasi. Fortunately, he was succeeded by his nephew, the famous Osei Tutu.

The reign of Osei Tutu

Assisted by his adviser and chief priest, Okomfo Anokye, Osei Tutu contributed to the growth of the Asante empire in five main ways. The first problem he tackled was the creation of a lasting union. By playing on the common fear and hatred of all the states for Denkyira, he and Okomfo Anokye were able to bring all of them together. It was with a view to making this union a permanent one that they 'conjured down from the sky' the now revered and sacred Golden Stool. They urged on the assembly that the Stool embodied their soul, strength, vitality, unity and their very survival, and that it should therefore be guarded at all costs. It was further agreed that its occupant was to be recognised as the *Asantehene*, the supreme political and religious head of the union of states, to be selected from the lineage of Osei Tutu and Obiri Yeboa. It is interesting to note that the Stool has to this day remained the soul and the symbol of the unity of the Asante nation and it is still guarded with the same dogged devotion.

Secondly, to strengthen the Union even further, by a shrewd use both of diplomacy and of magic, Osei Tutu got the members to agree that Kumasi was to be recognised as the capital and that once every year, all members of the Union were to attend the Odwira festival there. At this festival prayers were said for the entire nation, disputes or quarrels among chiefs were settled, and plans were concerted for the following year. The Odwira festival was thus instituted to unite these various peoples by a common celebration, and the rites associated with it 'rekindled the sentiments of solidarity and nationhood.'

Thirdly, Osei Tutu then went on to devise a constitution for the Union. At its head was the Asantehene who was also the head of the Kumasi state or division. Below him were the kings or Amanhene of the other component states or *aman*, all of whom had to recognise the court of the Union as the supreme court, attend the annual Odwira festival, contribute a contingent and pay tribute in cases of wars and national emergencies, seek recognition from the Asantehene by swearing the oath of allegiance to him, and give up the right of declaring war upon a member Omanhene at their pleasure. In all other spheres, these Amanhene were sovereign and independent.

Fourthly, as one of the main *raisons d'être* of the Union was the overthrow of the Denkyira rule, Osei Tutu paid particular attention to the military organisation of the Union. He is said to have introduced into Asante the Akwamu military formation consisting of the vanguard (*adonten*), the rear (*kyidom*), the left (*benkum*) and the right (*nifa*) wings. Each member state was assigned a place in one of the wings and each wing was placed under a commander who was at the same time the king of one of the member states of the Union. All the other *aman* adopted this square military formation while they retained their places in one of the wings of the Asante national army. If Osei Tutu borrowed this military organisation from the Akwamu, he and his successors certainly were able to develop it into an unprecedented peak of perfection and efficiency.

Finally, when he had formed the Union and endowed it with a national capital, a festival, a constitution, and an army, Osei Tutu started his wars of expansion. He first of all avenged his predecessor's death by inflicting a decisive defeat on the Domaa, who emigrated north-westward and founded the kingdom of Gyaaman. He then conquered Amakom and Tafo. His next obvious target was Denkyira, which he defeated between 1699 and 1701 when the final and decisive battle was won at Feyiase. This victory brought Asante dramatically to the attention of the Europeans on the coast for the first time. Indeed, the Dutch despatched an embassy to the *Asantehene*'s court as early as 1701. Next Osei Tutu conquered Akyem, but he was killed in 1717, in the campaign to suppress a revolt in Akyem.

If Obiri Yeboa was responsible for the establishment of the Oyoko kingdom of Kumasi, Osei Tutu should enjoy the singular honour of not only completing the work of his uncle, but also of initiating the process of converting that tiny Oyoko principality into the Asante empire. He was undoubtedly a brave fighter, a brilliant constitutional architect, and an able administrator, and he certainly deserves the place of honour and esteem that he has enjoyed since his death among the Asante.

Opoku Ware

According to traditional accounts Osei Tutu was succeeded by his grand-nephew, Opoku Ware. Again fortunately, he was a very able ruler, and as a fighter, was even more successful than either of his two predecessors. During his reign which extended from 1720 to 1750, the Asante conquered and annexed Tekyiman, Banda, Gyaaman, Gonja, and Dagomba, all in the north; Aowin, the Sefwi states and the Anyi state of Endenye in the west, Twifo in the south and Akyem, Kwahu, Akuapem and Accra though not Fante in the south-east, and Krakye and Krepi in the east. By the end of his reign, Asante was occupying an area much larger than modern Ghana. By bringing into their capital the craftsmen of the states they had conquered especially those from Bono and Denkyira, these kings of Asante were able to develop a civilisation noted for their golden regalia, rich and many-coloured Kente cloths, artistic gold weights and stools, colourful umbrellas and rich court music.

Why did the empire last so long?

By 1750, when Opoku Ware died, Asante had attained its widest territorial extent and stood at the peak of its power and glory; it remained the most dominant state in the area between the Comoe and Volta rivers for almost a hundred years. Indeed, it was not until the late 1820s that it began to disintegrate.

There are four main reasons why the Asante empire lasted so long. The first was that all the rulers of the second half of the eighteenth and the early decades of the nineteenth century (Kusi Obodum, 1750–1764; Osei Kwadwo, 1764–1777; Osei Kwame, 1777–1801; and Osei Bonsu, 1801–24) were able to provide the necessary leadership and inspiration and to suppress all the revolts and rebellions that broke out in the empire. These included those of Gyaaman in 1752, 1764, 1799 and 1818, Banda in 1764 and 1818, and Akyem Abuakwa in 1765 and very frequently in the nineteenth century.

The second reason for the survival of the empire was the strength of its army. Throughout the period under review, the Asante army remained strong and virtually invincible. This is clearly also borne out by the fact that all the rebellions during the period were quelled while the Fante confederation of states was also finally conquered by Osei Bonsu after a series of wars lasting from 1806 to 1814.

The third reason was the healthy nature of the economy of the Asante. The core of the empire did not only emerge in an area very suitable for agriculture, but it was the area that produced the two commodities in urgent demand both by the inhabitants of the savanna areas to the north and the Europeans on the coast. These were kola nuts and gold. Not only was the core of the empire producing a great deal of gold but as a result of the conquests the Asante also came to control all the other gold-producing regions such as Aowin, Denkyira and Akyem Abuakwa. From the beginning of the eighteenth century, Asante also began to export slaves southwards. The number of slaves who were mainly war-captives reached its peak during the second half of the century. These exports provided for Asante's import needs, including the arms and ammunition necessary for wars of expansion and the suppression of rebellions.

The final reason for the survival of the empire was that until the nineteenth century, Asante never experienced any interference in its internal affairs by any external power. Never throughout the period under review was Kumasi, for instance, invaded.

The fall of the empire

Unfortunately, from the end of the reign of Osei Bonsu in 1824, the great Asante empire began to fall apart, and by 1880 it had shrunk to virtually a third of its former size. What then brought about this rather unexpected turn of events? The causes were both internal and external. The first internal factor leading to the decline of Asante was the weakness of both the central and the provincial systems of administration. The Asante empire, at the peak of its power, consisted of three clear divisions: Kumasi, which was directly under the *Asantehene*; the territorial divisions or states or *Amantoɔ* such as Dwaben, Kokofu, Nsuta, Kumasi, Mampon and Ofinso, and the conquered states. Kumasi and the *Amantoɔ* formed what was known as metropolitan Asante. Provincial Asante was made up of all the conquered states such as Dagomba and Gonja to the north, Akyem, Akuapem, Akwamu, Ga, Denkyira and Wassa to the south.

In metropolitan Asante, it was only in the Kumasi state that the power of the *Asantehene* was supreme; when the council of the entire Union met, the *Asantehene* was not automatically supreme, enjoying autocratic or despotic powers over the other *Amanhene*. Rather, he was an equal, and the admittedly considerable influence he wielded was moral, as the occupant of the revered Golden Stool, rather than legal. Because of this, the extent of the *Asantehene*'s influence and power in metropolitan Asante came to be determined not by well-established constitutional practices but by the personality, ability and tact of the individual *Asantehene*.

Unfortunately, most of the nineteenth-century Asante kings after Osei Bonsu were not as capable and statesman-like as Obiri Yeboa and Osei Tutu. Rebellions and revolts therefore broke out periodically even within metropolitan Asante itself. For instance, in 1834 and again in 1875, Dwaben rebelled against the Asantehene, and on both occasions these rebellions led to civil wars.

The administrative set-up in provincial Asante was weaker still. None of the states conquered after Osei Tutu's reign was effectively brought into the Union. They were not given a place on the Union council and the Golden Stool had no significance at all for them. They did not even have direct access to the *Asantehene* and could see him only through one of the Kumasi *abirempon* (or wing chiefs) or the *Amanhene*. It is true that the great reformers, Osei Kwadwo and Osei Bonsu, did introduce some changes here too by imposing on the existing provincial administration a network of Asante resident commissioners hierarchically organised at regional and district levels; but the very fact that revolts and rebellion were so common in the nineteenth century shows that these administrative changes did not prove particularly effective. And the main reason was that, like their predecessors, the two reformers left the dynasties, the customs, the language and even the military structure of the conquered provinces intact. All that was expected of them was the regular payment of their annual tributes and the contribution of a military contingent when called upon to do so. Thus, since these states were not only by and large left to themselves, but were also treated as second-class members of the empire, they never identified themselves with Kumasi and the Golden Stool. On the contrary, they repeatedly attempted to regain their independence. Under these circumstances, the survival of the empire came to depend almost entirely on the military power of metropolitan Asante and it became obvious that if ever this power was weakened, the empire, especially provincial Asante, would fall apart.

The importance of the two main internal weaknesses of the empire should, however, not be exaggerated. Even though the *Asantehene* did not exercise absolute power in the Union, the Golden Stool was able to provide a strong unifying force which is as strong today as it was in the eighteenth century. Secondly, nearly all the eighteenth and early nineteenth-century rebellions of the provincial states were easily crushed. It can therefore be positively suggested that, left to themselves, the later nineteenth-century rulers of Asante could have maintained the territorial integrity of their empire. But from the second decade of the nineteenth century onwards, the Asante and their subjects were not left to themselves. On seven different occasions from 1811 to 1874 they came into a head-on collision with an external force – that of the British on the coast. It was this conflict which hastened the decline of Asante.

What brought about these clashes between the Asante and the British in the nineteenth century and what were the consequences? From the sheer frequency of the invasions of the coast by the Asante, many historians have described them as a warlike, aggressive and blood-thirsty people. This view is, however, totally erroneous. Throughout the nineteenth century, there was not one single invasion of the coast by the Asante which was not preceded by weeks, months or even years of negotiations. It was only when negotiations failed that the Asante took up arms. Nor were these wars for territorial expansion. On the contrary, the Asante were, in fact, on the defensive rather than on the offensive from the second decade of the nineteenth century onwards and their chief aim was to maintain intact the empire which they had inherited from their forefathers.

From their point of view, most of these wars were expeditions to punish rebellious states and to establish law and order. The Asante invasion northwards in 1818 was a punitive expedition against Gyaaman while those to the south in 1811, 1814, 1823 and 1826 were to suppress rebellions in Fante, Akuapem, Akyem, Wassa and Denkyira respectively. The Asante were also particularly anxious to maintain their grip on Elmina so that they could gain easy access to the coast and thereby ensure a regular supply of arms and ammunition. The wars with the British in 1869–70 and in 1873 were to prevent Elmina from falling into the hands of the British as a result of the Anglo-Dutch exchange of forts and the final departure of the Dutch from Ghana in 1872.

The British were not interested in territorial acquisition at this time either. Until after the 1860s, they were only interested in trade and in the introduction of western education and Christianity. But these interests could not be achieved as long as the Asante invasions continued. The British could, of course, have helped the Asante to tighten their hold on their coastal states and this would have lessened the number of invasions and ensured peace and order throughout the Asante empire. But they refused to do this because they were afraid to allow the powerful Asante to establish a firm hold over the coast. Their policy was therefore to help the coastal states to maintain their independence and they tried to achieve this first by acting merely as mediators between the coastal states and Kumasi, and later, from 1824 onwards, by taking to the battlefield when the effective occupation of the coastal areas, particularly the Fante areas, became a certainty. The first British war with Asante occurred in 1824, when the British were defeated and their governor, Sir Charles MacCarthy, was outwitted and killed. However, in 1826 and again in 1874 they decisively defeated Asante. On the latter occasion, Kumasi was entered, sacked and set on fire by a British army under the command of Sir Garnet Wolseley.

The effects of these wars were profound. The decisive defeats of Asante in 1826 and again in 1874 greatly weakened their military supremacy, while the flow of arms and ammunition was seriously interrupted. As one would expect therefore, the empire began to fall apart. All the northern states – Gonja, Dagomba, Krakye and Gyaaman – reasserted their independence and they were never reconquered. The southern states too – Akyem, Denkyira, Wassa, Fante and Accra – also declared themselves independent; they were recognised by the Asante in the Fomena Treaty imposed by the British in 1874.

The effect of these wars on the Fante states, was to draw them closer and closer together, culminating in 1868 in the formation of what could, with some justification, be described as the first proto-nationalist movement in modern Ghana, the Fante Confederation. As was the case in Asante, had it been left alone by the British, the Confederation would most probably have lasted. But mainly because of the rise of the new imperialism, to be discussed later, the British officials on the coast arrested the leaders of the Confederation in 1871 and imprisoned them. Though they were released shortly after, their arrest together with the subsequent intrigues of the British led to the collapse of the Confederation in 1872.

The British, partly as a result of these wars, became even more deeply involved in coastal political affairs. In addition, the departure of the Danes and the Dutch from Ghana in 1850 and 1872 respectively, conjured up prospects of increased British revenue from custom duties; all these factors together with the decisive defeat of Asante in 1874, led to the conversion of the so called moral protectorate of the southern states into the British Crown Colony of the Gold Coast in July of that year.

Thus by 1880 mainly as a result of these Anglo-Asante wars, the Asante empire had shrunk to metropolitan Asante and Brong-Ahafo, while the coastal states had become part and parcel of the British colonial empire.

8   The rise and fall of Oyo

The foundation of Oyo

The empire of Oyo was created by the Yoruba. Both the Yoruba language and archaeological discoveries prove that the Yoruba people have lived in their present area for thousands of years, and are not migrants from Arabia or Ethiopia as was earlier supposed. Like the Edo people of Benin, they developed and multiplied in the open savanna regions to the north, probably in the Nupe-Igala area, and spread into the different parts of present Yorubaland; by about 1000 AD they were living in communities, towns and city-states under clan and lineage heads and chiefs.

From the various oral traditions, it seems clear that it was at Ife that the institution of kingship and a centralised kingdom first emerged in Yorubaland through the conquest and unification of some of the existing communities and states in the area by a dynasty founded by the semi-legendary figure of Oduduwa. It was some members of this dynasty regarded as the sons and grandsons of Oduduwa who migrated from Ife at different times to establish kingdoms such as Egba, Ketu, Sabe, Owu, Ijebu and Ijesa as well as the Edo kingdom of Benin.

According to Oyo and Benin oral traditions, the founding dynasty of Oyo was likewise Yoruba and originated from Ife. Though both the period and the origin of Oyo's founding dynasty have been disputed in recent years by some historians, it still seems most probable that the first dynasty was indeed of Ife, hence Yoruba origin, and that Oyo was founded during the second half of the fourteenth century and had become firmly established by about 1400.

The expansion of Oyo

From its foundation to its fall in the early decades of the nineteenth century, the history of Oyo may be divided into three phases: from 1400 to c. 1610 or the pre-imperial period; from 1610 to c. 1790 or the imperial period; and from 1790 to c. 1836 or the post-imperial period of decline.

During the early part of the first period, the Alafin (kings) of Oyo were able to conquer and unite the small city-states and towns within the neighbourhood of Oyo between Nupe and the Moshi river to the north, the Ogun river to the west and Osun river to the south. Between 1500 and 1540, however, the Oyo rulers were defeated by the Nupe, and Oyo was sacked. They therefore had to abandon the capital and go into exile, first into Borgu; from there they moved from one place to the other under pressure from the Nupe or Tapa and the Borgawa, finally settling down at Ighoho in the 1550s.

It was not until the first decade of the seventeenth century that they were able to defeat the Nupe and to return and rebuild Old Oyo.

The second period from c. 1610 to 1790, was the imperial phase, when mainly through a series of brilliant campaigns, absorption and colonisation, Oyo became one of the largest, if not the largest, states to emerge in the southern savanna and forest regions of the Guinea coast. Oyo's expansion began soon after the return to the capital, Oyo Ile. Wars of expansion continued during the first half of the eighteenth century and resulted not only in the strengthening of Oyo control over south-western Yorubaland, but in the conquest of the Aja states of Porto Novo, Badagry and Weme and, above all, the kingdom of Dahomey which was attacked and conquered first between 1726 and 1730, and again between 1739 and 1748.

Thus, by 1750, as Akinjogbin has put it: '. . . the Alafin of Oyo was emperor of a territory that included the Oyo kingdom, the whole of Egba and Egbado, some part of Igbomina, the whole of Ajase kingdom (Porto Novo), the whole of Weme kingdom, the whole of Dahomey kingdom, and parts of Tapa (Nupe) and Ibariba (Borgu).' Oyo also controlled the sea coast from about Whydah to Badagry. During the 1770s and 1780s, although some states broke away as we shall see later, large areas of the Mahi country north of Dahomey were added to the empire by Abiodun, the last of the famous eighteenth-century Alafins of Oyo.

The third phase of Oyo history, from 1790 to 1836, is, as we shall see later, the inglorious one of decline and fall.

The civilisation of Oyo

Besides the huge empire that they founded, the most remarkable thing about the Yoruba was the very high civilisation that they developed. This is evident from the richness of their art. As far back as the fourteenth and fifteenth centuries, the Yoruba were producing works of art in bronze, ivory, wood and terracotta (baked earth). Most of these pieces which are coming to light now through archaeology have amazed scholars by their artistic beauty and naturalism, and are fetching fantastically high prices in the salerooms of Europe and America.

The centre of this highly developed art which probably dates back to the Nok culture (1000 BC–200 AD) was Ife, where the method of using bronze in sculpture by the *cire perdue* (or 'lost wax') process was probably first developed. Using this process the sculptors of Ife were able to make various heads of people, fullsize casts of kings, and any objects they fancied. This process spread from Ife not only into the neighbouring Benin kingdom but probably throughout West Africa.

The art of the Yoruba is also closely connected with their religion. In the first place, like most African peoples, the Yoruba believe in the existence of an Almighty God whom they call Olorun (Lord of Heaven), and in life after death; they worship the dead, believe in a future judgement and in the doctrine of the transmigration of the soul. But probably alone among all African peoples and rather like the ancient Hindus and Greeks, the Yoruba have various lesser gods or *orisa* of their own who are venerated and deified kings or heroes. The Rev Samuel Johnson, the famous historian, himself a Yoruba, has listed thirteen of these principal gods. The most important of them are Sango, the deified fourth king of the Yoruba; Oyo, the faithful and beloved wife of Sango; Ogun, the god of iron, war and hunting; Esu or Elegbara (the Satan or evil god); Egugun, and Ifa (god of divination). Each of these had its own cult or particular way in which it was worshipped, and these cults played an important part in the government of the empire. For instance, the head members of the Ifa cult had to give religious sanction for all state matters. The members of the Sango cult were sent out to the vassal states as political agents, since, being members of that cult, they were regarded as equals of the kings.

The government of Oyo

The system of government of Oyo was, like that of most other African kingdoms and empires, monarchical. In other words, at the head of the central government, was a king or Alafin, who was chosen from the royal family or lineage and the system of succession was patrilineal. From the beginning, the Alafin was succeeded by his eldest son, entitled the Aremo. However, from the middle of the sixteenth century, that is during the period of exile, the Aremo ceased to be the automatic successor and the Alafin was chosen by the *Oyo Mesi*, a non-royal group or council, from candidates from one of the three branches of the royal lineage presented by the *omo oba*, that is, the members of the royal lineage. In the 1730s, there was another change under which the Aremo was compelled to commit suicide on the death of his father. This law was not abolished until after 1836.

The oyo mesi

In his government of the empire, the Alafin was in theory an autocrat or an absolute king. His word was law; he was the supreme judicial authority and had the power of life and death over all his subjects. In practice, however, his power was limited, for he had to rule with the advice of seven notables known as the *oyo mesi*. They were non-royal chiefs who were chosen not by the Alafin but by their own lineages. They were in order of seniority the *basorun*, the leader, followed by, the Aqbakin, the Samu, the Alapini, the Laguna, the Akiniku, and the Asipa.

These chiefs were probably the heads of the wards of the non-royal part of the city of Oyo. They not only elected the Alafin but, in the words of Johnson, they also 'represented the voice of the nation, on them devolved the chief duty of protecting the interests of the kingdom'. The Alafin could not declare war nor conclude peace without their consent and they in fact exercised the right of life and death over him. Should their leader, the *basorun*, declare, 'The Gods reject you, the people reject you, the earth rejects you,' then the Alafin had to commit suicide. One of the effective checks on this power of the *oyo mesi* was that one of its members, the *samu* or the king's friend, had to die with him.

The *oyo mesi* also controlled some of the principal religious cults of the state such as the Oranyan, Egungun and Orisa cults. Above all the *oyo mesi* commanded the army of the Oyo capital with the *basorun* as commander-in-chief. Directly under the *oyo mesi* were also the *eso*, that is the seventy junior war-chiefs who served as the assistant commanders of the army. Controlling as they did both the succession to the throne and the army of the city, the *oyo mesi* were a very powerful group indeed and the stability of the Oyo state depended on a balance between the powers of the Alafin and those of the *oyo mesi*.

The administrative staff

The administrative and ceremonial tasks of the palace were conducted by the Alafin's large staff of officials or civil servants, rather wrongly called the king's slaves, who lived in the palace or in houses adjacent to it. These officials were divided into three categories: titled officers; *iwefa* (eunuchs); and *itari*. The eunuchs who were the highest in rank not only guarded the wives and children of the Alafin but the three most senior of them had other specific function: the first usually tried cases for the Alafin, the second was in charge of the Sango cult and of religious affairs generally, while the third was in charge of administrative matters and represented the Alafin on all occasions in civil as well as in military matters, and collected royal revenues. The several hundred *ilari* who were both male and female, served as the Alafin's bodyguard, as his messengers to the other parts of the empire and beyond, and as collectors of taxes at the city gates.

The third set of officials or civil servants were the 'titled officers' who were responsible for other administrative and ritual duties. Many of these officials were non-Oyo but were recruited from war-captives or were actual slaves. Among the female officials of the palace were the *iya oba*, (the king's mother), who could act as regent and the *iya kere* ('little mother') in charge of the Alafin's regalia as well as the female *ilari*. As the kingdom expanded, the number of palace officials grew and the Alafin tended to use them to counterbalance the influence of the *oyo mesi*.

Justice was administered in the empire in three sets of courts. The first court was that of the *bale* (or head of the compound) which dealt with disputes and thefts between the members of the same compound. The second court was that of the ward chief which tried cases between persons belonging to different compounds in the same ward. The court had no jurisdiction in criminal cases which it transferred after preliminary investigation and hearing. The third and highest court was the Alafin's court, which tried cases involving people of different wards, all appeal cases from ward courts, all criminal cases and all cases referred to the capital from the provincial towns. The court was often presided over by the *ona efa*. The Aremo also had his own court in which cases of his clients and relatives were settled.

Local and provincial administration

For the purposes of local and provincial administration, the empire was divided into two main parts, metropolitan Oyo or the kingdom of Oyo, and the non-Yoruba states which were conquered by Oyo and reduced to tributary status. Metropolitan Oyo consisted of the capital town, Oyo Ile, and the surrounding towns or city-states. The city of Oyo consisted of three parts: the *oke afin* or palace area; the area occupied by members of the royal lineage; and the area occupied by the free Oyo. The non-palace areas were divided into units, or wards. Each ward was made up of a number of compounds which in turn consisted of a number of lineages, each under its *bale* and the head or chief of each ward was chosen from the royal lineages of that ward by members of that lineage.

The rest of metropolitan Oyo consisted of two categories of towns or city-states. These were royal towns which were ruled in most cases by dynasties from the royal house in Oyo Ile with the title of *oba* and the ordinary towns which were ruled by dynasties not connected with Oyo Ile, with the title of *bale*. Each ruler was assisted in his administration by a council over which he presided. He owed allegiance to the Alafin and had to pay an annual tribute in person during the annual Bere festival. No *oba* or *bale* could pursue an independent foreign policy and, once selected, had to go to Oyo to obtain the Alafin's approval before he was installed; he could likewise be deposed at the Alafin's wish. Important legal cases had to be referred to the Alafin's court and each town had to send a contingent of troops to the Alafin at times of war. In all other matters, the provincial towns enjoyed autonomy.

Metropolitan Oyo was further divided into about eight provinces each under an important provincial ruler. At the annual festival of a provincial ruler, held immediately after the Alafin's Bere festival, the rulers of the towns in the province had to pay their homage and tribute to him. In war, it was the provincial or *ekun* head who had to assemble the troops of the towns in the province and act as their commander in battle. A newly installed subordinate ruler had to seek the approval of the head of his *ekun* before he proceeded to Oyo to seek that of the Alafin.

In addition to their obligations to the *ekun* and the Alafin, the towns in the provinces were assigned by the Alafin as fiefs to different officials and chiefs in the capital through whom they sent their tributes to and communicated with the Alafin, and whom they called *baba* (father). Members of the *oyo mesi* were assigned fiefdoms, as were some of the titled officers in the ranks of the civil service. The Alafin also permanently stationed official Oyo representatives called *asoju oba* or *ajele* in most of the provincial towns of the kingdom. They were appointed by the Alafin from among the palace officials to keep him informed of the affairs of the towns and to ensure their loyalty. The *ajele* were in turn supervised by the *ilari* of the Alafin.

To the extreme west were the conquered non-Yoruba and Aja states of Dahomey, Weme, Allada and Porto Novo (Ajage). These states had to pay annual tribute and occasional levies often in the form of livestock, firearms or local minerals; collection was supervised by an *ilari*. From the 1770s, the Egun states of Porto Novo and Badagry were similarly paying tribute to Oyo. Oyo could interfere in both the external and internal affairs of these states but it hardly ever did so.

The economy of Oyo

One of the principal reasons for Oyo's strength was its economy. The mainstay of the economy of Oyo was agriculture or farming in which the great majority of the people were engaged. In the northern parts of the kingdom, the main food crops grown were the savanna ones of cereals, especially millet and maize, while in the southern parts yams, oil palm, kola nuts, pepper and plantains were grown. In the northern part, cattle-rearing was also carried on mainly by Fulani pastoralists while some Yoruba employed slaves to raise cattle for them.

Besides agriculture and food production, Oyo also manufactured most of its everyday needs, such as iron tools, weapons, pottery and above all cotton cloth. Oyo cloth was of very high quality and was woven on narrow vertical and broad horizontal looms by men as well as women. Oyo Ile, Ijanna in the Egbado province, Ila in Igbomina and the Ijebu area were the principal weaving centres. Cotton was grown locally while the more prestigious and expensive cloths were made with silk which was a trans-Saharan import. The cloth was dyed with indigo which was also cultivated locally. Other manufactures included jasper beads for which Oyo Ile was famous, and leather articles such as sandals, bags and umbrellas. These crafts were produced on a household basis and craftsmen were organised, as in Hausaland, into guilds which controlled standards and prices. In all these economic activities, extensive use was made of domestic slaves who were well treated and regarded as members of the household.

In addition to agriculture and manufacturing, trade, both local and long-distant, contributed to the Oyo economy. Markets were held in all towns of any size where food crops, raw materials, manufactures and others were exchanged. Through inter-regional trade foodstuffs and manufactured goods such as cloth, kola nuts and sea salt, were sold in the savanna regions of the empire. In the Oyo markets, cowries were used. These were introduced before the seventeenth century from the Mande areas to the north-west and from that century onwards from both the north as well as the coast.

Even more important for not only the economy but also the military power of Oyo was the long-distance trade with the north as well as with the coast. From Oyo Ile, trade routes radiated north-eastwards through Ogodo or Raka to Nupe and thence through Kulfo to Hausaland and Borno; others radiated northwards through Kiama and Bussa to Borgu and north-westwards towards Timbuctu and the Niger Bend. Oyo's traditional exports to the north included pepper, camwood, kola nuts, cloth, ivory and slaves. From about the middle of the seventeenth century onwards, sea salt and European manufactured goods such as beads, woollen and cotton cloth, pewter, copper dishes and gunpowder were added. Imports from the north consisted first and foremost of horses and natron, especially from Borno; leather goods, cowries and textiles from Hausaland; copper, unwrought silk, Venetian beads and other fancies from North Africa and the Sahara.

Oyo also traded with the southern areas and from the seventeenth century onwards with the Europeans on the coast. The main trade route passed from Oyo Ile south-westwards through the Saki, Igboho and the Egbado towns at first to Offra and Jakin, the ports of Allada and in the eighteenth century to Badagry and Porto Novo on the coast; another passed southwards through Apomu and Ijebu Ode to Lagos, and the third south-eastwards to Benin. It would appear that the Oyo-Benin route was the oldest while the trade with the Europeans through the Allada ports of Offra and Jakin dates from the seventeenth century. The main commodities sent to the Europeans consisted of Oyo cloth and ivory, but mainly slaves. In return, Oyo received first and foremost salt, and a variety of European goods including cloth, earthenware, beads, rum, tobocco, iron bars, and fire-arms.

It is important to note that the great bulk of the revenue of the Alafin came from duties levied on the trade into and from the capital city as well as in the Egbado provinces in which an elaborate system of turnpikes was established at which tolls were collected. The Alafin also derived revenue from the trading activities of some of the members of his household, as well as from farming. Other sources of royal income came from the Sango cult, a share of war booty, death duties on the property of wealthy citizens, and tributes paid by provincial towns and conquered states. But it was principally from trading revenue that the Alafin maintained his specialist army, replenished his cavalry and the large staff of palace officials and servants, and also maintained his prestige through a very high standard of living.

The rise of Oyo

Such then was Oyo at the peak of its power and greatness. From the above, the reasons for the rise and expansion of Oyo and for its strength are not difficult to extract. Oyo owed its rise and expansion to four main factors: geographical, military, economic and political. Geographically, Oyo started emerging in the most northerly area of the land of the Yoruba-speaking peoples and therefore became the natural middleman between the Oyo and the Edo and other peoples to the south, and the Bariba, Topa (Nupe), Hausa and the Kanuri-Kanembu peoples to the north. This brought trade benefits and exposure to new ideas from the north as well as the south. In addition, Oyo's geographical situation next to Nupe and the Borgu states opened it to a great deal of political pressure and it seems most likely that the formation of the core of the empire around the town of Oyo Ile as well as the great development of its military strength must have been greatly stimulated by the need to unite to face this pressure, which persisted until the beginning of the seventeenth century.

The expansion of the kingdom into an empire in the seventeenth and eighteenth centuries was undoubtedly the outcome of two other factors, namely, the new army that Oyo developed and the intensification of trade with the north but even more importantly with the coast and Europe. By the end of the seventeenth century Oyo had developed a new army, which, unlike most of the existing armies in the region did not consist only of footmen or infantry but also included a cavalry wing of highly trained men armed with bows, arrows and spears which was borrowed by Oyo from its northern neighbours, the Nupe and the Bariba or Borgawa. That wing from then on became the main attacking force of the army. Since none of the states and kingdoms to the south of Oyo had a cavalry, it is not surprising that they proved no real match to Oyo till the 1780s. Military dependence on the cavalry is well illustrated by Oyo's pattern of territorial growth. Expansion failed in the eastern, forest areas in which the horses proved quite ineffective, whereas it succeeded in the western and Aja savanna areas where the cavalry wing proved invincible. The use of the cavalry, then, not only explains the expansion of the Oyo kingdom into an empire in the seventeenth and eighteenth centuries, but it also determined the direction of that expansion.

It was no mere accident, however, that Oyo expansion south-westwards followed the establishment of direct trading contacts with the Europeans in the seventeenth century. The development of the Atlantic trade, as was also the case of the states in modern Ghana, provided the interior Oyo with a motive for expanding southwards in order to effectively control the trade routes and trade directly with the Europeans. It also enabled Oyo to re-trade its European purchases in exchange for the commodities so necessary to maintain its military power, namely, horses and other cavalry equipment.

Finally, it is also important to take into account the abilities of some of the rulers of Oyo, especially those of the seventeenth and eighteenth centuries. Abipa who re-entered and rebuilt Old Oyo, Ajagbo (?1650–1687), Ojigi (1698–1732) who conquered Dahomey and the other Aja states, the *basorun* Gaha, who became the effective ruler of Oyo between 1754 and 1774, and finally, Abiodun (1774–1789) who brought the empire to the height of its greatness, were all exceedingly great and competent rulers.

The fall of Oyo

By the middle of the nineteenth century, however, the opulent and well-organised empire had completely disintegrated. The northern part had been captured and converted into the Fulani emirate of Ilorin; the southern part had broken up into a series of independent states competing among themselves for supremacy; Dahomey had declared independence and was attacking its former overlord; and the old capital, Oyo Ile itself, had been reduced to ashes, and the Alafin had been compelled to move a hundred miles south to settle in a town which developed into the present town of (New) Oyo. No empire or kingdom of the Guinea coast and southern savanna collapsed so dramatically and as completely as that of Oyo. The question, then, is what brought about such and inglorious and dramatic end to such a glorious and historic empire? The collapse of Oyo during the nineteenth century was caused by six main factors, three external and three internal.

Internal factors

Decline of military power

It is now generally agreed that the weakened state of the Oyo army by the end of the eighteenth century was due first to the many civil wars that raged in Oyo Ile between the Alafin and the *basorun* during the second half of the eighteenth century culminating in 1776 first in the deposition of Gaha, the *basorun* who had become the effective ruler of Oyo since the 1750s and then in the coup d'état against the Alafin in 1796.

The breakaway of the northern states of Borgu in 1783 and Nupe in 1791 also contributed to this military decline. The strength of the Oyo army lay in its cavalry wing, and the horses, as we have seen already, were obtained from the northern markets to which the Alafins lost access as a result of the breakaway of the northern states of Borgu and Nupe. Thirdly, horses were very expensive and because of a decline in Oyo's economy, the Alafins could not afford to buy them in any quantity. Thus, by the beginning of the nineteenth century, the Oyo army was already a shadow of its former self, a dangerous situation for a country whose economy had become primarily a slave-exporting one.

Economic decline

Parallel to this weakening of the army went the second reason for the fall of the empire, namely, a steady decline in the economy. As we have already noted, this had been based primarily on the trade with the north as well as the south. The assertion of independence by the Borgu and Nupe states, the Fulani conquests and occupation not only of Nupe but also of northern Yorubaland and the consequent instability as will be seen below, led to the dislocation of the traditional trade with the north. Such trade as remained was diverted through Borgu and Dahomey and Whydah outside the reach of Oyo.

Furthermore, the slave trade which during the eighteenth century had become the main backbone of Oyo's economy, also began to decline sharply due partly to the collapse of the port of Porto Novo, the main port through which the Oyo traders exported their slaves following the attacks of the kings of Dahomey on that port in 1803 and 1805, and the consequent shifting of trade to Lagos. The abolition of the slave trade by the British in 1807 and the subsequent activities of the British naval squadron on the west coast also steadily reduced the Atlantic slave trade. By the early decades of the nineteenth century, then, the economic resources of the Alafins were insufficient to support their empire.

Collapse of central authority

But the military and economic situations were worsened by the total breakdown of the central authority or government of the empire during the last decade of the eighteenth and the first two decades of the nineteenth century. This was one of the most important immediate reasons for the disintegration of the empire, and a fact that is now admitted by most historians. It is now believed that the breakdown was caused by two main factors. The first was the desire of some of the provincial rulers to break away from the control of the Alafin on the one hand, and that of the *oyo mesi* to curb the growing power of the Alafins on the other. The conflict between the *oyo mesi* and the Alafin had in fact been present ever since the late seventeenth century; it had led to the suicide, on *oyo mesi* orders, of six out of the nine Alafins who reigned between the 1680s and 1750s, and culminated in the final seizure of power by the *basorun*, Gaha, between 1754 and 1774. He was, however, deposed by the Alafin Abiodun (1774–1789) who was assisted by the provincial army.

With the end of the reign of the powerful Abiodun in 1789, it was to be expected that the *oyo mesi* would seek to redress the constitutional balance in their favour. On the other hand, the use of the provincial army and its leader, the *are ona kakanfo*, by Abiodun to overthrow *basorun* Gaha showed the provincial rulers that they could impose their will on the capital or even break away.

The situation was worsened by the second factor, namely, the personal ambitions and grudges of the three senior officers of the Alafin: Asamu the *basorun*, Lafianu, one of the senior chiefs of the *eso*, and Afonja, the Òba of Ilorin and the then *are ona kakanfo*. These three functionaries of the Alafin began to intrigue for his removal. The *basorun* and Lafianu organised a mutiny among the metropolitan troops while the *are ona kakanfo* plotted rebellion among the provincials. Both forces then got together and marched on Oyo in 1796 which they besieged until the Alafin committed suicide. Afonja had expected to be chosen as the next Alafin by the *oyo mesi* and when they chose another prince, Adebo, he and the other provincial rulers broke away from the coalition. Between 1796 and 1802 the central government broke down completely while the provincial rulers were busily creating independent kingdoms for themselves.

External factors

Intervention of the Fulani

Had there been no external interference, it is nevertheless likely that another Abiodun would have emerged to bring the *basorun* and the provincial rulers once more in line and to restore central authority. But this was prevented by the fourth of the factors accounting for the fall of the Oyo empire, namely the intervention of the Fulani.

By the second decade of the nineteenth century, the Fulani had conquered all the Hausa states; they had attacked Nupe, and were waiting for an opportunity to extend their conquests southwards across the Niger. This opportunity was provided by an invitation which they received from Afonja, the *are ona kakamfo*. In his efforts to carve out a kingdom for himself, Afonja appealed to the Fulani for help in 1817. Led by Salih known in Yoruba traditions as Mallam Alimi, the Fulani with their own aim of conquering the area for Islam, first assisted Afonja to achieve his ends. However, in 1823–24, they attacked and killed Afonja and seized power at Ilorin. From there, they invaded Yorubaland, took Oyo Ile in 1831 and Ota, Ikoyi, Gbogun, Saki and Ijanna between 1831 and 1833. In 1834, the Oyo made a last attempt to push back the Fulani but they were defeated in 1835; the Alafin was captured and killed, and the capital was taken, plundered and burnt and as Akanda puts it: 'it has lain in ruins ever since'. The court had to be moved about 150 kilometres south to the present site of New Oyo in 1836.

That the Fulani should have been so successful is not surprising. The Oyo army was a very weakened one without any cavalry wing, without any effective leadership and badly divided. It therefore proved no match for the Fulani army which was well-trained, highly inspired with an excellent cavalry wing and with its numbers increased by Hausa and Yoruba Muslims and ex-slaves.

The effects of this defeat by the Fulani virtually sealed the fate of Oyo. In the first place, the Fulani after converting the northern parts of the empire into their emirate or principality of Ilorin, constantly attacked the southern districts. It was only the brave and determined resistance of Ibadan at the battle of Osogbo in c. 1838 that halted the drive of the Fulani to the coast. Secondly, the Fulani occupation further dislocated the trade with the north.

While these events were taking place in metropolitan Oyo, the princes of provincial Oyo to the south also sought to aggrandise themselves at the expense of each other, and the inevitable result was a series of civil wars. It was refugees from these wars who founded both Ibadan and Abeokuta in 1829 and 1830 respectively. These two towns soon developed into very powerful, thickly-populated and well-organised city-states, and soon joined the Egba states – Ijaye, Ijebu and Ogbomoso – in the competition for supremacy and above all for the control of the trade routes and waterways to the south. These civil wars plagued Yorubaland throughout the nineteenth century.

Dahomey intervention

The other vassal state which took advantage of the situation, as we have seen, was Dahomey. In 1821 it made good its independence and Dahomey attacks or raids deep into Yorubaland continued throughout the century, naturally intensifying the anarchy in the southern districts.

British intervention

Thus by 1850, touched off by the collapse of the central authority, the weakened army and a declining economy and accelerated by the activities of the provincial princes and the Fulani, the disintegration of Oyo into a series of petty rival city-states and kingdoms had been completed. From 1865 onwards, another external power, this time from the coast, actively entered the field of Oyo politics. This was Britain. In the interests of the suppression of the slave trade and of promoting legitimate trade and missionary activities, the British had bombarded Lagos in 1851 and occupied it in 1861. However, the incessant civil wars in the interior, particularly between Abeokuta and Ibadan, steadily thwarted all British hopes of any lucrative commerce being developed between Lagos and those regions. At first they merely sent out envoys to arbitrate between the parties at war, as they did in Asante. But in 1865 when Abeokuta besieged the town of Ikorodu a few miles north of Lagos and, in spite of their requests, refused to raise the siege, the British moved in a battalion which pushed back the invaders. In the 1870s and 1880s they reverted to their old role as arbitrators and peace-makers, but in the 1890s, for reasons to be discussed subsequently, the British conquered and annexed the whole of Yorubaland. Thus, weakened and divided by the Fulani, harassed and raided by Dahomey, Oyo finally succumbed to the last of the invaders, the British.

9   The kingdom of Benin

In many ways the kingdom of Benin which emerged in the mid-western region of Nigeria among the Edo peoples of Nigeria was historically one of the most important of the states and empires of the southern savanna, forest and coastal regions of West Africa. In the first place, it was the first of the kingdoms to emerge in the forest and Guinea areas of West Africa. Secondly, it did not owe its rise and early development to either Islam or the European presence on the coast. Thirdly, unlike Oyo, Benin never abandoned her capital city which has remained in continuous existence in the same place for about a thousand years. Its second dynasty, the Oranyan or Eweka dynasty, founded in the thirteenth century has also remained in power ever since. Its cultural artefacts are world famous, and Benin probably exerted a greater influence on the socio-political institutions of the states and peoples of southern Nigeria than did Oyo or any other state.

The pre-twentieth-century history of this old and fascinating state falls into two main phases: the first is known as the Ogiso period from the beginnings to about 1300; the second began with the founding of the Eweka dynasty.

It is evident from the few available sources that by the tenth century a centralised kingdom, or rather city-state, had already emerged in the very area of the city of Benin today, under a ruler with the title of Ogiso. Not much is known about these early rulers except Ere, who was the eldest son and successor of Igodo, the founder of the dynasty. According to Chief Egharevba, the outstanding traditional historian of Benin, it was Ere who founded many villages and created the five elders of the kingdom, who were later to constitute the *uzama* group or council as we shall see below. He is also believed to have introduced a number of royal regalia, and to have instituted the *ughoron*, a specialist group of royal historians. Above all, he established the guild system by organising woodworkers, carvers, leather workers, hunters, weavers and pottery-makers into separate associations.

Many rulers followed Ere about whom history is still silent. It is known, however, that some rulers of the period extended the frontiers of the kingdom by founding villages over which they sent their children to rule as hereditary chiefs or *onogie*. However, some time between 1000 and 1300, the last Ogiso was banished for his cruelty and after an interregnum and a period of instability, the five elders of the *uzama* got together and appealed to the Oni of Ife to send them a new ruler. According to both Benin and some Yoruba traditions, this request was granted, and Oduduwa sent one of his sons, Oranminyan or Oranyan. He married the daughter of a Benin chief and had a son, Eweka. It was this Eweka who became the first Oba and the real founder of the Benin dynasty. And it was this dynasty which developed the city-state of Benin into the famous kingdom. By the end of the sixteenth century when the kingdom was at the height of its power and fame, it extended from Lagos in the west to the Niger in the east and to the Yoruba areas of Ijesha and Ekiti to the north, and its artists and craftsmen were creating those wooden, terra cotta and bronze masterpieces for which Benin has become so famous today.

The rise of Benin

The rise of this famous empire was the outcome of a number of factors. These were the geographical location of the kingdom, the development of long distance trade, the social organisation of the Edo people, the emergence of a new dynasty of the divine kingship type, the ability and creativity of the early rulers of the new dynasty, and finally, the lack of any effective political resistance to the Benin army in the fifteenth and sixteenth centuries.

The area in which the nucleus of the empire was founded was most suitable for the emergence of a centralised kingdom. In the first place, the dense forest area between the Ogun and the Niger rivers compelled the Edo people to live in communities and villages close to each other instead of being widely scattered about as in the more open savanna areas. Indeed, recent archaeological investigations have revealed that the city of Benin was originally a series of small communities and villages each with its farmland but close to each other. It was obviously easier to form such close villages into a centralised city-state or a kingdom than widely scattered ones. Secondly, unlike Asante, Dahomey and Oyo, Benin emerged in an area not far from the sea. This enabled it to play an important and lucrative role in the commercial relations between the coastal inhabitants to the south and the savanna peoples to the north. Thirdly, the forest provided protection from attacks, especially by the cavalry of the Oyo or Fulani or Nupe armies. Indeed, Benin never ever faced any serious external attack until the very last decade of the nineteenth century.

The second important contributing factor was the development of long distance trade. The Edo people developed trading contacts with the coast people mainly in salt and fish and participated in the trans-Atlantic trade between those areas and the coastal regions of modern Ghana on the one hand and with the savanna and Sahara regions to the north, long before the coming of the Europeans. The very lucrative middleman role which the Benin rulers and their Edo subjects played in long distance trade must have provided the necessary incentive towards and means for centralisation and expansion.

The third important factor was the nature of Edo society. Unlike the Yoruba, the Edo did not live in towns or urban centres but in small communities and villages close to each other. Each community or village for purposes of administration was divided into three age grades, the elders (*edion*), the adults (*ighele*) and the youths (*iroghae*). The grade of elders, the oldest of whom was the head of the village or community (*ɔdiɔnwere*), was responsible for the making of laws, settling of disputes and religious affairs and rituals. The adult grade constituted the warrior and executive group while the youth grade performed public works like clearing the roads and footpaths. It is obvious that any individual or family or clan group with the ambition and the power could easily unite such small independent villages and communities into a kingdom.

The fourth factor in the early rise and development of Benin was the establishment towards the end of the thirteenth century of a new dynasty in place of that of the Ogiso. Though oral traditions suggest that the institution of kingship was introduced or borrowed from Ife, it is also clear that the political system was adapted to suit Edo culture and world-view. This is evident from the fact that, unlike most of the chieftaincy titles in Oyo, those in Benin were not confined to certain lineages, but rather appointed by the Oba and open to any person of talent and ability, as was typical of Edo society. Secondly, the Edo principle of primogeniture, that is automatic succession by the eldest son, was adopted and later became the rule governing succession to the Oba office. The religious and divine nature of the institution became even more emphasised here than among the Yoruba, as is evident from the high incidence of human sacrifices and the complex nature of gods, priesthoods and rituals that surrounded it. This adaptation of the Yoruba monarchical system to suit Edo institutions and beliefs must have contributed to the stability and lasting survival of the new Benin dynasty.

The most important factor, however, was the ability of the rulers of Benin during the fifteenth and sixteenth centuries. The first of these famous founding fathers was Ewedo who was the fourth Oba in the new dynasty. It is believed that until his reign, the obas were controlled by the Uzama. Ewedo set himself the task of reducing the power and control of the *uzama*. First of all he built a new palace on a site where it has remained till now and which was outside the area inhabited by the Uzama. He went on to stop the Uzama from having swords of state carried before them into the palace, or through the street, which then became the exclusive privilege of the Oba. Thirdly, he created a number of non-hereditary posts for his leading supporters thereby beginning the new class of *eghaevbo* chiefs; the leader of this group was entitled to crown the oba, whereas the *uzama* had traditionally had the full role of kingmakers. Finally, he is also believed to have introduced many divinities into Benin, thereby increasing the spiritual powers of the monarchy. In all these ways, he considerably reduced the power of the *uzama* and made the king at least *primus inter pares* (first among equals), and potentially the dominant ruler of the Edo people.

However, it is agreed by all that the greatest of the early Benin kings was Ewuare, who reigned during the second half of the fifteenth century. Following a protracted civil war he inherited only a small town as his capital while the kingdom covered an area with a radius of only about fifteen miles of the capital. Ewuare was to change all this. He completely redesigned and rebuilt the capital. He divided it into two parts separated by a long broad street encircled by a huge earth wall and a ditch. The smaller part of the city, containing the palace and the houses of most of the palace chiefs, was called the 'Ogbe'. The larger part in which the town chiefs and most of the guilds lived was the 'Orenokhua'. The guilds included those of physicians, diviners, smiths, carvers, carpenters, bands, drummers, executioners and cloth weavers.

To boost the position and ritual nature of the monarchy, Ewuare instituted a number of festivals and divinities and also persuaded his subjects that he had supernatural powers. Of the festivals, the most important was the annual *Ique* festival which was meant to celebrate the mystical powers of the Oba. Furthermore, to ensure that succession to the obaship remained with his heirs, he adopted the Edo principle of primogeniture and created the post of

Edaikhen or heir-apparent; the new title was conferred on his eldest son whom he had chosen to succeed him. Ever since Ewuare, the eldest son of the oba has borne the title Edaikhen. By all these changes Ewuare considerably increased the power of the monarchy at the expense of the *uzama*.

Having done this he turned to the other task of converting the city-state into a large kingdom. This he did by a series of campaigns using his well-trained troops in the course of which he conquered the south-eastern Yoruba areas of Ekiti, Ijesha and Ondo. He also marched eastwards and conquered the Ibo communities on the west side of the Niger. According to Egharevba, he 'fought against and captured 201 towns and villages' in all these areas. In view of all these achievements to which one might add his encouragement of the arts, the Benin historian, Egharevba, has every right in calling Ewuare 'the Great'.

Although there was a period of instability following Ewuare's death, he was eventually succeeded by his eldest son Ozolua, who also proved an able ruler, successfully re-establishing order, increasing the power of the monarchy and adding new territories to the kingdom. During the sixteenth century, succeeding rulers such as Esigie, Orhogbua and Ehengbuda confirmed the continuity and strength of the dynasty, and the growth of the kingdom; they also added to its wealth by exploiting the trading opportunities with the Portuguese who had now established a presence in the city and old port of Benin. The quantity and quality of the brass works produced during the sixteenth century bears eloquent testimony to the wealth and prestige of the kingdom.

The final reason for the early rise and relatively rapid expansion of the Benin kingdom was the fact that the Benin rulers did not encounter much resistance either among the neighbouring or distant Edo and non-Edo peoples. The northern Edo, the Igbo to the west of the Niger and the southern Edo and the Itsekiri all lived in independent communities and villages rather than centralised states; they therefore could not offer much resistance to the Benin armies. The political conditions in the north-eastern parts of Benin and eastern Yorubaland (except Owo) were similar. In Akoko, for instance, every town or village was a kingdom in its own right and were often at war with each other. It is not surprising then that the Benin armies so easily conquered them in the fifteenth and sixteenth centuries. This same political fragmentation meant that Benin never experienced any external invasion to delay its period of imperial expansion.

It should be clear, then, that the early rise and expansion of Benin was the outcome of this unique combination of geographical, socio-political, economic and human factors. By the end of the sixteenth century, when Oyo was still a 'state in exile', when the Akan states were still in their most elementary stages, and when the foundations of the parent state of Dahomey, namely Alladah had just been laid, Benin had already developed into a large empire dominating the entire area between Lagos and the Niger.

The government of Benin

How was this kingdom governed and what was the nature of its economy? The kingdom of Benin, like that of Oyo, consisted of two parts. The first was the kingdom proper, or metropolitan Benin, which was the capital or principal town of Benin City and a number of subject towns, villages and hamlets, around the city. The second consisted of the states, towns and kingdoms that had been conquered and converted into tributary states, in other words, provincial Benin. At the head of both parts of the empire was the Oba or king of Benin, who, unlike the Alafin of Oyo, was not selected for this office, but succeeded automatically as the eldest son. Similarly the Oba could not be deposed, as could the Alafin by the *oyo mesi*.

Although he wielded enormous religious power and was regarded by his subjects as semi-divine, in practice, the Oba of Benin exercised his powers and governed the metropolitan kingdom in co-operation with not just one group of senior title-holders or estates, as in Oyo, but rather three. These were the *uzama* (hereditary nobles and kingmakers), the *eghaevbo n'ogbe* (palace chiefs), and the *eghaevbo n'ore* (town chiefs). For major matters of state, such as the declaration of war or passing of new laws, the Oba had to consult a state council made up of the three groups. It was this council which passed laws and carried out executive and judicial functions at the central government level. The Uzama were the highest ranking and the oldest of the orders dating from the Ogiso period. They were originally five in number – Oliha, Edohen, Ezomo, Ero and Ehola – but were increased to seven by Ewuare the Great by the addition of the Oloton and the Edaiken (heir apparent). During the early period of the second dynasty they were extremely powerful but the oba steadily reduced their powers and by the seventeenth century, though they still retained their rank, they had lost all effective power and played virtually no part in the day-to-day administration of the state. However, they still attended the Council of State with the Oba and acted as arbitrators in the event of disputes within the state council. They were also in charge of the shrines of the kingdom. On their own estates, however, they enjoyed all the powers: they could confer titles on their subjects and administer justice in their own courts.

Next in rank to the *uzama* was the *eghaevbo n'ore*, or the order of palace chiefs. The chiefs of this order were the principal administrative officers of the state and the Oba's closest advisers, and they lived in the palace quarters of the town. Besides their specific duties relating to palace administration and to the Oba himself, (such as looking after the Oba's finances, his wives and his children, and arranging appointment) these officials could be sent out to gather information, investigate complaints and represent the Oba at village rituals. They were also responsible for the guilds of the city. Finally, they were also assigned many fiefs, or districts, to administer and they could also undertake private trading.

None of these posts were hereditary: indeed all were open to all freeborn commoners from any part of the kingdom and not confined to particular lineages or families as was the case in Oyo. Moreover, the Oba could create new titles any time and confer them on whomsoever he pleased. Taking a title or being initiated into a grade was a very expensive exercise since fees had to be paid to all title holders of the orders except the *uzama*.

The third order was that of *eghaevbo n'ore* (town chiefs) whose leader, the Iyase, has been described as being both Prime Minister and leader of the Opposition. With only one exception, all the posts or titles of this order, like those of the palace chiefs, were in the Oba's gift. In other words any freeborn commoner not heir to any hereditary office and who had acquired wealth and prestige through trade or warfare or farming, could be appointed as a member.

Besides being members of the supreme council the town chiefs performed many important religious, military and administrative functions. In the first place, the four senior members had each day to perform the rite of *zematɔn* which was to purify, renew and release the mystical powers of the Oba. Like the palace chiefs, they controlled many fiefs and therefore the Oba depended on them for tribute, labour and troops. Furthermore, no state chiefs appointed by the Oba could be installed without their approval since it was their leader, the *iyase* who had to perform the installation ceremonies. Finally, the Oba needed their support to prevent him from coming too much under the control of the palace chiefs. It is evident from all these roles that the Oba could not impose his will on or dictate to the town chiefs and the interest of the state could best be served by active co-operation among the Oba, the town chiefs, and the palace chiefs. However, since nearly all of the town and palace chiefs were appointed by the Oba, it appears the balance of power still rested with him.

The government of provincial Benin

It would appear from the evidence that, as in Oyo, there was no single system for the administration of provincial Benin, and that some vassal states were governed more effectively and directly from Benin, while others were not, depending on their distance from the capital. The rulers (*enigie*) of the nearest Ishan states to the north-east had to be approved by the Oba, had to participate in the wars of the Oba, had to pay annual tribute and above all were grouped into fiefs and assigned to fief-holders living in Benin City. In other words, they were governed in the same way as states and towns within Metropolitan Benin. On the other hand, the distant vassal states of the north-western Edo peoples, such as the Akoko, Ivbiosakon and Afenmai were very loosely governed. It would appear that most of them were left alone so long as they paid their tribute regularly. The equally distant Urhobo and Isoko principalities to the far south were similarly loosely governed.

Lagos and the Itsekiri kingdom were also associated with Benin in different ways. Like the others, they also paid annual tribute to the Oba. But they were also attached to Benin by dynastic ties since the royal houses of both states were of Benin origin. Indeed, for centuries, up to the middle of the nineteenth century, the dead kings of Lagos were taken to Benin for burial. \

Benin's rule over the Yoruba vassal states to the north-west, especially that of Owo, was very strict. A resident Benin official was stationed in Owo, through whom the Olowo of Owo sent his annual tribute to Benin. Owo also had to send its princes as hostages to the Benin court. As Akintoye has pointed out, these princes were then educated at the Benin court and this explains why Owo's culture and palace rituals show so much Benin influence. In Akoko, too, Benin resident officials known as *balekale* were stationed especially in the larger towns, and every Akoko town paid tribute to Benin.

In Ekiti, Benin control over the southern areas was tighter than over the northern parts. In the latter areas, Benin military outposts were established, *balekale* were stationed, and annual tributes were paid.

From the above, it is clear that Benin really had no uniform system for the administration of its provincial domain, and that the degree of control varied according to the distance from the centre and the strategic importance politically or commercially of the area.

The economy of Benin

Like the economy of Oyo, that of Benin was based first and foremost on agriculture, then on crafts and industry, and above all, on local and long-distance trade. Situated as it was in the fertile forest areas with ample rainfall and many rivers, Benin was naturally an agricultural country, and a majority of its people earned their living as farmers. Yam was Benin's principal food crop and it was grown mainly by men. Other crops were pepper, groundnuts, corn and melons which were cultivated mainly by women. Oil palm trees belonged to the village as a whole. The Edo people paid their tribute to the Oba in the form of agricultural products. Many of the Oba and title-holders bought slaves whom they established in villages to establish farms for them.

Arts and crafts and industrial activities were also widely practised and were very carefully organised into guilds and controlled by the Oba. Indeed, the town section of Benin City was divided into forty or fifty wards, each occupied by a special group or guild of craftsmen, such as bronze-casters, smiths, carvers, leather-workers, cloth-weavers, hunters, pot-makers etc. Each guild had its own internal political organisation based on the grading of its male members and headed by an ɔdiɔnwere. They produced iron tools, cloth, beads, ivory, which were sold locally and also exported far and wide – as far as modern Ghana and Hausaland.

There is no doubt that trade formed an important feature of Benin's economy and became more important with the arrival of the Europeans from the end of the fifteenth century onwards. Benin trade was of two kinds. The first was the internal trade which consisted of exchange of goods in local and inter-regional markets. The second, which grew in importance with the years, was the long distance trade. Right from the beginning, this was divided into two sectors, trade with the north and that with the south or the Atlantic. Trade between Benin and the sea coast must have started right from the beginning since the two were not too far apart and this was extended as far west as the coast of modern Ghana even before the arrival of the Europeans. The long-distance trade with the Yoruba and Hausa states and the Sahara to the north, also dates to about the thirteenth century, if not earlier, as is evident from the fact that the copper used in the making of the Benin bronzes dated to the fourteenth century was probably imported from the Sahara.

The Oba and all the title-holders as well as the free citizens took part in this trade, and it was one of the main means of gaining wealth in pre-colonial Benin. Secondly, right from the beginning, the long-distance trade was very rigidly organised and controlled by the Oba. It was controlled by trading associations of which the Oba of Benin himself was the patron and one of the leading palace chiefs was president or *ɔdiɔnwere*. The best-known of these associations were the *ekhen-egbo* (literally, traders to the forests, – i.e. Owo, Ekiti and Akoko), *ekhen-oria* (traders to Ishan), *ekhen-irhuen* (traders to the Ivbiosakon area in northern Afenmai) and the traders to the coast who dealt with European and Itsekiri merchants. Any person who wanted to take part in the long-distance trade had first to join one of these associations which held regular meetings to discuss trading matters and measures for protection of traders in distant areas.

Trade to the coast was particularly closely controlled by the Oba through some of the palace officials. Certain exports such as pepper and ivory and imports such as fire-arms and powder were the exclusive monopolies of the Oba and heavy dues were imposed on visiting ships for the Oba. Moreover, no foreign traders from the interior were allowed to operate in the kingdom of Benin itself. All this rigid state control was calculated to ensure that the political elite, in other words, the Oba and the hereditary and non-hereditary chiefs, remained rich and therefore powerful.

The main goods exported by Benin northwards into Owo, Ekiti, Akoko and beyond, were salt, coral beads, brass utensils and iron implements. From the sixteenth century onwards, European goods such as cloths of various colours, calicoes, linen, iron bars, beads, cowries, and looking-glasses were added. Later tobacco, chains and necklaces and much later guns and gunpowder joined the list.

From the north, Benin traders brought back home-made cloths, leather goods, ivory, palm oil, Ilorin beads and such savanna products as locust beans (*iru*). The most important of these commodities consisted of two main types of cloth, the expensive and prestigious Benin cloth and the inferior blue one. Most of these cloths were produced mainly by women in the Ijebu, Ekiti, Igbomina and Nupe countries. It is important to note that these cloths and beads were re-exported as far as the coasts of modern Ghana, Gabon and Angola, and this movement of goods was intensified with the arrival of the Europeans. Slaves were also among the imports from the north. Trade between Benin and north-eastern Yorubaland through Okeluse dating from very early times grew in importance with the centuries and this explains why Benin established such a tight control over that area.

In the sixteenth century trade with the Europeans on the coast also continued to grow in importance; even more so in the seventeenth and eighteenth centuries with the appearance of the Dutch, English and French merchants. The ban on the export of male slaves up to the seventeenth century was lifted and slaves, mainly war captives or those obtained from raiding, steadily became the leading export of Benin from the seventeenth century onwards.

These long-distance trading activities and especially the waterside trade, brought a great deal of wealth first to the Oba and the political elite and then to the ordinary people.

Why did Benin last so long?

Unlike most kingdoms and empires of West Africa, Benin did not decline after attaining the peak of its power by the end of the sixteenth century. The two following centuries were marked by periods of decline followed by those of revival and a few of the states, such as Ijaw and Itsekiri, broke away. The kingdom, however, remained intact and the first half of the nineteenth century in fact witnessed a revival of its power and the strengthening of its control over the north-eastern Yoruba states. Benin was still a relatively strong and stable kingdom when it was conquered by the British in February 1897. The last question then is why this kingdom lasted so long.

The first and probably the most important reason was that partly because of geographical factors – the forest which prevented attack by the cavalries of the savanna states, and partly because of the absence of any strong kingdoms on the border, Benin never experienced any external attack. The fact that the fall of the kingdom was eventually due to an external attack – the British conquest in 1897 – seems to prove the importance of Benin's safe geographical location. The second reason for its strength and survival was its economy. Based as it was on agriculture, industry and local and long distance trade, the Oba and the political elite were able to amass enough wealth to maintain the considerable administration of the state.

The third and an equally important reason was the nature of the unwritten constitution of Benin which ensured a more workable balance among the Oba, the palace and town chiefs than that of, say, Oyo. Because of the very fact that most of the offices and titles of the state were non-hereditary but appointed by the Oba, no powerful lineages and family groups with large followings could develop as happened in the case of Oyo. Secondly, because the chiefs did not have the right to appoint or destool the Oba, their control over him was very limited. On the other hand, since the Oba had to rely on them for soldiers, labour, tribute, as well as for administrative services both in the kingdom and in the conquered states, and for the rituals needed to prop up his position, the Oba could not ignore the views of those people. The unwritten constitution of Benin therefore ensured a better balance of political forces with the scales tipped slightly in favour of the Oba, than say that of Oyo which tipped the scales slightly in favour of that of the oyo mesi.

The final reason for the survival of the kingdom was, as Bradbury has pointed out: 'the immense value attached to the kingship, which, over the centuries, had accumulated a great aura of mystery, fear and respect.' Over the years, partly because of the great emphasis on rituals and festivals by the priests and the chiefs, and because of his exclusive exercise of the power of life and death over his subjects, the mystical powers of the Oba became accepted by the people who regarded him as virtually divine. They therefore came to believe in the supernatural powers of the Oba and developed attitudes towards that institution which were 'a complex of affection and awe, pride and fear, but the overriding notion was one of fearfulness'. All this certainly constituted great support for the institution of monarchy which has still not entirely lost its strength and vitality.

10 The kingdom of Dahomey

In many interesting ways, the history of Dahomey is strikingly similar to that of Asante. First, like Asante, the kingdom of Dahomey was created by a clan or ruling dynasty known as Fon or Aja, which continued to rule until the very end of the nineteenth century. Secondly, Dahomey, like Asante, began as an inland kingdom and started to expand southwards only later. Abomey in Dahomey and Kumasi in Asante are almost on the same latitude. Thirdly, both Dahomey and Asante began to emerge in the seventeenth century and in the second half of the eighteenth century both grew into strong states. The kings Agaja II and Tegbesu IV were not only contemporaries of Osei Tutu and Opoku Ware, but also as brave and as victorious.

There were, however, also some notable differences between the kingdoms. The internal organisation of Dahomey, its central and provincial systems of administration, its military organisation and its sources of income, were, as we shall see presently, fundamentally different from those of Asante. Secondly, while by the last quarter of the nineteenth century the empire of Asante had completely declined, Dahomey was still at the peak of its power, and was exercising control over the Europeans who were trading on the coast. Thirdly, Dahomey was much smaller in area than Asante.

The rise of Dahomey

The founders of Dahomey were part of the Aja people, who also include the Ewe of Ghana and Togo, the Fon, the Gun and the Popo of Dahomey. According to their oral traditions, the ancestors of all these people lived in Tado. From there, while the Ewe migrated westwards to modern Togo and Ghana the Aja migrated south-eastwards and founded the kingdom of Allada, probably in 1575.

The Aja migration from Allada took place most probably during the early decades of the seventeenth century as a result of a succession dispute, and many historians have dated it to about 1620. They settled peacefully, they say, on the Abomey plateau about sixty miles from the coast, with the permission of the chiefs of the area. On the death of their leader, his son and successor, Dukodonu, seized power from the local chiefs, who failed to resist since they were so disunited, and thereby established the kingdom of Dahomey with himself as its first king. His two immediate successors, Wegbaja his son (1650–1685) and Akaba (r. 1685–1708) not only succeeded in keeping power in their hands but they were also able to conquer the neighbouring districts mainly to the south and south-east of Abomey. Thus, by the beginning of the eighteenth century, Dahomey, like Asante, had been firmly established.

At this stage, however, it was only a small inland kingdom on the Abomey plateau of between forty-two and sixty-two towns and villages with a strongly centralised monarchy. It was not until the eighteenth century that the kingdom grew into a very strong and sizeable state, mainly because of the activities of its kings, of whom the first and the greatest was Agaja.

The reign of Agaja (1708–1740)

A contemporary of Osei Tutu and Opoku Ware of Asante, Agaja began his reign by reorganising the army and setting up a military school for Dahomey boys who became disciplined and trained soldiers. Secondly, he instituted the *agbadjigbeto* which was a combination of a sort of war intelligence and public information service. Agaja used this for spying on other countries and for spreading propaganda within Dahomey. He then embarked on his wars of expansion. After subduing the north-western districts, and conquering the state of Weme (1716), in the 1720s he turned southwards to the coast with a view not to taking part in the slave trade but rather to stopping 'by stages the slave trade in the Aja country and substituting for it a general trade in agricultural produce.' In 1724 he very easily conquered and annexed the parent state of Allada and three years later that of Whydah. To tighten his grip on these coastal states, Agaja abolished their ruling dynasties and placed the government of both in the hands of two of his most senior ministers, the *migan* and the *yovogan*. Agaja created the latter post himself in 1732 to control the activities of the Europeans on the coast.

Agaja's conquests of these coastal Aja states attracted the attention of the Alafin of Oyo. Between 1726 and 1730 Oyo attacked Dahomey four times because of their anxiety about Dahomey's intentions regarding Oyo's trade routes to the coast. It says a lot for the prudence of Agaja that he realised that the best way to preserve his kingdom was to move the capital from Abomey to Allada and to enter into a treaty with Oyo. This he was able to accomplish in 1730. Agaja agreed to pay an annual tribute to Oyo, to recognize Oyo's suzerainty over the kingdom of Ajase Ipo (later to be known as Porto Novo) and undertook not to attack any of the other Aja tributary states such as Weme, Epe and Badagry. But he was left alone to manage the internal administration of his kingdom. By so doing, Agaja saved the young kingdom from any further invasions by Oyo. Thus by the time of his death, though Dahomey and become a tributary state of Oyo, it was well-established and enlarged with the whole area down to the coast under its direct control.

Agaja's successors, Tegbesu IV (1740–1774), Kpengla V (1774–1789), and Agonglo (1789–1797) did not add much to the area of the kingdom they inherited nor were they able to end its tributary status. Tegbesu in fact devoted himself to improving the economy of the state by actively participating in the slave trade and ensuring that the Europeans traded at Whydah. Although he was initially successful in this, from the 1760s onwards trade through Whydah decreased to the advantage of other coastal centres such as Porto Novo. By the end of his reign in 1774. Dahomey's economy had declined. Furthermore, its tributary status had been further tightened by an additional treaty with Oyo in 1748. Dahomey's fortunes continued to decline:

the withdrawal of all the Europeans from the port of Whydah was a further blow to dwindling trade. Of the two kings to follow Tegbesu one was assassinated and the other overthrown by a coup d'état.

But in 1818, as a result of the coup, Gezo took over power in the kingdom and helped not only to restore its fortunes but to complete its growth into a very strong kingdom. Taking advantage of Oyo's preoccupation with its wars against the Fulani, Gezo broke free of Oyo completely in 1823. He then pushed northwards and conquered large parts of the Mahi country in the 1840s. In the east he attacked the Egbado areas in the 1830s and 1840s. He launched a huge campaign against Abeokuta in 1851 and forced Ketu to come under Dahomey's protection. Besides his wars of conquest, Gezo promoted agriculture, set up oil palm plantations, and encouraged palm oil production. He also encouraged arts and crafts. In 1848, however, he died of smallpox in the middle of his campaigns. His successors, Glele (r. 1848–89) and Behanzin (r. 1889–94) continued to attack the western provinces of Oyo and though they succeeded in capturing Ketu, they failed to subdue Abeokuta. Behanzin also attacked the south-eastern districts and this brought him into conflict with the French who defeated him in 1894.

The survival of Dahomey

While Oyo and Asante had lost their military strength and declined by the last quarter of the nineteenth century, Dahomey was still stable, dominant and aggressive. This was due to a number of internal as well as external factors.

The first factor was its extent. Dahomey even at the peak of its power, was in area much smaller than Asante or Oyo. The kingdom was only about 160 kilometres from north to south and from east to west it never extended anywhere beyond 80 kilometres; it was indeed much narrower near the coast where it was about 45 kilometres wide. Thus Dahomey occupied an area of only 6 400 square kilometres, about a tenth of the size of the modern Republic of Benin. It was therefore much easier to defend or hold together than the sprawling empires of Oyo and Asante.

The development of one of the most efficient systems of government known in West Africa was another crucial factor. To begin with, its system of succession to the throne, which was introduced by Tegbesu, dictated that only princes born of royal wives during their father's reign were eligible. This rule automatically eliminated several potential candidates. Since the number of children born to a king during his reign was limited, especially if he came to the throne at a mature age, rival claimants for the throne became relatively few. Moreover, usually the reigning monarch selected his successor before his death. This system greatly minimised disputed successions and civil wars, which, for instance, plagued Asante during the second half of the nineteenth century, or Oyo, or Dahomey's sister kingdom, Porto Novo.

Once elected, the king of Dahomey, unlike the Alafin of Oyo, the king of Asante, or even the Oba of Benin, was not a *primus inter pares* – that is, the first among equally powerful chiefs. He became an absolute monarch whose word was law throughout the kingdom and who controlled all political and military appointments. The inheritance of all property was validated through his court, and, through his officials, the king monitored events of all kinds throughout his kingdom. Dahomey was also fortunate in having throughout the nineteenth century very able, highly enlightened and courageous rulers in the persons of Gezo, Glele and Behanzin.

The kings of Dahomey were assisted by a cabinet which consisted of the *migan*, (prime minister); the *meu*, (finance minister) created by Tegbesu, who supervised all the chiefs and was also responsible for Allada; *yovo-gan* (viceroy of Whydah); the *to-no-num* (the chief eunuch and minister in charge of protocol), the *tokpo* (minister of agriculture), the *agan* (general of the army) and the *adjaho* (minister for the king's palace and chief of police). The interesting and unique feature of the cabinet is that each of these posts had its female counterpart who complemented him but reported independently to the king.

Furthermore, Dahomey also had a large army consisting of full-time soldiers, and a militia which could be summoned at any time. This army was believed by nineteenth century European observers to be the strongest and best organised on the west coast. During his reign, Gezo increased the number of the full-time soldiers from about 5 000 in 1840 to 12 000 by 1845. This army consisted not only of men but also of women, the famous Amazons 'devoted to the person of the king and valorous in war'. This unique female section was created and organised by Gezo and consisted of 2 500 female soldiers divided into three brigades. Commanders of this army were also top cabinet ministers in charge of the central government thus enhancing the position of the army in decision making.

The provincial system of government was also interesting and unique. The kings of Dahomey, unlike the rulers of the other empires, usually abolished the ruling royal families of the states they conquered, and suppressed their laws and customs; they then imposed the laws and customs of Dahomey, and appointed governors for such states. In other words, they pursued a policy of 'Dahomeanisation' and total integration of the conquered states. The whole kingdom was divided into six provinces each under a provincial chief below whom came the governors and village chiefs, all appointed by the king. Communication between the king and the provincial governors was swift and was ensured by a strong body of runners, stationed at relay posts throughout the kingdom. This institution was comparable to the *ilari* system of Oyo and was introduced by Tegbesu. Not only could provincial governors be summoned to Abomey at any time, but to ensure that full reports of their activities reached the court, each one had a spy attached to his office.

The policy described above meant, first, that unlike Asante and Oyo, Dahomey was not surrounded by enemies who awaited favourable opportunities to shake off their allegiance. Secondly as Dahomey laws and institutions took root, the whole kingdom became an homogeneous entity, able to withstand and absorb shocks. Hence, while the defeat inflicted on the Asante by the British and on Oyo by the Fulani led to their disintegration, the defeat of Dahomey's invading armies by Abeokuta in 1851 and 1864 did not. Thirdly, it meant that anybody could become a citizen of Dahomey, including even Europeans.

Another unique and modern feature of the government of Dahomey was its sources of income. The kings derived their income not only from customs duties, tolls, proceeds of the royal estates and from their monopoly of the slave trade and certain European imports such as gold, coral, arms and ammunition, but also from other sources unknown in the other kingdoms of West Africa. The first was the tax on income or head-money paid according to the rank, reputation and the income of the person. Secondly, agriculture, the basic industry, was taxed. The farmers in each village were counted by officials of the minister of agriculture and the tax paid in kind by each was fixed according to the assessment made of the villagers' total production. Livestock were also counted and taxed. Hunters, farmers, salt-makers, craftsmen and even grave-diggers were also taxed. The kings of Dahomey regularly conducted a population census to get an accurate estimate of the number of people to be taxed and also to be conscripted into the army when necessary.

All these internal factors listed above combined to make Dahomey a highly organised and stable polity. However, the last factor underlying Dahomey's survival until the 1890s was external: unlike Asante and Oyo, Dahomey was not subjected to any serious external attacks and invasions until the 1890s. To the north and west of Dahomey were the tiny Mahi, Watyi and Atakpame principalities which had neither the organisation nor the resources to invade Dahomey. To the east was Oyo which, as we have seen, was disintegrating throughout the nineteenth century and too preoccupied with her own civil wars and problems to embark on any invasion. On the contrary, it was Dahomey that assumed the offensive from the 1820s onwards.

While the African states could not attack Dahomey, the European nations would not do so either for various reasons. First, until the 1890s no single European nation ever became dominant on the coast of Dahomey. The French, the English, the Dutch and the Brazilians were all trading there, and rivalry among them prevented them from taking any joint action against the kings of Dahomey, while the latter were able to play one off against the other and dictate the terms of trade. Secondly, none of the European powers really had any cause for actively interfering in the internal affairs of Dahomey except the British, since the kings were able to ensure peace and order and keep the trade routes open. However, since the kings of Dahomey persistently refused to abolish the slave trade, the British, who were genuinely interested in the question, did have cause for intervention and most of the British officials on the coast, the consuls of the Bights of Benin and Biafra as well as the governors of modern Ghana, did in fact urge the British government to intervene. But the British government persistently refused to sanction any attack since they were convinced that Dahomey, unlike Lagos which they attacked and annexed between 1850 and 1861, was so powerful a kingdom that its conquest would be difficult and very expensive.

It seems clear then that the survival of Dahomey until the early 1890s was due to its own inherent strength and vitality coupled with the fact that she did not face any serious external attacks until then. But the former was certainly the more decisive factor since it was the main consideration that put the British off, and had it not been for the French conquest in 1894, the old dynasty would be reigning in Abomey to this day. The circumstances that led to the French conquest will be discussed later.

11 Lower Niger states and peoples

Origins and migrations

From the available evidence – oral tradition, archaeology and the study of language – it appears that the various peoples of south-eastern Nigeria have lived in the area for thousands of years, but there has been considerable migration of people within the region, particularly from the interior southwards towards the coast. There is also evidence of migrations both eastwards and westwards across the Niger river. The oral traditions of a number of peoples in the area about their origins indicate links with Benin. For example, the Itsekiri of the mangrove swamp coastlands west of the Niger have an oral tradition that their kingdom was founded when Ginuwa, prince of an unpopular Oba of Benin called Olua, escaped from Benin and settled near the mouth of the Benin river at Ijala. There is another tradition that the Itsekiri state was founded by a Yoruba migration. Among the Urhobo of the immediate interior there are similar variations; most of the Urhobo clans trace their origin back to Benin but others say they migrated from Ijoland and the latest arrivals claim Igbo origin. It is quite possible that all these traditions of origin contain elements of historical fact. The various Ijo groups have varying traditions but they agree broadly on two points: they were pushed south from their original homes into the delta by the Igbo and Itsekiri; and they have lived in the delta for a very long time.

The Ibibio, like the Igbo, have no traditions of having lived anywhere else apart from their present homelands in the rainforest belt of south-eastern Nigeria. This must mean that both peoples have lived in their present location for thousands of years. The Efik of Calabar, who are really a branch of the Ibibio, appear to have resided close to the Uruan clan of the Ibibio for at least a century before migrating east of the Cross river and founding new settlements, probably in the early seventeenth century. The first of several Efik settlements on the Calabar river was at Ikot Itunko, called Creek Town by British traders. The purpose of the Efik migrations was probably to secure vantage points for the new Atlantic trade, which we shall turn to in more detail later in this chapter.

The oral traditions of many Igbo groups reveal a pattern of much internal migration, as a way of solving population pressures and disputes. When migrants established new homes they would become part of the community they settled in, but preserve the memory of their origins. Igbos moved out of Igboland to settle and trade in the delta. At the same time, non-Igbo peoples moved into Igboland. Indeed, various groups appear to have moved south of the Benue into the Igbo forests to escape slave-raiding.

The traditions of the formation of Igbo states along the Niger indicate the close relationships between the various communities of the region. The city-state of Aboh, on the west bank of the Niger at the neck of the delta, has two rival traditions of its origin in the late fifteenth century: one, that it was founded by a losing contender for the throne of Benin; the other, that it was founded as a result of the downstream migration of families from Idah, the capital of the Igala kingdom to the north between Igboland and the Niger-Benue confluence. Whatever the truth, it is obvious that the motive for founding Aboh was to command the trade of the three major channels of the Niger delta which meet the river nearby; the Nun south towards Brass, the Forcados west to Warri and Benin, and the Engenni eastwards to Bonny. The migrants, whoever they were, ruled over the Igbo-speaking Akri they found at Aboh. Likewise, the town of Ossomari on the east bank, founded in the sixteenth century, has a clear tradition of connections with Igala, at least with regard to the origin of its rulers. Two further city states were founded along the Niger at about this time, namely Onitsha and Asaba.

The traditions of the foundation of Arochukwu close to the west bank of the Cross river once more illustrate the interaction and intermingling between the peoples of the region. The Aro, an Igbo group, over a period of several generations up to the mid-seventeenth century, took over the area from the original Ibibio inhabitants after forming an alliance with the Akpa, a group from east of the Cross river. Arochukwu grew up as a community of villages of Igbo, Akpa and Ibibio origin. The Long Juju, the oracular shrine of the Igbo High God Chukwu, may have been acquired from the Ibibio, but some oral accounts claim that the shrine was originated by the Aro themselves.

Trading economies

It is important to note that the economy of south-eastern Nigeria was expanding and becoming more complex long before the arrival of European traders in the sixteenth century. Before 1500 the region had developed a variety of economic activities and many communities were engaged in long-distance trade. In the Niger delta fishing and salt-making were the major sources of livelihood. Salt was produced in the towns at the mouths of various branches of the Niger by filtering a solution of ash from the roots, shoots and leaves of mangrove trees and by evaporation of sea water. Portuguese traders shortly after 1500 reported that Bonny was manufacturing salt and exporting it to the Igbos in the hinterland in exchange for foodstuffs. In fact, all along the coast salt and dried fish were being sold to the interior in exchange not only for yams, kola nuts, palm oil and livestock but also for pottery of an advanced type, elaborately woven cotton cloth, swords and other goods made out of skilfully worked iron and copper. The archaeological excavations being carried out at Igbo-Ukwu since 1959 have revealed the skill and beauty of Igbo workmanship and the extent of the network of long-distance trade that the region was part of. We know that as early as the ninth century Igbos were making iron swords and bronze and copper vases and ornaments of outstanding quality. The evidence of Igbo-Ukwu is that the rulers there wore beads from Venice and India imported via the trans-Saharan trade, and the copper worked there was imported from the Sahara. The exports sent north in return were probably ivory and kola nuts and possibly slaves.

It is not true to say that the trading states of the lower Niger and the Cross river arose as a result of the Atlantic slave trade that grew up after 1500 and reached its peak between 1650 and 1800. We have seen that trading states arose as part of a much earlier pattern of economic activity. It is true, however, that the existing trading-states did take a major part in the slave trade and in some of them slaves became the leading export. (See Section 3 for the general causes and results of the slave trade as it affected West Africa.) At this stage two questions will be answered. What were the main features of the organisation of the slave trade in south-eastern Nigeria? and what were the social and economic effects of the slave trade on this region?

Most of the slave-raiding in the region was carried on in Igboland and beyond, most of the slave-trading was done at the coast. The most common method of obtaining slaves was kidnapping by armed gangs though some slaves were sold as criminals, or as a result of debt or famine. There is plenty of evidence of such raids in traders' accounts as well as in the autobiography of Olaudah Equiano. Igboland was an obvious target for Igbo, Ijo, Ibibio and Efik slave-raiders and traders because it had a dense population and was politically divided into many small states and therefore lacked the strong central government needed for defence. The slave-raiders often had the added advantage of possessing firearms, the use of which became general in the Delta in the eighteenth century. Europeans were not allowed into the interior to obtain slaves directly, and the African slave-traders became more and more prosperous as middlemen. They would march their human merchandise to the coast to be sold to Europeans sometimes in the ports but often offshore. The slaves were branded with the letters of the trading company that bought them.

In the eighteenth century the slave trade was dominated by the English who drew the bulk of their slaves from the lower Niger. The loss of people was a heavy blow to the region. Captain Adams, who sailed on ten slave-trading voyages to West Africa between 1786 and 1800, stated that 20 000 slaves were sold annually at Bonny and 16 000 of them were Igbo. He estimated that over a twenty-year period 320 000 Igbos were sold to European slave-traders at Bonny and another 50 000 at Elem Kalabari and Calabar. The majority of these slaves were young, fit people whose presence at home was essential for stable economic development. In addition to those Igbos and others who were sold to Europeans we must add a sizeable number who were put to work as labourers, canoeists and trading assistants in the city-states and their trading colonies and plantations. Their fate was far more endurable than that of their countrymen who were shipped to the Americas: The histories of Alali and Jaja in Bonny showed that a few could rise to positions of wealth and authority. However, even in the Delta city-states slavery was a misfortune and slaves remained city-state victims of social inequality.

There is evidence that several of the coastal towns grew in size and wealth as a result of the slave trade. It is quite possible, however, that the slave trade also prevented the natural growth of these towns from their pre-slave trade beginnings, and as a result, the rulers could only maintain and develop their towns by organising an artificial, enforced, involuntary influx of slaves. The goods the European slave-traders brought with them for exchange did nothing to help the economic development of the region either; in fact it did much to hinder it. Many of the goods they introduced such as cotton cloth, iron bars, copper and salt, were already being produced by the peoples of the region. The imports undermined the existing industry and trade of south-eastern Nigeria. Spirits and tobacco harmed people's health and firearms increased the incidence of war and kidnapping. The excessive imports of cowrie shells by European traders devalued existing local currencies.

South-eastern Nigeria did not benefit immediately from the abolition of the slave trade by Britain in 1807 (see Section 3). It was not until after 1845, when Britain signed a treaty with Portugal and Brazil, giving her the right to stop the Brazilian slave-ships that had largely replaced the British slavers in the Delta, that the Atlantic slave trade began to decline.

The rise in the vegetable oil trade did, however, enable the Niger Delta to become by 1850 the major exporter of palm oil to Europe. British imports of palm oil from West Africa rose from 1 000 tons in 1810 to 40 000 tons in 1855. Of this total, it is estimated that the delta exported 22 500 tons, most of it from Bonny and Elem Kalabari. The bulk of the palm oil was produced in the rain forest belt of the southern Igbo, Ibibio and Efik. The palm oil trade increased the financial links between the coastal states and the interior communities. The interior producers married their daughters to coastal middlemen and sent their children to Bonny to be trained in international trade. The Delta states appointed reliable family heads as produce buyers on commission, and advanced them barter goods on credit for business activities further inland.

The Delta states and Houses

The House system of the Delta city-states assisted their continued economic development in the nineteenth century. The city-states were confederacies of Houses, each containing hundreds or even thousands of people. Each House had its own fleet of trading and war canoes, the latter being put at the service of the state in wartime. House heads were second in rank to the king, and sat in the council of state. In the eighteenth century only princes could become House heads but in the nineteenth century promotion came increasingly to men of lowly or even slave origin. Houses realised that they must promote men of ability or they would collapse before their trading rivals. Besides being efficient trading bodies, the Houses were also ideal organisations for absorbing and uniting people of different origins and social status.

Social mobilty in the Houses led to the rise of 'new men' – commoners or ex-slaves – able to challenge the authority of traditional rulers in the Delta. A typical 'new man' was Olomu, a member of the commoner Ologbotsere family of Itsekiriland. In the 1840s Olomu emerged as a powerful commercial rival to the Itsekiri royal family, expanding his palm oil trade on the Benin river while the royal family's economic fortunes declined on the Forcados. Civil wars between the royal family and various commoner families led to a political revolution in 1848, when the monarchy's powers were brought under control. It was agreed that a 'Governor of the River' (the Benin river) would rule and the governorship would alternate between the royal and Ologbotsere families. Olomu was governor from 1879 to 1883. Olomu was a brilliant soldier, sailor, diplomatist, trader and administrator. He founded a new town at Ebrohimi from which he organised trading expeditions up the Ethiope and Warri rivers into Urhoboland. Here he increased his influence through a marriage alliance with the daughter of the head of the Evrho clan and a friendship with Ovwha, head of the Agbarho clan. Olomu's force of slave sailors armed with guns secured his political and commercial domination over a wide area of the western delta. Olomu's son Nana continued his father's policy of expanding the Ologbotsere family's role in the palm oil trade by a combination of diplomacy and force.

With the palm oil trade Bonny came to be dominated by ex-slaves of Igbo origin. Bonny had already become virtually an Igbo state, due to the influx of Igbo slaves causing Ijo to give way to Igbo as the language of the state. The Pepple royal family (founded in the early eighteenth century) and several House heads were of Igbo origin. Bonny was dominated from 1830 to 1861 by the ex-slave Alali, head of the Anna Pepple House. Alali was appointed regent on the death of King Opobo in 1830 because the new king, William Dappa Pepple, was a minor. In 1836 Alali bravely imprisoned some British traders after the British navy seized a Spanish slave-ship in Bonny harbour. The British sent a warship and Alali was forced to resign. For eighteen years Alali concentrated on trade, but another incident involving the British gave him the opportunity to return to power. In 1854 King Dappa Pepple, who was owed money by British traders, seized a British ship. Alali allied with the British to overthrow the king and thus became one of a regency council of four ex-slaves. Within this council, Alali once more became the effective ruler of Bonny. However, he refused to take orders from the British consul and the British restored the king. Alali appears to have taken poison either to avoid arrest or out of shame at the humiliation of his country.

The most famous and most successful of all the 'new men' in the delta was undoubtedly Jubo Jubogha, called Jaja by Europeans. He was born in Igbo-land in 1821, sold as a slave to a Bonny trader in 1833 and elected head of the Anna Pepple House to succeed Alali in 1863. Jaja's qualifications were his astonishing organising ability and intelligence, his mastery of the English language which greatly assisted his trading with the British and his good relations with his fellow Igbos, the oil producers on whom his House's prosperity relied. As a House head, Jaja paid off Alali's huge debts to foreign firms, absorbed other Houses, extended Anna Pepple's operations in the hinterland and widened its circle of European buyers. These successes aroused the jealousy of the Manilla Pepple House, whose head, the ex-slave Oko Jumbo, was encouraged by King George Dappa Pepple to attack the Anna Pepple House in a civil war in 1869. Jaja was unready for war and sought peace. He took advantage of a truce to resettle his House with all its people at a new settlement he called Opobo to the east of Bonny. Opobo was in a perfect position to cut off Bonny from its trading empire on the Imo and Qua rivers and ensure Jaja's control of the area. Jaja was already linked with the Igbo rulers along the Imo by marriage alliances, but he also strengthened his new position as an independent ruler and king by exercising his ritual authority as a priest of the traditional religion, in order to bind his palm oil producers to himself rather than to Bonny. Bonny soon went into decline and fourteen of Bonny's senior Houses moved to Opobo in order to survive and to share in Opobo's profitable trade. In the 1870s Jaja took over parts of the Imo valley, made trade alliances with the Aro, chartered European ships for direct trade with Europe, sent his sons to be educated in Britain, opened a western-type school in Opobo and built European-style houses. Jaja, however, remained opposed to Christianity. In religion he was a traditionalist but as a ruler he was modern and progressive.

The inland communities

Among the inland communities, the Aro were the most successful in commerce, and the religious and political influence they wielded was considerable. They quickly adapted to the palm oil trade and became major suppliers to first Bonny and then Opobo, using the same routes they had developed earlier during the slave trade. At the same time they kept the internal slave trade going to provide for their need for slaves for carrying loads and performing agricultural work. As religious authorities, the Aro traders, like the Awka smiths of central Igboland, administered an oracle that gave them authority over a considerable area. Like the oracle of the god Agbala at Awka, the oracle of the god Arochukwu was consulted by people from all over Igboland and even wider afield for political, religious and judicial purposes, not least as courts of appeal to prevent disputes developing into wars. This religious authority was an important influence enabling the Aro to maintain their commercial monopoly along the routes to the coast and further inland into Igboland.

Systems of government

The Aro did not establish centralised political authority in their 'sphere of influence', but their history provides interesting proof that under certain conditions centralised government was not a necessary condition for economic achievement during this period in West Africa. The Igbo in general have often been classified as a 'stateless' society, but this is misleading. Their lack of political unity before colonial rule was due partly to the need of different Igbo communities over a wide area to develop different political systems to suit different environments. Indeed, some of these communities did develop centralised government. For example, the Igbo along the Niger evolved centralised states with what has been called a 'presidential-monarchy' form of government. They adopted the monarchical ideas and practices of the neighbouring non-Igbo states like Benin and Igala, such as the titles, regalia and ceremonials of kingship, but at the same time the western Igbo kings were more like presidents than monarchs because their powers consisted simply of presiding over their *ama ala* (councils of elders) and village assemblies. In practice, in the allocation of political power there was little difference between these Igbo kingships and the hundreds of village republics throughout central and eastern Igboland, where every householder regarded himself as a king. In one respect, however, central Igboland's government was different from that of the west: in the central village republics government depended on the kinship system, whereas in the west title systems were as important. The south-eastern Igbo, including the Aro, governed to a large extent through secret societies like their Ibibio and Efik neighbours, and the north-eastern Igbo adopted the age-grade system of their non-Igbo neighbours in the upper Cross river valley. The secret societies and the age-grades helped to link villages and clans and even cut across Igbo and non-Igbo ethnic divisions in some areas. In Arochukwu there was a crowned head, the *eze aro*, whose powers were little more than ceremonial, real power resting with a council of representatives from the different Aro villages, while the religious power of the oracles played a unifying role. So, too, did the *Igbanda*, a system by which two or more villages with no formal ties of blood relationship created one by performing certain rituals at their common boundary – mixing their blood, eating together and planting a live tree on the spot, thus pledging to settle all disputes between them by peaceful negotiation.

Decline and its consequences

We have seen that the changeover from the slave trade to the palm oil trade in the early nineteenth century brought new opportunities for the trading states and peoples of south-eastern Nigeria. However, in the late nineteenth century the palm oil trade began to decline. Europe soon found many alternatives to palm oil as an industrial lubricant, a fuel and a raw material for the manufacture of candles and soap. Tallow, linseed oil, copra and ahale oil were just as useful in soap-making, for example. In the 1860s the price of palm oil fell as cheaper alternatives entered the world market. Faced with falling prices, the Delta city-states had to obtain larger quantities of palm oil in order to maintain their middlemen profits. Bonny in desperation invaded Elem Kalabari's markets and Elem Kalabari fought Brass for control of Uguta. Elem Kalabari lost both wars and slumped into serious decline. Bonny survived for a while but the secession of Jaja ruined Bonny. In Calabar, New Town emerged victorious in a war with its rivals over control of palm oil.

Weakened by these wars with each other, the city-states at the same time had to face the most serious threat of all, the commercial invasion of the Niger north of the delta by British palm oil trading firms. In 1854 Dr Baikie discovered that quinine could cure malaria and British firms were now able to act quickly to undermine the middleman position of the city-states by obtaining palm oil more cheaply and directly from the producers. Macgregor Laird established posts at Aboh, Onitsha and Lokoja. When Brass inspired the townspeople to destroy Laird's stores at Aboh and Onitsha, the British navy bombarded the towns. By 1878 four British firms were trading up the Niger. In 1879 George Goldie united them into the United Africa Company and set up a hundred posts guarded by twenty gunboats. Colonial rule was about to come to the lower Niger and Igboland.

12 The kingdoms of Sierra Leone

The history of the peoples of present-day Sierra Leone from the fifteenth century to the late nineteenth century reveals long and continuous processes of state-formation, economic adaptation and development of complex systems of government and social control. It also shows the very close interaction and co-operation between the various ethnic groups in the region.

Who were the earliest peoples of Sierra Leone? This question can be answered by outlining the language divisions of the country. Two broad groups of languages emerged: the West Atlantic group, including the languages of the Temne, Limba, Bullom, Sherbro, Fula, Kissi, Gola and Krim peoples; and the Mande group, including the languages of the Mandingo or Mandinka, Mende, Koranko, Kono, Loko, Vai, Susu (or Soso) and Yalunka. The Mande languages are closely related but the West Atlantic languages are not very similar to one another; they are grouped together because of the geographical unity of the peoples who speak them, rather than for linguistic reasons.

Until the sixteenth century the vast majority of the people of Sierra Leone belonged to communities speaking West Atlantic languages. The Bullom lived along the north-western coast and the Krim along the coast south of them. The Temne lived in the western interior and the Kissi in the east, with the Limba occupying much of the northern interior. At this time only a few Mande-speaking peoples had migrated into Sierra Leone. But by the early nineteenth century the pattern of settlement had changed dramatically. Large numbers of Mande-speakers, particularly the Mende, had occupied much of the south-east and older-established Mande-speakers like the Susu and Koranko had expanded further into the area from the north. At the same time, West Atlantic language-speakers had expanded their territory and the Temne had taken over much of the centre of the country, thus driving a linguistic wedge between the Mande-speakers of the north and those of the south.

Some of the West Atlantic peoples have no traditions of migrations. The Bullom of the coast and the Limba of the interior say they have always lived in their present homelands – which suggests that they moved to them a very long time ago. By the time the Portuguese arrived in the late fifteenth century the Bullom were dealing in gold, bought from traders from the empire of Mali in exchange for salt. The Bullom sold gold and extraordinarily beautiful ivory carvings to the Portuguese, in return for large metal basins and cotton cloth. However, this trade stopped after the Mane invasions in the sixteenth century.

The Mane invasions

There are various and conflicting traditional accounts of the Mane or Mande invasions of Sierra Leone in the first half of the sixteenth century. One version implies that the Mane were Mande soldiers from Mali cut off from their homeland by a Songhai offensive and forced to return home by a great march southwards and westwards that brought them to the southern Sierra Leone coast. Another account describes the Mane as a group of Mandinka led by their queen Masarico and exiled from Mali. Whoever the Mane were, it is possible that they had some previous knowledge of the lands they invaded because for several centuries Mande traders from Mali had been buying sea salt from the coastal peoples of Sierra Leone. Mande-speaking Susu traders had begun to settle at the coast just north of Sierra Leone as early as the thirteenth century. By about 1540 the Mane had settled among the Gola and Kissi close to the present day Liberia/Sierra Leone frontier, in the Cape Mount area. From here, they launched a series of invasions, some twenty years apart, into the rest of Sierra Leone. The Mane were assisted in their conquests by the fact that the non-Mande peoples had in general not developed political institutions beyond the village level and the small and divided communities could offer no effective resistance. However, when the Mane struck inland to fight the Susu and Fula, they were defeated and pushed back to the coast.

What were the results of the Mane invasions? In the first place, there were a number of political changes in Sierra Leone. New kingdoms were set up, owing allegiance to the parent Mane kingdom in the Cape Mount area. The great soldier-king (or *farma*), Tami, established a kingdom among the Temne and Baga in about 1560. Several communities not under Tami's direct rule, such as the Limba, acknowledged his authority and sent tribute to him at Koya, his capital. As ruler of a confederacy of states Tami set up an administration of officials to help him govern. Next most powerful after the *farma* was the *naimbana*, ruler of the *rogbannah* secret society, the significance of which we shall examine later. The chief counsellors were the *pa kapr*, the *nainsogo*, four queens and some lesser officials. All counsellors were elected and held their positions for life. When Tami died in about 1605, the Mandinka title *farma* remained as the title of the kings and the Temne added *bai*, their own title, so that later kings were entitled *bai farma*. Tami and his followers adopted Temne culture and his descendants because Temne; this was the general pattern among the new states where the actual population numbers of the Mane were far outweighed by the local people. Indeed, the Mane kings generally intermarried with their subjects and their descendants identified with or were absorbed by them. By the middle of the seventeenth century, although some kings and chiefs were of Mane origin, the Bullom, Temne and Loko kingdoms were no longer 'Mane states'.

The Mane invasions brought economic changes to Sierra Leone. Initially there was an increase in the slave trade as the Mane sold prisoners of war to the Portuguese, who followed the Mane invaders up the coast like vultures flying over a battlefield – one Bullom ruler sold himself as a slave to the Portuguese to save himself from the Mane. In the seventeenth century the slave trade declined in Sierra Leone, because the Mane invasions had stopped and the sale of local products such as beeswax, camwood and ivory became much more important. The slave trade revived in the eighteenth century as a result of the fighting in the Fula Muslim *jihad* to the north. On the positive side, however, the Mane improved the durability of iron tools in their area of conquest. It is probable too that it was the Mane who introduced cotton cloth-weaving to the coast, although the weaver's loom may well have been brought by the Susu or Koranko before the Mane invasion.

The Mende and Temne migrations

Another Mande-speaking group – the Mende – migrated into Sierra Leone from the Liberian hinterland in the eighteenth century. The Mende migrated and formed states in a very different manner from that of the Mane. Most of them migrated slowly and peacefully, clearing land for farming. They were also great elephant hunters and towns would be founded at places where elephants were killed, such places being regarded as sacred. The Mende traded not only in ivory but also in their own cloth which they sold in exchange for salt at the coast. From the late eighteenth century, the Kpa Mende, with their strong military traditions that were not found among the other Mende groupings altered the pattern of Mende migration and state formation with their aggressive wars against the Temne. A determination to gain larger shares in the slave trade and ivory trade at the coast seems to have been the motive that drove the Kpa Mende across the Moa river and into Temne country some time before 1800.

Temne traditions point to an origin probably in the mountainous Jallonkadu (part of which is Futa Jallon). The Temne had migrated to the Sierra Leone interior by the fifteenth century and originally settled north of the coastal Baga and Bullom. In the seventeenth century the Temne expanded gradually from the Koya area to the coast. In the late eighteenth century Temne country was invaded by the Kpa Mende from the east. The Temne beat off this attack by obtaining help from their Fula trading partners. In gratitude to the Fula trader Masa Keleh, the Yoni Temne recognised one of his successors (as head of the Fula among the Yoni) as their own king, with the title of *fula mansa*. The Fula became integrated into Yoni society through intermarriage. To the north-west, the Temne came into contact with the Koranko around Kholifa and Konike and together they created a Koranko-Temne or eastern Temne community. Yet another multi-ethnic state had been created. The Temne provided the political leadership and the Koranko brought the Temne into some of their social institutions, such as the *doweh* secret society, which soon spread to all Temne and was called Ragbenle.

Political organisation

The states of the Mende, Temne and other peoples of Sierra Leone had by the nineteenth century developed clear patterns of political and military organisation. The small Mende states began to merge into a number of larger confederacies, such as the Kpa-Mende confederacy and the group of states under the authority of the powerful King Makavoray of Tikonko. The confederacies emerged out of several needs: to protect people from the raids of coastal slave-trading states ruled by the mixed race rulers like the Caulkers, Clevelands and Rogers; to secure and maintain control over trade routes between the further interior and the coast, and to compete successfully in the growing palm oil trade.

The largest Mende confederacy was that of the Kpa-Mende originally centred on the town of Taiama – actually sixteen towns together making up a metropolis, built on high ground above the banks of the Taiama. There were nine stockaded towns and seven open villages where farms provided food for the fortress towns. A king exercised clear authority over all the settlements but within each of them a chief carried out much of the day-to-day administration. Many of the inhabitants of the open villages were slaves but they were 'slaves of the House' in the West African not the American pattern: they were given farms, they often married into the master's family and they could become headmen, or even chiefs. Mende chiefs and kings were elected and chosen on merit by the elders after a long process of consultation. Kingship was not hereditary. It was important to select a man with a proven record in warfare and or trade. Such a man was Gbanya Lango, king of the Kpa-Mende confederacy. Gbanya extended his authority to the Bullom towns along the upper Bumpe, moved his capital to Senehun, the Bumpe river-head, where palm oil and other goods could be collected and sent down river to the coast, and as the leading organiser of Mende professional warriors in the second half of the nineteenth century he hired out mercenaries to whoever could afford to 'buy war' from him.

A Mende ruler, apart from having to protect his subjects in war and famine, had to play a central role in ceremonies and rituals, entertain strangers and judge cases as president of a court of elders. In return, his subjects were obliged to perform labour for the ruler, such as making a rice farm (*manja*) for him, keeping his compound in good repair or building a new one, and clearing the roads. The ruler was entitled to a portion of the rice and palm oil produced in every extended family (*mawe*). Among the officials of a Mende ruler was the speaker, who had three principal functions: to act as the ruler's deputy when he was ill or absent; to act as the main intermediary between the ruler and his subjects (all complaints and disputes were first brought to the speaker); and to pass on the ruler's orders to subordinate officials. Thus the speaker in a Mende state was a kind of prime minister.

The Temne were divided politically by the beginning of the nineteenth century into twelve or more kingdoms, each independent of the other. Kings were elected, as among the Mende, by the elders (in practice the senior grade of the local lodge of the secret society). Rulers were believed by their subjects to be sacred and they underwent long and complicated installation ceremonies. In theory, once elected, a Temne king could not be deposed and could even act as a tyrant; in reality, his powers were limited in various ways. After election, a king was confined in *kantha*; he would be secluded with his subordinate officials for several months to be made aware of his duties and responsibilities to his people. Subordinate officials could not be deposed either; therefore, the king was obliged to listen to their views and advice and to try to work with them in a co-operative manner. Top policy decisions were made not by the king alone but by the king's council or by the *poro* society. The council contained officials who resembled modern cabinet ministers, for example, the *kapr kabin* or speaker who acted as a prime minister, the *kapr masm* or chief priest, the *kapr loya* or chief prosecutor, the *kapr soya* or army commander, the *kapr kuma* or custodian of the kingly articles of office and the *kapr fenthe* with responsibility for health. The council also included subordinate officials, *mamy* queens and leading officials of secret societies.

Co-operation between Temne kingdoms took the form of military alliances; defensive towns and villages were organised, with strong stockades, along Mende lines, and the people armed with cutlasses, sling-shots, stone clubs and guns of various types bought from the French or the British or made by the skilled Temne blacksmiths. Temne military organisation led to the rise of military rulers such as Kebalai, a prominent leader in one of the alliances, who began his military career in 1865 and was elected king of Kasseh in 1886, assuming the title of *bai bureh*. In 1892 Kebalai led a Temne-Lokko-Limba alliance in a major campaign against Karimu, a Soso leader in the pay of the French who were trying to expand in Guinea. Kebalai's organisational skills and tactics and the discipline of his soldiers took them to victory. The alliances led by Kebalai helped to build wider loyalties than the local kingdom among many Temne.

The secret societies

The secret societies played a major role in the government and the economic and social life of the peoples of Sierra Leone. The most important of these were the *poro*, known largely among the Temne, Kono, Mende and other peoples at or near the coast, the *gbangbe* and *doweh* among the Koranko in the north and some of the Temne, the *gbangbani* among the Limba, the *wunde* of the Kpa Mende and the *bundo*, a female society found among virtually every ethnic group. The societies were secret only in the sense that meetings were held in private and the contents of discussions were not revealed. In some communities every man of standing had to join the society and in others every adult male, regardless of status and wealth, was required to join. Membership was therefore democratic, but effective power was given to the kings, chiefs and other rich men in the higher grades. A secret society had neither a centralised organisation nor a continuous all-the-year-round existence, but it managed to serve vital political, economic and social functions. The *poro* was organised as a collection of local 'lodges' independent of each other, and members were called together only to perform specific tasks at irregular times. Therefore a secret society could not provide a basis of political unity across state boundaries. However, it was politically useful. For example, it upheld the authority of rulers but at the same time helped to check the abuse of power by rulers. The societies were responsible for the installation ceremonies of rulers and their subordinates and thus bestowed on them a semi-divine status that enhanced their authority. On the other hand, the religious side of the societies checked the powers of the rulers, who were bound to observe moral and religious laws.

Major decisions such as those of war and peace were made by the societies not by the rulers or their councils. War was banned while a society was in session. If, at other times, a society decided on peace, then it would send out armed men to act as police and kill anyone found out of doors and confiscate his livestock and grain. Society members would act as secret agents and police in their localities. In the economic field, the societies exercised control of everyday affairs such as local trade and market prices and charges for load-carrying. Their social functions were to organise the schooling of initiates, public religious ceremonies and popular entertainments of dance and music, and to look after the shrines of the ancestors. In all these various ways, therefore, the societies assisted rulers in the tasks of government and helped to unite separate communities behind common customs and practices.

The effects of Islam

Like the secret societies, the coming of Islam affected the social and political development of Sierra Leone but, unlike in neighbouring areas to the north (Senegambia) and the east (Mali and its successor states) the impact of Islam was less profound. There is evidence that Muslim Mandinka, Fula and Susu traders were active in Sierra Leone as early as the thirteenth century. However, it was not until the eighteenth century that Islam made any real headway in Sierra Leone. Until then, the traders who settled in Sierra Leone and the Mane invaders appear to have lost their Islamic religion as they became absorbed by the far more numerous non-Muslims. Nevertheless, the Muslims left their mark in the adoption by the local peoples of terms like *almamy* (headman), *sakara* (sacrifice) and *tabule* (drum). Muslim Mandingo and Fula were welcomed by the rulers and people as clerks, because of their literacy in Arabic, or as charm makers.

Islam was far more successful in parts of Sierra Leone after the Fula *jihad* in the eighteenth century, which dates from about 1725. After the Fula built a strong Islamic state in Futa Jallon the Solima Yalunka of the further interior accepted the Fula as their overlords and joined the Fula in spreading the *jihad* to the Koranko and Limba peoples, some of whom were converted and began to live in new Muslim towns and villages. However, Fula rule proved to be too harsh not only for the Koranko and Limba but even for the Solima. In the 1770s the Solima failed to support the Fula in a war against the Sankaran, and the Fula killed all the Solima in Futa Jallon; the Solima retaliated by killing all the Fula in their country. The Solima, led by their leading warrior, Tokbo Asana, and aided by the Koranko, joined the Sankaran led by Konde Brima and invaded Futa Jallon itself. However, the Fula launched a successful counter-offensive and destroyed the Solima towns. The defeated Solima moved further south and in 1780 founded a new capital at Falaba, a strong fortress in the mountains. Most of the Solima gave up Islam during the war against the Fula but some of their leaders remained Muslims.

Islam spread more peacefully and with greater success in the north-west part of the country. The Susu were converted to Islam by the Mandinka after an early eighteenth-century *jihad* led by Modi al-haji. The Susu then moved into the areas around Kambia and Port Loko at the same time as the Temne but the two peoples settled together peacefully, because the Susu accepted Temne overlordship. The Susu founded the town of Saindugu on the south bank of Port Loko creek, spread out to build other settlements, intermarried with the Temne and took Temne children into their Koranic schools. In time, however, the Susu aroused the jealousy and enmity of the Temne because of their success in purchasing firearms in great quantities and their involvement in the slave trade and other forms of commerce. By 1816 the Susu *almamy*, Brima Konkoura Sanko, had become so powerful that the Temne led by Moriba Kindu Bangura, the son of a Temne king, attacked Saindugu. Most of the Susu around Port Loko were captured and sold into slavery. The Susu presence in the area for about a hundred years had, however, led to widespread and permanent conversion to Islam by the Port Loko Temne. The Susu contribution to the spread of Islam in Sierra Leone continued when in the 1820s a Susu scholar, Foday Tarawaly, set up an Islamic school at Gbile on the Scarcies river. By 1850 the school had expanded into a university with several hundred students. However, Temne invaders from Dixing destroyed the university in 1875. The Mandinka conqueror, Samori Toure, overran parts of the Sierra Leone hinterland in the 1880s and there was mass conversion to Islam. Samori's rule lasted for only a few years but its effects were lasting, as the areas he conquered have remained Muslim.

Some observers have blamed the spread of Islam for the growth of the external slave trade in Sierra Leone in the eighteenth century and the internal slave trade in the nineteenth century. This kind of accusation is unjust and unhistorical. The Muslims who entered Sierra Leone in the eighteenth century were largely traders and they simply provided the Christian European traders with what they wanted: slaves. In the nineteenth century the internal slave trade was carried on by Muslims and non-Muslims alike. The growth of the slave trade, in Sierra Leone as elsewhere in West Africa, was a consequence of economic not religious factors.

13   The coming of the Europeans

In the last two sections we traced the history of the principal states and empires of West Africa. We referred on a number of occasions to the effect which the activities of some European nations had on the fortunes of the states, and we saw that the Europeans were partly and in some cases wholly responsible for the fall of the forest and coastal kingdoms. Had it not been for the activities of the French in the last decade of the nineteenth century, the Aja dynasty, for instance, would probably be reigning in Dahomey to this day. The questions posed by these references to European nations particularly in the second section are these: which European nations were involved? When and why did they come to West Africa? What was the nature of their activities before the last quarter of the nineteenth century? Why did they so actively and consistently interfere in the affairs of the West African states during that quarter and eventually partition practically the entire African continent among themselves? What did they do after their conquest and occupation of West Africa? And, finally, what was the reaction of the Africans to all this? These are the questions that we shall try to answer in this third section.

The first Europeans to come to West Africa were the Portuguese, who began their activities in the second decade of the fifteenth century. They were soon followed, from the 1450s onwards, by the Castilians or the Spanish as we call them today. But these Castilians gave up their West African interest when the Americas were discovered between 1492 and 1504. The English and the French also began to operate on the west coast from the last two decades of the fifteenth century. Their activities were, however, carried on only by a few individuals and the real challenge to the Portuguese position in West Africa did not begin until the arrival of the Dutch from the 1590s and the formation of their West Indies Company in 1621. Twenty years later, the Dutch had conquered all the Portuguese trading posts and castles on the west coast, including Elmina, and had established a monopoly over the West African trade.

From the 1650s onwards, the English and the French also intensified their activities on the west coast. Operating through chartered companies, they had effectively ousted the Dutch from their leading position by the end of the seventeenth century. The Danes (1642), the Swedes (1647) and the Prussians (1682) entered the West African coastal scene. The activities of the Swedes and the Prussians were not particularly successful, and were terminated in 1661 and 1732 respectively. But the other five powers – the Portuguese, the Dutch, the French, the English and the Danes – continued to operate on the west coast until the Danes withdrew in 1850 and the Dutch in 1872.

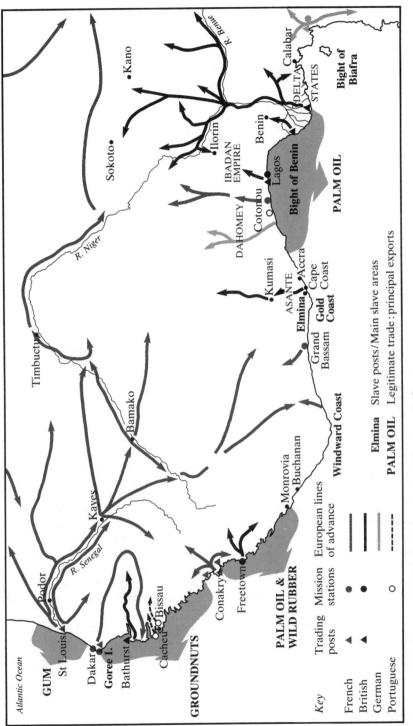

European Contacts with West Africa in the Nineteenth Century

Factors affecting European expansion

Why did European expansion to West Africa not begin until the fifteenth century, and why did the Portuguese take the lead in this? There are three main answers to these questions. The first was technological. The problem of building ships capable of undertaking long-distance voyages on the vast oceans was not satisfactorily solved until early in the fifteenth century when the *caravel* was invented. This was a sailing ship that used large triangular sails instead of oars. Secondly, the problem of finding one's way about on the high seas was also solved about the same time when the observation of latitude from the altitude of the polar star was improved and the compass was developed and refined. Finally, the astrolabe and a rudimentary quadrant for measuring the altitude of heavenly bodies were invented in the same century.

The second reason was economic. Until the fifteenth century, the European countries had had to rely on a bewildering number of middlemen – Malayan, Indian, Egyptian, and Italian – for the supply of goods and spices that they needed from India and China; consequently the prices of these goods became increasingly high. The discovery of a maritime route to the markets of the East, which would not be under the control of Muslim powers, became more and more urgent as the price of spices and other oriental goods soared. Gold also became a very scarce commodity in Europe in the fifteenth century mainly because of the increasing practice of minting coins in gold rather than in silver. The discovery of the sources of the gold that was coming to the markets of North Africa, of which the Portuguese became eye-witnesses during their attack and conquest of Ceuta in Morocco in 1415, was certainly one of the factors that precipitated the systematic exploration of the coast of Africa so soon after the Ceuta expedition.

The third reason was political. Throughout the fourteenth and fifteenth centuries, all the eastern European countries had to face constant threats of invasion from the Ottoman Turks; these came to a head with the capture of Constantinople in 1453. France and England were from 1337 till 1435 engaged in a series of wars which have become known as the Hundred Years War. In the sixteenth century, western Europe was plunged into the religious wars sparked off by the Reformation, which raged intermittently till the middle of the seventeenth century. The Dutch were also involved in their wars of independence against Spain, which continued until the end of the sixteenth century. It is significant that they began their overseas activities only after these wars had ended. In the Iberian peninsula, Castile was waging a crusade against the Muslims and this did not end until 1492 when it expelled them from its soil. Faced with these political problems in Europe, these powers could hardly promote overseas adventures.

Portugal took the lead in these activities first and foremost because it was the first country to solve most of the technical problems already referred to. Secondly, unlike the other European kingdoms, it was not confronted with any internal difficulties or external threat by the beginning of the fifteenth century. On the contrary, it had expelled the Muslims as early as 1262 and was in fact enjoying peace and stability by the end of the fourteenth century. Moreover, the new Aviz dynasty which came to power in 1385 had not only entrenched itself by the beginning of the fifteenth century but was also prepared to finance overseas activities, while Prince Henry, one of the sons of the founder of this new dynasty, was only too anxious to organise and direct such activities.

European aims and interests

What then were the aims of all the European nations in coming to the west coast of Africa and how far had these aims been achieved by about the end of the eighteenth century? It is clear from the available evidence that all the European nations wanted to learn something about the unknown regions of West Africa and to discover the sea route to India; secondly, right from the beginning, the Portuguese at least, wanted to convert Africans to Christianity; thirdly, some of them wanted to establish colonies and, finally, all of them definitely wanted to trade with the Africans. The aims, broadly speaking then, were scientific, religious, political and economic.

By the end of the eighteenth century, the scientific objective had been accomplished to a considerable extent. Under the inspired patronage and direction of Prince Henry, the Portuguese began their exploring activities in about 1417 and a year later explored the Madeira Island. They reached Cape Bojador in 1434, Cape Blanco in 1442, the mouth of the Senegal and the Cape Verde Islands in 1444, and the coastline of modern Sierra Leone in 1460. About ten years later, they had reached the coast of modern Ghana; they pushed on from there to Benin in 1475, and to the mouth of the Congo in 1482. They rounded the Cape of Good Hope in 1488 and ten years later, that is, just before the close of the fifteenth century, they reached India. These exploring activities were, however, confined almost entirely to the coastline and neither the Portuguese nor any of the European nations who followed them to West Africa bothered much about the interior.

In the field of religion, although all the European nations sooner or later became interested in the conversion of the Africans to Christianity, very little had been accomplished by the middle of the eighteenth century. In the 1450s, some kings of the regions of the Senegal and the Gambia were converted and in 1458 an abbot was sent to them from Portugal. When the Portuguese built their strong castle at Elmina in 1482, they also built a church for the Africans, and four years later, some missionaries were despatched to Benin. However, though the Portuguese continued to pay some attention to missionary work in the sixteenth and seventeenth centuries, particularly in the Senegambia, Benin and Congo areas, nothing permanent had resulted from these activities as far as the West African mainland was concerned by the middle of the eighteenth century.

The Dutch, who superseded the Portuguese in the seventeenth century, became interested in missionary work and even started the practice of sending Africans to be educated in Europe. The best-known products of this system are Jacob Capitein and William Anton Amo. The latter gained a master of arts degree and a doctorate in German universities and even lectured at the universities of Wittenberg, Halle and Denvar before he returned to Axim, his home town in Ghana, in about 1747. But in general nothing came out of the Dutch attempts at missionary work.

The French and Spanish Capuchins and French Dominicans also sent out missions to the west coast between 1637 and 1704; and the protestant churches joined in the eighteenth century with a mission sent out to Elmina in 1737 by the United Brethren or the Moravian Church and another by the English-based Society for the Propagation of the Gospel to Cape Coast in 1751. But by the middle of the eighteenth century the seeds of Christianity sowed on the West African mainland had completely failed to germinate. This was partly because of the high rate of mortality among the missionaries but mainly because the interest in missionary work was by and large sacrificed to commerce.

The Portuguese, the French and the English all showed some interest in colonisation. The Portuguese, however, confined this interest to the off-shore islands. Thus, they colonised the Canary Islands, Madeira, the Azores, Cape Verde Islands, Fernando Po and São Tomé. The French also attempted to found settlements at the mouth of the Senegal between 1687 and 1702 but this was unsuccessful. They were followed by the British who founded the crown colony of Senegambia in 1763, but this was abandoned in 1783. It seems then that by the middle of the eighteenth century, the political objectives had not been realised either.

In spite of the limited nature of the success in the field of exploration, and the failure in the religious and political fields, the Europeans not only remained on the west coast, but their numbers increased. This was simply because they found their economic or commercial activities very lucrative. The Europeans dealt first in sugar, then pepper (or 'grains of paradise'), ivory, wax and gold. The coastal areas from where these various commodities were obtained were named after their produce, hence the Grain Coast, the Ivory Coast, and the Gold Coast. The trade in gold was particularly lucrative, and by the beginning of the sixteenth century, the value of gold exported mainly from modern Ghana has been estimated at £100 000 per year, which was equivalent to one-tenth of the world's total supply of gold. It was the very lucrative trade in gold which attracted so many of the European nations to the coast of modern Ghana and brought about the erection of numerous forts and castles, some of which are still in use. From the second half of the sixteenth century onwards, however, the slave trade began to overshadow the others and in the eighteenth century, it became the main preoccupation of all the European nations on the west coast. The rise, volume, nature and effects of this trade in slaves across the Atlantic forms the subject of the next chapter.

14   The Atlantic slave trade and its effects

The Atlantic slave trade had, as we have seen, become the main interest of the European nations in West Africa by the beginning of the eighteenth century. Its beginnings however, seemed almost innocent. In 1441, Gonzalves, one of the Portuguese explorers, returned to Lisbon with a party of ten Africans whom he presented to Prince Henry. The prince received them with great pleasure since he hoped to convert them to Christianity, educate the most talented among them and send them back to their countries as missionaries. Though Henry's hopes never appear to have been realised, more and more Africans were brought to Portugal and sold. A contemporary chronicler has recorded that by the time of Henry's death in 1460, between 700 and 800 slaves were being exported annually to Portugal. Henry himself is said to have condemned the sale of Africans, but the kings and princes of Portugal after him gave it their blessing and even participated in it. Between 1486 and 1493 an average of 448 slaves belonging to the Portuguese crown were annually imported into Portugal.

The nature of the slave trade

If this export of slaves had been confined to Portugal or even to the Iberian Peninsula, it would most probably have stopped soon. Unfortunately, the export was extended across the Atlantic to the Americas. When the Spaniards penetrated North and South America between 1492 and 1554, they began to establish plantations and, above all, to exploit the fabulous mineral resources. An acute problem of labour supply arose because the indigenous people proved quite unequal to the tasks required of them and their population began to decline sharply. The Indian population of Mexico, for example, dropped from about 20 million in 1519 to only about one million by 1608. Naturally the Spaniards, who were already used to African slave labour, found the export of Africans to the new world the solution to the labour problem confronting them. It is interesting to note that the first batch of Africans exported to the Americas in about 1501 was sent from Lisbon, and it was not until about twenty years later that slaves were transported directly from the west coast to the Americas.

As more mines were opened up and more plantations were set up, so the demand for slaves increased. Between 1530 and 1600 an average of 13 000 slaves a year were being exported to the Americas. This number rose to about 27 500 a year in the seventeenth century, 70 000 in the eighteenth century and by the 1830s it had soared to 135 000 per annum. This phenomenal increase was due to the steady colonisation of North and South America and above all to the introduction of the plantation system of sugar growing in the New World from about 1640 onwards.

Most of these slaves were exported from the region between modern Ghana and the Cameroons, hence that coastline became known as the Slave Coast. Some were also obtained from Angola and the Congo. The slaves from Ghana were known in the Americas and the West Indies as 'Coromantine' Negroes, a name derived from the coastal port of the same name where the English built their first lodge probably in 1631. They were considered the most courageous, the most proud and the most unyielding of all the slaves and were often the leaders of slave mutinies. Edward Long, who wrote a history of Jamaica in 1774, called them 'haughty, ferocious and stubborn', and mentioned a slave uprising 'in which thirty-three Coromantines, most of whom had been newly imported, murdered and wounded no less than nineteen whites in the space of an hour.' The Jamaica House of Assembly, when describing a series of slave revolts during the middle of the eighteenth century, reported that 'all these disturbances have been planned and conducted by the Coromantine Negroes who are distinguished from brethren by their aversion to husbandry and the martial ferocity of their dispositions.'

How were all these numerous unfortunate Africans enslaved and purchased? African scholars and politicians today must be honest and admit that the enslavement and sale of Africans from the seventeenth century onwards was carried out by the Africans themselves, especially the coastal kings and their elders, and that very few Europeans actually ever marched inland and captured slaves themselves. Africans became enslaved in four main ways: first, criminals sold by the chiefs as punishment; secondly, free Africans obtained from raids by African rulers and a few European gangs or from kidnapping; thirdly, domestic slaves resold; and fourthly, prisoners of war.

Though the sale of criminals as punishment was not new in Africa, with the beginning of the slave trade this practice became grossly abused. Many kings formed the habit of punishing any and every offence by selling the accused. Again, as some historians have recently pointed out, 'subversive plots against the local government became surprisingly common in sea-coast towns off which the slavers dropped anchor. The king almost always discovered a number of dangerous conspirators, and they naturally had to be sold. To eliminate all possible danger, the king also sold the conspirators' wives, their children and their brothers.' Debtors were also sold.

The greatest sources of the supply of slaves, however, were raids conducted for the sole purpose of catching men for sale and, above all, inter-group and inter-state wars which produced thousands of war captives, most of whom found their way into the New World. Captain John Hall, who voyaged to Africa in 1772 and 1776, reports that an appearance of a slave ship at Old Calabar was the signal for the Africans to go upstream in their war canoes, and they usually returned two to three weeks later with their canoes full of slaves.

All these slaves were bartered for European merchandise such as guns, gunpowder, textiles, rum, beads, tobacco and iron and copper bars, and the total cost of a slave increased with the years. It was between £3 and £4 between 1660 and 1690, £10 by 1700, £18 by 1730 and £27 by 1800. The net sale price of a slave in the West Indies during the second half of the eighteenth century was about £40.

The effects of the slave trade

What general effects did this hideous traffic have on West Africa? Curiously enough, some European historians contend that the parts of West Africa which suffered the most from the slave trade were later among the most advanced and densely populated areas in the region – hence the slave trade acted in certain circumstances as a stimulus to the growth of population and development of political institutions. Such an argument is invalid on both counts. Firstly, the affected areas were remarkable for their population density even at the height of the slave trade; it should also be remembered in this connection that the great increase in West Africa's population generally really took place in the last hundred years, if not the last fifty. Secondly, as we have seen quite clearly in earlier chapters, the rise of the great kingdoms of the forest and coastal areas of West Africa were in no way dependent on the slave trade.

The slave trade did not confer benefits of any kind on West Africa. On the contrary, it was, to use the words of one historian of the 1890s, 'an unmitigated misery – a crime unredeemed by one extenuating circumstance.' In the first place, it led to an unpardonable destruction of population. Nothing has become as controversial now as the total number of people lost to Africa. According to the latest studies, about 15 400 000 were exported from Africa across the Atlantic. This figure does not include those who died during the raids and the march to the coast. What is particularly lamentable is that the victims were the most virile and active of the people of West Africa – the young and healthy men and women. In March 1722 the directors of the African Company in London instructed their agents in Cape Coast Castle that they should get ready cargoes of 600 slaves each who should 'all be good merchantable Negroes, viz. two-thirds males, one-third females, six-sevenths of each cargo to be about sixteen and thirty years of age and upon no account to exceed thirty, one-seventeenth boys and girls of which none should be under ten years of age'.

Secondly, the raiding and wars which the trade generated and steadily intensified caused a great deal of misery, bloodshed and destruction; whole villages and towns were burnt down and as many people were killed as were caught. These raids and wars created an atmosphere of general insecurity, which impeded inter-regional trade, orderly progress and cultural activities. Thirdly, though civil and inter-state wars were known in Africa before the coming of Europeans and only scholars anxious to glorify the African past would deny this, there is no doubt that the demand for slaves increased the incidence of such wars. Furthermore, these wars became more and more demoralising than the pre-European wars because, as a recent African historian has pointed out, they were motivated by commercial greed not by self-preservation nor imperial ambitions; they also became more and more fatal and bloody, because of the use of firearms. Fourthly, by encouraging the importation of manufactured products such as cloth, beads and iron goods the slave trade tended to eliminate the indigenous industries which had existed before and thereby impeded the industrial development of West Africa. The wonder is that some of the manufacturing skills survived and are being revived today.

The slave trade was also mainly responsible for the late development of the production of cash crops in West Africa since the European governments saw this as a positive trade, especially from the 1740s onwards. For instance, in 1751 the British Board of Trade peremptorily ordered Thomas Melvil, the Governor of the Cape Coast Castle, to stop the development of cotton cultivation among the Fante for commercial reasons which are most illuminating:

> The introduction of culture and industry amongst the Negroes is contrary to the known established policy of this country, there is no saying where this might stop, . . . it might extend to tobacco, sugar, and every other commodity which we now take from our colonies; and thereby the Africans, who now support themselves by wars, would become planters and their slaves be employed in the culture of these articles in Africa, which they are employed in, in America.

As we shall see presently, after the abolition of the slave trade, West Africa was allowed and indeed assisted to produce these very cash crops but again forbidden, as it were, to produce manufactured goods, which she was to continue to receive from Europe.

Finally, far from promoting the development of some indigenous institutions, the slave trade rather retarded their growth. This was particularly true in the field of jurisdiction. In addition, the slave trade brutalised all the people who took part in it, black as well as white, and it brought to Africa a vast disruption of its culture. On the whole, then, the slave trade remains one of the greatest crimes committed against Africa, and one of the most disastrous episodes of its history.

15   The abolition of the slave trade and its effects

Reasons for the abolition

There is still a great deal of controversy over the circumstances which led to the abolition of the slave trade in Britain. Some historians attribute the abolition of the slave trade to purely humanitarian or moral and religious considerations. Others argue that the slave trade and slavery were abolished mainly for economic reasons. One such writer, Conton, a Sierra Leonean, states: 'the slave trade was abolished largely because it had now become more profitable to seek in West Africa raw materials and markets rather than slaves'. Finally, some historians maintain that it was a combination of both economic and humanitarian considerations that brought about abolition.

From a careful study of the evidence and after an examination of most of the recent studies on the subject, this writer is still of the opinion that the slave trade and slavery were abolished for both humanitarian and economic reasons. In the first place, it should not be forgotten that the attacks on the slave trade did not really begin in Europe and England until the eighteenth century – the very century when in the realms of literature, philosophy and religion, emphasis was being placed on the equality, brotherhood and liberty of man. The slave trade was condemned alike by philosophers and economists such as Jean-Jacques Rousseau and Adam Smith, literary figures such as Samuel Johnson and Daniel Defoe, and by evangelists such as John Wesley.

Secondly, all the people who actually organised and launched the attack on the slave trade and remained persistently in the forefront of the campaign were men who were personally committed to the evangelical and humanitarian ideas of the day. They included such well-known abolitionists as Granville Sharp and William Wilberforce and later Fowell Buxton and James Stephen. It was these people who formed the Society for the Abolition of the Slave Trade (in May 1787) and the British Anti-Slavery Society (in 1823) and it was these two Societies which conducted the campaign against the slave trade. They organised branches throughout the country with a view to arousing public opinion against the trade, and from 1788 persistently tabled motions in Parliament until their ends were achieved by the abolition of the slave trade in 1807 and of slavery in 1833.

However, if moral and humanitarian pressure alone had been sufficient, the slave trade would have been abolished in 1792 when the House of Commons did in fact pass a motion agreeing to the gradual abolition of the slave trade. By that time, a majority of the members had clearly become convinced that the sale of Africans was evil and inhuman. Nevertheless, they argued for reform of the slave trade rather than wholesale abolition which they feared would bring about the economic ruin of both Britain and her West Indian colonies. The fact that the British parliament agreed to abolish the trade in 1807 and slavery in 1833, indicate considerations other than humanitarian ones, and from a study of the conditions at the time, it becomes quite clear that these considerations were economic.

By the end of the eighteenth century, the British West Indian islands had had all the slaves they needed and in fact about fifty per cent were being re-exported to the islands of the other European powers. It meant, therefore, that abolition would not be totally ruinous to them. Secondly, even some of the British West Indian planters began to support the campaign for abolition of the slave trade from the beginning of the nineteenth century, because they were alarmed by the competitive development of the new fertile French and Dutch islands, which the British had conquered during the wars fought between 1792 and 1802. Undoubtedly, one of the reasons leading to the passing of the Abolition Bill in 1807, was this division that occurred in the ranks of the West Indian planter interest in parliament. Thirdly, since Brazil and Cuba were producing sugar in greater quantities and more cheaply during the second half of the nineteenth century, British West Indian sugar could not be sold on the continental markets. There was therefore a surplus of sugar in England and one writer has argued that it was the accumulation of unsold sugar in Britain and the subsequent need to stop further over-production that led to the passing of the Abolition Bills in 1807 and 1833.

However, economic conditions in the West Indies alone were not sufficient to bring about abolition. This is evident from the fact that between 1772 and 1774, the British government refused to give royal assent to bills passed by the assemblies of Massachusetts, Virginia and Jamaica aimed at abolishing or reducing the volume of the slave trade. The colonies were told that they would not be allowed 'to check or discourage in any degree a traffic so beneficial to the British Nation'. That the slave trade was a prop of the British economy at the time cannot be doubted. The textile, sugar-refining, shipping and iron industries of Britain all depended directly or indirectly on the slave trade to the West Indian islands.

Between 1800 and 1830 this situation changed radically, mainly as a result of the industrial revolution. The textile industrialists, for instance, needed far more raw cotton than the British West Indian islands could produce and they were obtaining their supplies from the southern parts of the United States. The sugar refiners also needed far more crude sugar than they could get from the West Indies and they began to look to Brazil. Shipowners were also now deriving far more profit from conveying raw cotton and unrefined sugar from Brazil and the United States to Europe and Britain than from conveying slaves to the West Indies. Indeed by 1805 only two per cent of British export tonnage was employed in the slave trade. Moreover, as more and more manufacturing machines came into use the demand for more raw materials increased and many industrialists as well as humanitarians now began to argue that Africans, instead of being exported to the West Indies, could be more profitably employed in Africa to produce such commodities as palm oil (needed for lubricating the new machines), groundnuts and cotton. Manufactured goods could also be sold in African markets.

By the early nineteenth century, therefore, it had become clear that the slave trade had ceased to be a prop to the British economy, and that Africa could serve Britain more effectively by producing cash crops rather than by supplying labour to the West Indian colonies. This realisation was the main force behind the abolition of the entire slave system between 1807 and 1833.

Thus, the strong economic forces at work in the West Indies and in Britain contributed at least as much to abolition as humanitarian and moral considerations.

Effects of abolition

The abolition of the slave trade had far-reaching social, economic and political effects in West Africa. The first social effect was the suppression of the slave trade in West Africa. After achieving the legal abolition of the slave trade, the humanitarians and abolitionists put pressure on European governments to achieve world-wide abolition of the slave trade and its effective suppression in West Africa. As a result of this pressure and the favourable response it received, almost all the European countries had passed acts abolishing the slave trade by the 1830s. In spite of these acts, however, the volume of the new illegal trade had in fact increased mainly because of increased demand for slaves in Cuba and Brazil. The abolitionists, therefore, urged the British government to send naval vessels to the west coast of Africa to capture any vessel carrying slaves illegally to the Americas and to occupy any areas where the slave trade was still dominant. The British government agreed and introduced a number of measures calculated to suppress the slave trade. They instituted a naval patrol, concluded treaties with some European powers granting them right of search, set up the Courts of Mixed Commission in Freetown to try offenders, and concluded anti-slavery trade treaties with African rulers. The naval patrol of the west coast, which began as early as 1808, continued until the 1860s when the Atlantic slave trade finally ceased.

The second social effect was the promotion and spread of Christianity and western culture in West Africa. The abolitionists were convinced that the slave trade was a crime against humanity and a sin before God and therefore that it should not be merely abolished but it should also be atoned for by bringing western civilisation, education and Christianity to Africa. Between 1792 and 1804, they were instrumental in the formation of a number of missionary societies to promote Christianity and western education in Africa. In 1795, the Wesleyan Missionary Society sent out a party of mechanics and preachers to Sierra Leone, and it extended its activities to the Gambia in 1821, to Ghana in 1834, and to Yorubaland in the 1840s. The Glasgow and Scottish Missionary Society also entered the field in 1797 and the Church Missionary Society in 1806. These three societies were joined by many others from all over the world between 1820 and 1860. These new societies included the North German or Bremen Missionary Society, which operated in Togo, the Basel Evangelical Missionary Society from Switzerland in eastern Ghana, the United Presbyterian Church of Scotland in Calabar, the Society of French Missions in Ivory Coast, Dahomey and Benin, and finally more than ten missions from the United States of America which operated in Liberia.

These societies, however, did not confine themselves to building churches, preaching the gospel and converting Africans to Christianity. All the missionaries paid attention to the development of agriculture and 'legitimate' trade as a substitute for the slave trade. They introduced new crops, set up plantations and experimental farms and taught new methods of producing and preparing commodities such as cocoa, coffee, or spices for export. Some of the societies also formed trading companies to buy these products and sell worthwhile goods to the Africans. The Basel Missionary Society in Ghana formed the Basel Trading Company (now known as the UTC) in 1859, while the Church Missionary Society (CMS) formed the West Africa Company in Nigeria in 1863. They also introduced new architecture suitable for the tropics, and were certainly the first to introduce bricklaying, stone houses and corrugated-iron roofing to the west coast.

The greatest contribution of the missionary societies, however, was in the field of education. They all set up schools as well as training colleges. By 1841, the CMS had twenty-one elementary schools in Sierra Leone and in 1845 and 1849 respectively it founded the first two secondary schools in West Africa; one for boys and the other for girls. As early as 1827 it established the Fourah Bay College which exists to this day. By 1846, the Wesleyans had set up four girls' schools and twenty boys' schools in Ghana and in 1876 it opened Ghana's first secondary school, now known as Mfantsipim. In Nigeria, mission schools were established from the 1840s onward, first in Badagry and Abeokuta, then in Calabar, Bonny and Onitsha. In 1859, the CMS founded its grammar school in Lagos, the first secondary school in Nigeria.

Finally, the missionary societies and the humanitarians also devoted some time to linguistic studies with a view to rendering the African languages in written form and teaching their converts how to read the Bible in their own language. By 1880, most of the leading West African languages such as Temne, Twi, Ga, Yoruba, Hausa and Efik had been reduced to writing; grammar books and dictionaries had been prepared, and the Bible had been translated into some of these languages. Some Missions also established printing presses – for example, the Presbyterian Press in Ghana and the CMS Press in Nigeria – to print and distribute religious literature.

The influence of the missionaries produced a new type of African – literate, Christian, having European taste in clothing, food, drink and music, exposed through reading to ideas and influences from abroad but still shouldering his responsibilities to his extended family and his traditional authority. However, the missionaries looked down on everything African – African art, music, dancing, systems of marriage and even of naming – and their converts had to renounce all this. Mission activities, therefore, created divisions in African society and suppressed the development of indigenous African culture. In their educational work, they also tended to concentrate on reading, writing and arithmetic to the neglect of industrial and technical training. All the same, Africans do owe a debt of gratitude to these missionaries and the abolitionists.

Economically, the abolition of the slave trade created an economic vacuum on the coast and all kinds of attempts were made to fill it by developing what came to be called 'legitimate' trade, that is trade in natural products, such as palm oil, groundnuts, cotton, minerals, coffee, rubber and timber.

Both European and African traders first turned their attention to palm oil, which was urgently needed in Europe for lubricating the newly-invented machines and for making soap with which the factory workers could wash themselves. Africans were now encouraged to obtain oil as well as kernel from the nuts for export. This revived activity was very successful first in the regions of the Niger delta from where the quantity of palm oil produced increased rapidly throughout the century – from 1 000 tons in 1810 to 5 000 in 1820, to 10 000 in 1830 and to 30 000 tons by 1850. Palm oil was also exported from Ghana from about 1820 onwards, and by 1840 it formed the third leading export, the first two being gold and ivory.

The next product to become an important export item was groundnuts, which were also needed for soap, particularly in France. In 1830, ten baskets of groundnuts were exported for the first time from the Gambia. Twenty years later, the quantity had increased to the huge figure of 8 600 tons per year, and groundnuts have remained to this day the Gambia's main source of revenue. Senegal, the country most associated with groundnuts today, and Sierra Leone followed the Gambia, and, much later, northern Nigeria also began to export groundnuts in large quantities.

The production of gum, coffee, cotton and timber were also encouraged with varying degrees of success, and from 1880 rubber and cocoa were introduced as cash crops. Gum, the traditional export from Senegal, became increasingly important from the 1820s onwards. By 1860, largely through the efforts of the missionaries, cotton had become the third principal export of Western Nigeria; after 1860, however, northern Nigeria became the more important cotton-growing region. Coffee was also cultivated with some success in Liberia. The timber industry began in Sierra Leone in 1816 when the first cargo of timber was shipped to England; by the 1840s it was a major export commodity.

During the last two decades of the nineteenth century, attention was particularly focused on rubber and cocoa. The tapping of wild rubber trees became particularly successful in Ghana, Sierra Leone, Guinea and Nigeria, and by 1890 Ghana had become the third largest producer of rubber in the world. However, the reckless tapping of rubber trees combined with the competition from Malayan rubber meant that West Africa's rubber boom was short-lived. Ghana's cocoa industry began effectively from 1879 when Tete Quarshie planted the seeds from pods brought in from Fernando Po. In 1891, the first shipment of cocoa, weighing 80 lb, and valued at the meagre sum of £4 sterling, was made. From this modest beginning, the industry grew steadily until it became what it is today – the backbone of Ghana's economy. Cocoa-growing was also encouraged in western Nigeria and today it constitutes an important export commodity.

These various attempts to develop 'legitimate' trade in West Africa were not confined to the coastal regions. The European traders tried to exploit the Niger as a commercial highway after the discovery of its mouth by John and Richard Lander in 1830. Indeed, as soon as the Lander brothers returned to England with the news of their discovery, two companies were formed, one in England and the other in America with the aim of establishing a permanent trading centre at the confluence of the Benue and the Niger. Though the first two failed, the third (1854) expedition sent out by the companies, in many ways marked the turning point in the development of the Niger as a commercial highway. The steam vessel constructed specially for this expedition was able to explore over a thousand kilometers of the Niger in the short period of eleven weeks. This confirmed what had been demonstrated by the earlier Niger expeditions in 1832 and 1841, that the Niger could be nevigated by properly constructed vessels. More significantly, not one crew member of this expedition died, mainly because quinine was used to the first time not just as a curative but also as a preventive medication.

With the problems of navigation and health solved, many traders, mainly British, now began to develop trade with the interior along the Niger. Between 1857 and 1859, three trading stations were established on the Niger at Aboh, Onitsha and at Lokoja. The value of the produce collected at these stations increased from £1 800 sterling in 1857 to £2 750 in 1858 and to £9 000 in 1859, and this trend continued throughout the century. The French made a similar advance on the Senegal river especially during the governorship of Faidherbe from 1856 to 1860 and from 1863 to 1866.

The replacement of the slave trade by legitimate trade had far-reaching social, economic and political consequences. The first and most important was that instead of being treated as a commodity by the Europeans, the African became regarded as a human being with material and spiritual needs to be satisfied, and who himself had commodities to sell. Secondly, as a result of this increasing commercial activity, two classes of Africans began to emerge; a middle class consisting of private traders and businessmen, and a working class consisting of people employed by the various European trading firms and companies. Thirdly, more and more traders and trading companies were attracted from European countries to West Africa. By 1840, at least ten British and eight French companies were operating on the west coast. From 1840 onwards, they were joined by a number of firms from Germany. By 1870, there were about six of these German firms, mainly from Hamburg, which were already monopolising the trade in Togoland and the Cameroons. This keen rivalry was not confined to the coast. By the early 1880s, there were as many as five British and two French firms operating on the Niger. The former companies were later amalgamated into the United African Company, which was chartered in 1886 and renamed the Royal Niger Company. The economy of West Africa became even more firmly tied to that of Europe than before and this has never changed since.

Finally, the abolition of the slave trade had some political consequences. The first of these was the founding of the new colonies of Sierra Leone and Liberia. It was mainly with a view to solving the serious social and political problems caused in both Britain and the United States as a result of the presense of an increasing number of poor and unemployed freed slaves that Sierra Leone and Liberia were founded by the English and American abolitionists in 1787 and 1821 respectively. The British government took over Sierra Leone in 1807 mainly to use it as the base for the suppression of the Atlantic slave trade and the resettlement of freed slaves while Liberia was granted its independence by its founders, the American Colonization Society, in 1847.

Secondly, it led to the annexation of parts of the coast by Europeans, usually in response to appeals by missionaries, traders, and naval officers. It was partly in response to such appeals that the British became directly involved; as we have seen, in the Asante-Fante wars culminating in the annexation of southern Ghana in 1874; it was for the same reason that they bombarded Lagos in 1850 and annexed it in 1860. The French also annexed Porto Novo and Cotonou in the early 1880s mainly to facilitate the activities of the traders.

Thus, the abolition of the slave trade involved Europe even more deeply in the affairs of West Africa. By 1880, Europeans were not only preaching the gospel and building schools in West Africa but they were also actively trading in a wide range of natural products; and as a result of these activities they had in some instances even assumed direct political control.

16 The scramble for and the partition of Africa

Reasons for the scramble

Up to 1880 the activities of European traders and missionaries had been confined mainly to the coast and the Niger, Gambia and Senegal river basins; most of the West African states of the period were enjoying an autonomous, if sometimes uncertain existence. However, during the short period of twenty years between 1880 and 1900, European political domination was extended to every corner of West Africa and by the end of that period, only one state, Liberia, was still a sovereign and independent state. All the other kingdoms and states had become colonies of the European imperial powers. What brought about this loss of African independence and the establishment of European rule not only in West Africa but throughout the whole continent?

To answer this question, we should first recognise the scramble as a world-wide phenomenon, affecting all the tropical areas throughout the world, powered therefore not so much by conditions within Africa as some recent historians have argued, but by the economic, social and political forces operating in Europe during the second half of the nineteenth century. It is these factors which explain why the 'scramble' for Africa took place at the time it did.

The first economic reason for the scramble was the need for new markets for surplus manufactured goods caused by the spread of the industrial revolution from England to France, Russia, Germany and Italy during the second half of the nineteenth century. As each country became industrialised, she began to produce far more goods than could be absorbed locally, and therefore began to look for a solution to this problem of the overproduction of goods. This was found in the imposition of high tariff duties on manufactured goods imported from abroad and in the acquisition of colonies whose markets she could dominate. Secondly, the demand for raw materials became also very acute and competitive and it therefore became the aim of the industrial countries to control the sources for the production or supply of such raw materials as cotton, rubber and minerals. Indeed, according to one American historian, Carlton Hayes, what actually started the push into Africa and the sunbaked islands of the Pacific 'was not so much an over-production of factory goods in Europe as an undersupply of raw materials.'

A third economic factor in the race for colonies was the investment of surplus capital. As more and more profit accumulated in the European countries, the need for new areas where surplus capital could be more profitably invested became felt. Lenin, the great Russian leader, attributed the rise of the new imperialism solely to this need and has described imperialism as the 'highest stage of capitalism'. Although eventually the imperial powers invested the bulk of their capital outside their colonies in independent countries such as the United States, Brazil and Canada, the prospect of investment in colonial territories proved a strong motivation for acquiring them.

The political forces of the day greatly strengthened the economic forces. After the Russo-Turkish war of 1877–78, a balance of power in Europe was created which made it impossible for any European nation to expand its territories within Europe. A line of least resistance had therefore to be found. For Russia this was Central Asia; for the United States, it was the wild West; for the western European countries, it was Africa, Asia and even Latin America.

This expansion along the line of least resistance was made almost inevitable by the second and the greatest of the operating political forces, namely, the force of nationalism. Just as the second half of this century is destined to go down in history as the era of African nationalism, so the second half of the nineteenth century has gone down as the era of nationalism in Europe. That period saw the emergence of two major European nation-states – Germany and Italy – which shared the nationalistic ambitions of the other European powers. These ambitions included the partition of Africa mainly because colonies formed one of the important symbols of a nation's greatness and prestige just as atomic bombs, skylabs and space satellites are today. The more colonies a nation-state had, the more powerful and great it was considered to be. Thus, after humiliating defeats by Germany in the Franco-Prusian war of 1870–71, France turned its attention overseas to demonstrate that it was still a great power. As a French scholar proclaimed in 1882: 'Colonisation is for France a question of life and death, either France will become a great African power or she will be no more than a secondary European power'. The Germans also talked of getting 'a place in the sun', while later Italy also entered the race for colonies mainly for reasons of prestige. There is a great deal of truth in the view that just as African nationalism today is mainly responsible for the liquidation of colonialism in Africa, European nationalism partly accounts for its establishment.

Existing social factors were also important reasons for the acquisition of colonies. The industrial revolution and the capitalist system produced not only surplus capital but also surplus working power. As more and more machines came into use, more and more people found themselves out of work. In the 1870s alone, it was estimated that there were about a million paupers in England, while there were even more people in Germany and Italy without jobs. The acquisition of colonies meant that surplus population could be settled and could maintain contacts with the mother country. Such settlements were made in north, eastern, central and southern Africa but climate conditions and diseases such as malaria jointly prevented such European settlements in West Africa.

The Berlin Conference

With France, Britain, Germany and Portugal all very actively staking out claims on Africa's west coast from 1879 onwards, the scramble had reached an advanced state by July 1884. It was to lay down rules to govern this race and to avoid the possibility of an open conflict that an international conference was held in Berlin from 15 November 1884 to 30 January 1885 under the chairmanship of Bismarck. On 26 February 1885, the Berlin Act which laid down the 'rules' for partition was signed. The first of these rules was that any power which wanted to claim any territory should notify the other signatory powers 'in order to enable them, if need be, to make good any claims of their own'. The second was that any such annexations should be followed by effective occupation in order to become valid. The third was that treaties made with African rulers were to be considered as valid titles to sovereignty. The fourth was that every imperial power was to be free to extend its coastal occupations within certain limits into the interior and establish spheres of influence. It was also laid down that there should be freedom of navigation on the Congo and the Niger rivers.

Stages of the Scramble and Partition

There were three stages in the scramble for and the partition of Africa. The first stage was either the signing of a treaty between the African ruler and the European imperial power (usually involving the exchange of protection for exclusive rights of trading and other activities), or the unilateral declaration of annexation of an African state or area as a protectorate. The second stage was the conclusion of a treaty among the imperial European powers defining their spheres of interest and laying down boundaries. The third stage was the movement of troops by the imperial powers to conquer and occupy the areas that had been demarcated. The first two stages were then known as the partition 'on paper'. The third stage is usually referred to by Eurocentric and colonial historians as the 'phase of pacification' but this is a totally wrong description. This was rather the phase of the partition on the ground and was marked by brutal invasions and conquests of African states by imperial armies.

Between 1880 and 1890, the French concluded treaties with Ahmadu of the Tukulor empire, Samori Toure of the Mandingo empire, the king of Dahomey and a number of Baule principalities such as Tiassale and Niamwe in Ivory coast. During the same period, the British also signed similar treaties with many of the rulers of the states of present-day northern Ghana, with many of the Yoruba states, the Oil Rivers and the Oba of Benin – all in Nigeria. They also offered a treaty of protection to Prempe the king of Asante in 1891 who firmly but politely rejected it. The French unilaterally annexed the coastal areas of Little Popo and Porto Novo in 1883 while Germany also annexed the coastal areas of both Togo and the Cameroons in June 1884.

These treaties and annexations were then followed by bilateral treaties between the imperial powers laying down various boundaries of the areas claimed on the basis of the previously concluded treaties. Thus the Anglo-German Treaty of April and May 1885 and between 1890 and 1893, defined the spheres of action of the two powers in different parts of Africa; the Anglo-French treaties of 1890 and 1898 laid down all the boundaries of their colonies in West Africa while the Franco-Portuguese Treaty of 1886 settled the boundary problems between the two powers.

On the basis of these various treaties, all the imperial powers then moved in troops to conquer and occupy the areas they had acquired on paper. Thus, from 1885, the French began their occupation of West Africa by landing a well-equipped army which in a series of campaigns captured Cayor in 1886, the Soninke empire of Mamadu Lamine in 1887, Koundian in 1889, Segu in 1890, Yauri in 1891, Timbuctu in 1894, Dahomey between 1890 and 1894, the Tukulor empire between 1888 and 1890, the Mandingo empire of the great Samori between 1891 and 1898, and Bauleland between 1890 and 1901. The British also launched an invasion of Asante which resulted in the capture and exile of Prempe in 1896. In Nigeria, they captured Ijebu in 1892, Benin in 1897, the Itsekiri kingdom in 1894, Ilorin and Nupe in 1897 and the Sokoto empire in a series of bloody campaigns between 1900 and 1904. In Togo, between 1895 and 1899, German action included thirty-five military campaigns, fifty combats and skirmishes and the storming of many towns. Thus by the first decade of this century, the partition on the ground had been completed and all West Africa with the sole exception of Liberia, had been occupied by the European powers.

African reactions to partition and conquest

What were the reactions of the Africans to this European partition and occupation of their lands? From the available evidence, the Africans reacted in three main ways. Some of them submitted or surrendered without a fight, some allied with the Europeans in the hope of maintaining their sovereignty or even gaining some territories at the expense of their African neighbours or former masters while the overwhelming majority opposed or resisted the Europeans in defence of their independence and sovereignty.

In French West Africa, M'Backe of Sine and Guedel M'bodj of Salum in the region of Senegambia readily submitted and placed their countries under the French. In British West Africa, all the states in Yorubaland including Abeokuta, Ibadan, Oyo, Ekiti and Ijesha, with the exception of Ijebu, also submitted without a fight, probably after realising the futility of resistance.

Some of the African rulers on the other hand, chose to ally with the imperialist invaders. Typical examples of such rulers were Tieba of Sikasso and Toffa of Porto Novo. Both allied with the French against Samori and the kings of Dahomey respectively. These rulers who chose to ally with the European invaders have been called collaborators by some historians. However, this term gives the wrong impression that such African rulers sacrificed the interests of their own people to those of the Europeans. In fact, at the time of the French annexation of Porto Novo in 1883, Toffa was himself facing three enemies, namely, the Yoruba to the north-east, the Fon kings of Dahomey to the north and the British on the coast. He therefore saw the arrival of the French as a god-sent opportunity for him not only to maintain his independence but even to make some gains, especially at the expense of the kings of Dahomey. This was why he chose to ally with the French. As we shall see below, Lat Dior of Cayor and even the great Samori also at one time or the other allied with the French in the hope of preserving their lands. These alliances do not deserve the negative description of 'collaboration'.

There is no doubt, however, that an overwhelming majority of Africans chose to oppose or resist the European imperialists. There are two main ways in which the Africans carried out their policy of opposition or resistance or confrontation as some historians prefer to call it. These were opposition by the use of diplomacy and opposition by use of force, and some African leaders used both. A typical example of West African leaders or rulers who chose the method of diplomacy to oppose the imperialists and retain their sovereignty was Prempe of Asante. He politely rejected the British offer of protection in 1891. Indeed, as he wrote to the British governor on that occasion: '. . . My kingdom of Asante will never commit itself to any such policy [i.e. come under the protection of the British]. Asante must remain as of old at the same time to remain friendly with all white men'.

When he again rejected the British offer to station a resident in his capital town of Kumasi in 1892 and felt the pressure on him still increasing, he despatched a high-powered diplomatic mission to the Queen of England in November 1894 'to lay before Your Majesty certain divers matters affecting the good estate of our kingdom.' The British government not only refused to see this mission on its arrival in Britain, but promptly despatched a full-scale military expedition under Sir Francis Scott which entered Kumasi in January 1896. Prempe, still sticking to his diplomatic weapon, refused to fight and he was arrested and deported first to Sierra Leone and then to the Seychelles Islands in 1900.

Unlike Prempe, a great majority of the Africans resorted to force alone or a combination of force and diplomacy in defence of their independence and sovereignty. Lat Dior of Cayor raised an army and fought against the French from 1882 until 1886 when he was killed in battle. Ba Bemba of Sikasso also opposed the French until 1894 when he killed himself rather than surrender his sovereignty to the French. When his policy of alliance with the French failed, Ahmadu of the Tukulor empire resorted to arms in 1889 and after inflicting a number of defeats on the French in 1890, he retreated to Masina in January 1891 and from there went into voluntary exile in Hausaland. The people of Benin fought the British until they were defeated in 1897. Nana of the Itsekiri kingdom beat back the British attack on him in April 1894 but was defeated in the second attack in September.

Numerous other rulers and their armies fought off the newcomers for as long as they were able, but there is no doubt that the greatest of the African opponents of European imperialism was Samori Ture. Having raised an army which he equipped with the latest weapons and trained along modern lines, Samori Ture first fought with the French between 1882 and 1885, then concluded a treaty with them in 1886 and again in 1887. He resorted to warfare again in 1888 when the French broke the treaty by assisting some of his rebellious subjects, and concluded a treaty of friendship with the British in 1890 which enabled him to purchase more arms from Sierra Leone. Having reorganised and re-equipped his army, he resumed the fight against the French in 1891 and defeated them at the battle of Dabaduqu in September 1891. However, he suffered a very severe defeat in January 1892 and therefore retreated eastwards where he created a new empire in the basin of the Bandama and Mono rivers and part of modern northern Ghana. He was, however, attacked there by a French expedition from the Baule country in 1895 and from 1897 by the British from Wa. He was eventually captured in a surprise attack by the French at Gelemou on 29 September 1898 and was deported to Gabon where he died in 1900. His capture ended what has been described as 'the longest series of campaigns against a single enemy in the history of French Sudanese conquest.'

The reasons for African failure

The final question to be answered then is why the Africans failed to beat back the European invaders and defend their lands and independence. The first reason for African failure was that thanks to the activities and reports of European explorers and missionaries in Africa, the imperial powers knew far more about Africa than Africans did about Europe by the 1890s. Secondly, each European imperial power was richer by far than any African state or even a number of states combined; each therefore could wage a much longer war than any African state could afford and so the defeat of an African state was only a matter of time. Thirdly, rather contrary to expectations, the imperialist invaders had a greater number of troops than the Africans, since the former could employ thousands of Africans as soldiers, carriers and so on. Very often it was only the officers who were Europeans. Fourthly, and a very important factor, the Africans failed to form alliances or unite against the European invaders. Had say Ahmadu, Lat Dior and Samori united against the French, the outcome of the wars could have been different. However not only did they fail to come together but they allowed the French to ally with one against the other, as we have seen already. Thus divided and often at war with each other, the Africans proved no serious opponents. The final and easily the most important reason was the fact that the African armies were armed with their old weapons of bows, arrows, spears and very outmoded guns, while the European soldiers were armed with the most up-to-date arms such as repeater rifles, maxim guns and machine guns. Moreover, the imperial powers used steamers and trains to move their troops to and fro while the African towns situated on the coast or banks of rivers could be bombarded from ships. It is most significant that the West African leader who succeeded in opposing the European invaders for the longest period, Samori, was the one who was able to obtain and use some of the up-to-date weapons.

In view of all these imperial advantages, the surprise is not that Africans failed to defend their independence but that they put up such long and determined resistance.

Thus, by the 1900s, the whole of West Africa, and indeed, the entire continent of Africa with the sole exception of Ethiopia and Liberia, had been appropriated by the European imperialist powers to meet their selfish economic, political and social ends, and Africa had lost her freedom and sovereignty.

17 The colonial powers and West Africa

In the previous chapter we saw that the most important reason for the scramble for and the partition of Africa was the need felt by the imperial powers to obtain raw materials and to acquire markets for the sale of manufactured goods. All the imperial powers also insisted that each colony should support itself financially, that is, that it should pay for its own administration. It was mainly for the achievement of these two objectives that a number of political, social and economic measures were introduced as soon as the conquest and occupation stages were completed.

These measures were influenced first and foremost by how the colonial powers regarded their colonies and secondly by their attitudes towards the Africans whom they ruled. The British and the Germans on the whole regarded their colonies as complete entities and treated each one, therefore, separately. The French and the Portuguese, on the other hand, regarded their colonies as integral parts of the metropolitan countries and therefore as mere provinces overseas. Thus, while the British did envisage a day when each of its colonies would become an independent state in its own right, the French did not recognise the possibility until the late 1950s; and the Portuguese never changed their unrealistic attitude.

Secondly, even though all the colonial powers regarded the black race as inferior to the white race, the British certainly showed a great deal of respect for the Africans and for many aspects of their culture and institutions, while the French and the Portuguese condemned practically everything African as primitive and barbaric. While the British therefore sought to improve and modernise African culture and institutions, the French and the Portuguese adopted the policy of assimilation, that is turning Africans, mainly through western education, into black Frenchmen (*evolués*) or black Portuguese (*assimilados*) who were then, and only then, accorded all the rights and privileges of French citizens.

To become a French citizen or *evolué*, the African in a French African colony until 1946 had to have fulfilled are of the following requirements: to have been born in any of the four *communes* or municipalities in Senegal (Saint-Louis, Gorée, Rufisque and Dakar); to have held with merit a position in the French service for ten years; to provide evidence of good character and possess a means of existence; to have been decorated with the Legion of Honour or the Military Award. And once an African became a French citizen, he was subject to French law and had access to French courts. Above all this meant that we was exempted from what has been rightly described as 'the most hated feature of the colonial system in French West Africa', the *indigenat*. This was a legal system which enabled any French administrative officer to sentence any African for up to two years without trial. Further advantages of French citizenship were that one could commute compulsory labour for monetary payment, and finally one could be appointed to any post in France and in the colony. In the Portuguese colonies, the African had to be well educated, a Christian and to have abandoned such African practices as polygamy. Once his application was accepted and he became a Portuguese citizen, he was saved from the indignity of having to carry a pass book and exempted from compulsory labour.

However, this practice of converting Africans into citizens was, on the whole, a failure. As late as 1937, out of a population of fifteen million in French West Africa, only 80 000 had become French citizens, and of these 78 000 were citizens simply because they were born in the four communes or municipalities of Senegal. In the Portuguese colony of Guinea only 1418 out of a total African population of 550 457 had become *assimilados* by 1950.

There were two main reasons for this failure. First, the Portuguese totally and the French to a great extent neglected higher education for the Africans, who could therefore not qualify for citizenship rights. Secondly, the few qualified Africans themselves refused to apply for citizenship for fear of being ostracised by their fellow Africans. Article 80 of the 1946 Constitution of the French Union or the first 'loi Lamine Gueye', abolished the distinction between subjects and citizens and allowed all the Africans to become citizens, but the Portuguese stuck to their stupid and degrading policy to the end.

Systems of administration

Initially, the administration of most of the colonies was left in the hands of military officers and chartered companies but civilian administrations replaced them in the 1920s. Unlike the French, but in conformity with their attitudes towards their colonies, the British set up separate administrative machines for each of their colonies. At the head of each colony was a governor, who was responsible to the secretary of state for colonies in the British government. He administered the colony with the assistance of a partly nominated legislative council and an executive council of officials. Most of the laws for each colony were drawn up by the governor and his council and not by the British government in London.

In contrast to this, but again following from their attitude to their colonies, the French and Portuguese colonial powers set up highly centralised and authoritarian systems of administration. Between 1896 and 1904, the French formed all their eight colonies in West Africa into the Federation of French West Africa (AOF) with its capital at Dakar. At the head of the federation was the governor-general. He was under the minister of colonies in Paris; he took most of his orders directly from France and governed according to laws mostly made in Paris. At the head of each colony was a lt-governor who was assisted by a council of administration. He was directly under the governor-general rather than the minister of colonies and he could make decisions on only a few specified subjects. Similarly, in the Portuguese colonies, all policies and nearly all laws were made by the metropolitan or home government. The governor-general and his subordinates merely carried them out, calling for local advice when they needed it, but never bound by it. Finally, at the head of the German colony of Togo was an imperial

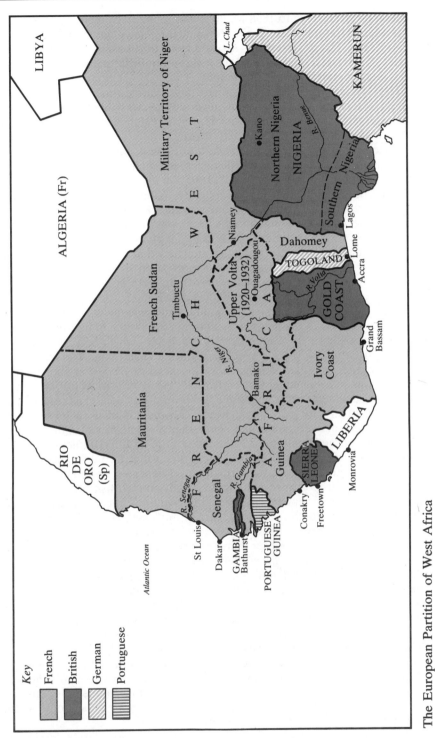

The European Partition of West Africa

commissioner from 1885 to 1898 when he was replaced by a governor and the seat of administration or the capital town of the colony was transferred from Sebe to Lome. The governor was assisted from 1904 onwards by an advisory council. This council contained at least three unofficial members who were usually German merchants in the colony.

The system of local government also varied under the different regimes. Under the British system, each colony was divided into regions under regional or chief administrators, each region into provinces under provincial commissioners, and each province into districts under district commissioners. Each district was made up of one or more traditional states, and the day-to-day affairs, local ordinances, jurisdiction over certain specific cases, development programmes and sanitation all came in theory under the traditional rulers and their councils of elders. Where considered appropriate jurisdiction was to be carried out in accordance with customary law and practice. The district commissioner's duty was merely to supervise these activities and advise the rulers. This was the so-called system of 'indirect rule' to which the British became so attached that they extended it from Northern Nigeria where it was first fully practised to all their colonies. In some cases they even created chiefs where there were none as in Igboland in Eastern Nigeria and some parts of Northern Ghana.

Much praised as the system of indirect rule was by the British, it had many serious flaws. In the first place, although the system of indirect rule was to leave 'in existence the administrative machinery which had been created by the natives themselves', in practice it did no such thing. The traditional paramount ruler or sultan was no more the head of the social and political order but was rather a subordinate of the British overlord, who used him to implement such unpopular measures as compulsory labour, taxation and military enlistment for two world wars. Those traditional rulers who had armies lost control over their armies while they also had no say in the conduct of foreign affairs and legislation. The courts of the traditional rulers were also brought under those of the British and every subject could appeal to the British courts. Furthermore the British could depose traditional rulers and replace them with their own nominees. Finally, the British often interfered with existing paramountcies by breaking some of them up and raising subordinate chiefs to the status of paramount chief as they did in Sierra Leone. In all these ways then, the system of indirect rule did weaken the traditional administration rather than preserve it.

Secondly, far from merely supervising and advising the traditional rulers, the British district officers, in practice often dictated to them and treated them as employees of the government. Thirdly, for fear that the traditional ruling families would become 'denationalised', members of the royal families were in most cases not encouraged to attend the new schools that were introduced. Indeed, in areas such as northern Nigeria and Northern Ghana, the introduction of western education was officially discouraged. Under the system of indirect rule, therefore, the traditional rulers were not given the sort of education that would enable them to cope with the new problems of providing concrete wells, building roads, bridges, dispensaries and even schools. This failure made them even more dependent on the district commissioners and British technical officers.

However, the greatest fault in indirect rule was that it completely excluded from local government the African educated elite whose number increased over the years. This greatly annoyed members of that group and turned them against not only the British overlords but also the traditional rulers.

Thus, the system of indirect rule failed to promote the welfare and development of the ordinary, people while it made the traditional authorities not only backward-looking but also very unpopular both with the educated elite and the ordinary people from whom they collected taxes on behalf of the British. The system was maintained until after the Second World War because the British found it a relatively cheap and very easy system to use. As one authority has described it, it was the most indirect method of ruling directly.

The French and the Portuguese on the other hand, adopted in theory a policy of direct rule through appointed officials. Like the British, they all divided their colonies into regions, and districts. The French, for instance, divided their colonies into *cercles* under *commandants du Cercles*, each cercle into subdivisions under *Chefs du Subdivision*, and each subdivision into cantons under African chiefs. However, the term 'chief' as used by the French was quite different from that of the British. Indeed, the French adopted a policy of deliberately destroying the great traditional paramountcies and by 1937 only about fifty of them were remaining, most of which had been deprived of their prestige. The criteria that the French used in appointing their chiefs was not birth but rather education and familiarity with the metropolitan administrative practice. Canton chiefs could be transferred from one province to another, as such they acted as civil servants executing orders and laws emanating from the metropolitan country.

The Germans also divided southern Togo into four districts each under a district commissioner. In the coastal areas, they administered directly through appointed literate African clerks who also acted as government head-chiefs over a cluster of villages. In the inland areas, however, they, like the British, administered through the traditional rulers.

All the colonial powers backed up their administration with a legislature which by and large overruled customary law, especially in criminal cases or political offences against colonial law. Added to this was the institution of a standing army such as the British Royal West African Frontier Force (established 1897) and police force used initially to conquer and later to monitor control in the respective colonies.

The colonial economy

Having established effective systems for administering the colonies and for maintaining law and order, the colonial powers turned their attention to the principal reason for their presence in Africa, namely, the production of raw materials and the acquisition of markets for the sale of their manufactured goods. To assist this development, it was important to provide an infrastructure of roads, railways, ports, telegraph and postal services to ensure easy communication and efficient transport of goods and machinery. Attention was first focused on railways, and indeed the last decade of the nineteenth century and the first three decades of the twentieth century saw the construction of most of the railways in West Africa today. Road development intensified after World War I when the Americans flooded the West African markets with cheap Ford cars. Harbours like Dakar, Freetown, Takoradi and Port Harcourt were also constructed during the first three decades of this century.

While this infrastructure of railways, roads and ports was being provided, the various colonial administrations increasingly took part in the economic work being performed by the European trading companies and missionaries, namely, that of promoting the production of cash-crops such as groundnuts, palm oil and kernel, cotton, coffee, rubber, banana, pineapple and cocoa. By setting up botanical gardens where instruction was given to farmers and from where seedlings could be obtained, by importing new varieties of old crops and introducing new ones, by assisting the companies to borrow money from abroad, by setting up agricultural colleges and, finally, by introducing the compulsory cultivation of certain cash crops such as cotton and coffee as the French in particular did in French West Africa (AOF) from 1921 onwards, the colonial administrations greatly stimulated agricultural activities in their colonies. By the 1930s, the success of their efforts was reflected in record export tonnages of coffee and groundnuts from AOF and cocoa from Ghana. Thus, the volume of cotton exports from AOF rose from an average of 189 tons in 1910–14 to 3 900 tons in 1935–9, while that of coffee soared from 5 300 tons in 1935 to 495 000 in 1936. The volume of groundnuts exported from Senegal alone increased from 500 000 tons in the 1890s to 723 000 in 1937. However, the greatest success story was that of cocoa production in Ghana whose volume of exports rose from only 80 lb in 1881 to 2 million lb in 1901 and 88.9 million lb in 1911. This made Ghana the leading producer of cocoa in the world, and the quantity continued to rise until it reached the record figure of 305 000 tons in 1936.

In their promotion of these agricultural activities, however, the colonial rulers adopted different attitudes towards the mode of production or the way in which these crops were produced. Mainly because of the opposition of the Africans themselves and because of the failure of the earlier attempts by British companies to set up plantations, the British on the whole disallowed Europeans from setting up plantations, and left the production of these cash-crops in the hands of the Africans. The African farmers established small farms using mainly family labour supplemented by hired migrants or labour. The French, Portuguese and the Germans, on the other hand, allowed both Africans and Europeans in the agricultural field, and in places like Ivory Coast, Guinea and Togo, large plantations were established by Europeans. Furthermore, while the French declared all vacant lands to be the property of the state, the British and the Germans left the land under the control of the Africans, for reasons to be discussed later.

Another industry which witnessed a phenomenal development during the colonial era, especially in British West Africa, was the mining industry. However, with the establishment of large-scale mining, first of gold and iron, then of coal, manganese, bauxite, platinum and diamonds. The two world wars stimulated the production of manganese and bauxite respectively and output soared. The value of minerals exported from Sierra Leone (iron, gold, diamonds, platinum), for instance, rose from £252 sterling in 1929 to £1.6

million in 1940 while that of gold from Ghana rose from £1 million in 1911 to £5.6 million in 1946. However, unlike agriculture, the mining industry became the exclusive monopoly of European mining companies.

In exchange for the export of these agricultural and mineral products, a number of goods were imported from the metropolitan countries. They were primarily manufactured goods such as textiles, foodstuffs (flour, sugar, alcoholic drinks etc.), building materials, motor vehicles and bicycles, factory machinery and various household goods. A host of trading firms and companies began to appear on the West African economic scene at first from the metropolitan countries then from the 1890s onwards from the Middle East. By the 1930s the whole import and export business in West Africa was dominated by three big companies. The first was the United African Company (UAC) formed by the amalgamation of the Royal Niger Company and the African and Eastern Trade Corporation Ltd. in 1920. By the 1930s, UAC was controlling fifty per cent of the overseas trade of West Africa. The second was the Compagnie Française de l'Afrique Occidentale (CFAO) which was founded in 1887 and the third was Societé Commerciale de l'Ouest Africain (SCOA) founded in 1906. By 1927, the CFAO had thirty-three branches and over one hundred and fifty trading centres. By the 1920s, too, the Levantine firms were dominating the retail field in West Africa.

Another significant economic change introduced by the colonial rulers with a view to facilitating economic relations between the metropolitan countries and their colonies were new monetary systems. In place of the system of barter and commodity currency such as iron bars, cowries and pieces of cloth that had been used in West Africa from time immemorial, each colonial power introduced new coin and paper currencies. In AOF and in the Portuguese colonies these currencies were the same as those of the metropolitan countries, but in the 1940s the French introduced a separate franc for AOF. The British introduced different currencies that were, however, tied to sterling at certain rates of exchange. In 1912 the West African Currency Board was set up to supply currency to British West Africa. In 1913, it issued special coins of the denominations of two shillings, one shilling, sixpence and threepence. Three years later, currency notes of the denominations of £1,10/-, and 2/- were issued.

In the wake of currencies came commercial banks. It was the French who established the first successful bank in West Africa. This was the Banque du Sénégal established in St Louis in 1854. In 1901, it was replaced by the Banque de l'Afrique Occidentale (BAO) which was planned significantly to serve the whole of AOF. The first bank established in British West Africa was the Bank of British West Africa (BBWA) founded in 1894 by a number of private businessmen. By 1910, it had opened branches throughout British West Africa and even in Monrovia in Liberia. In 1917 the second bank, the Colonial Bank, (later known as Barclays D.C. & O.) also started operations in West Africa. These two banks dominated the banking industry in British West Africa until the time of independence.

Finally, as part of the policy of making the colonies financially self-supporting, both direct and indirect systems of taxation were introduced. Indirect taxation consisted of the imposition of duties or tariffs on imported goods, and in most cases this constituted the main source of income for the colonies. Direct taxation, applied more by the French and Germans than the

British, consisted of the imposition of taxes on houses, fees paid for licences to carry on certain commercial activities, poll tax (paid by individuals), income tax (paid on the income earned by workers and employees), and finally labour tax (of say twelve days per annum paid by each adult either in cash or in labour, which was quite different from compulsory labour).

Colonial trade figures illustrate the apparent success of the economic policy of both the French and British. The value of exports from British West Africa rose from £13.8 million sterling in 1912/13 to £231.6 million in 1950, and those from French West Africa from £5.3 million to £79 million. The value of imports into British West Africa increased from £11.9 million sterling to £158.7 million and into French West Africa from £6.3 million to £125.2 million. However, as we shall see the benefits of this expansion were not equally distributed between the Africans and the imperial powers.

Social change

Colonial economic policy also brought about a number of social changes. Expansion in the various areas mentioned above was assisted by compulsory African labour, which was used to a greater or lesser extent by all the colonial powers. Though the British restricted compulsory labour mainly to their mining activities, the practice was far more widespread in the French and Portuguese territories. There were various systems: Africans could be recruited into road-gangs for building and maintenance work which they were obliged to carry out without pay for a certain number of days per year; a form of contract labour which forced many Africans to migrate, particularly from Upper Volta to Ivory Coast where they worked on the large European plantations for minimal wages; finally, particularly during the two world wars, Africans were compulsorily recruited into the French army. Punishments for dodging compulsory labour included flogging and imprisonment.

However, in addition to the extraction of cheap or free manual labour, the colonial rulers needed a certain source of educated middle-level manpower, in order to effectively administer their colonies and carry out their various commercial activities. Furthermore, some standards of hygiene and health had to be maintained in the interest of increased productivity. The British also hoped to improve upon the culture and institutions of the Africans while the French and the Portuguese wanted to replace them with their own in the interest of efficiency. All the colonial powers therefore introduced measures in the social field to achieve these ends.

The first measure hit upon was western education, and all the colonial rulers continued the work begun by the missionaries and abolitionists of promoting European education in their colonies. The British, the Germans and the Portuguese tended to leave these educational activities in the hands of the missionary societies and merely assisted them with annual grants, while the French assumed direct responsibility for education from 1907 onwards. There is no doubt that, during the colonial period, there was some expansion in the facilities for education. For instance, the number of school children in French West Africa increased from about 11 000 in 1912 to 106 000 in 1951, while in British West Africa 1 295 000 children were attending school by

1951. It is evident from these figures that there were greater facilities for education in the British than in the French colonies, though education in French West Africa was not only free but also of a better quality, a product of their assimilationist policy.

In the field of health and sanitation, some attempts were also made; hospitals, dispensaries and health centres were built; vaccination and inoculation were also introduced; health boards were set up in some towns, and Africans were trained and appointed as health inspectors to ensure certain standards of hygiene. Pipe-borne water and electric lighting were also laid on for some towns. Furthermore, attention was paid to research into tropical diseases; the French set up the Pasteur Institute in Dakar as early as 1896 while the British also established the schools for Tropical Medicine in Liverpool and London in 1899. By the 1940s there was usually one up-to-date hospital, generally situated in the capital town, in almost all the colonies.

The impact of colonialism of West Africa

What were the effects of all these changes introduced by the colonial rulers in West Africa? They were positive, even if accidentally so, as well as negative. The first political effect of colonial rule was the establishment of peace and order especially from the 1910s onwards after the initial brutal wars of conquest and resistance. This greatly contributed to the social and economic changes that have been analysed above. The second was the emergence of the states of West Africa as we know them today. The boundaries of all these states and hence their areas, were, as we have seen already, laid down by the colonial rulers during the period of the scramble. With the exception of the German state of Togo, part of which was later added to Ghana, these boundaries have not been changed since. Thirdly, new systems of justice and administration were introduced which have continued to be maintained. Fourthly, colonialism gave birth to a new nationalism in West Africa, that is a common sense of identity and consciousness which cut across the pre-existing clan, ethnic and regional feelings.

There were, however, some negative political effects too. The first and most important was the artificial nature of the states that emerged. The boundaries that were laid down often divided the same peoples, resulting in social disruption and tension. Thus the Ewe were divided by the Ghana-Togo border, the Akan by the Ghana-Ivory Coast border, the Senufo by the Ivory Coast-Mali border, and the Yoruba by the Dahomey-Nigerian border. Moreover, some of the states that emerged such as the Gambia and Togo were often very small with extremely limited natural resources, while others such as Nigeria were very large with large resources. Thirdly some of these states were landlocked that is, without access to the sea, such as Niger, Upper Volta and Mali. All these factors have created very serious problems of development for the modern states of West Africa.

Colonial rule also weakened the traditional institutions of chieftaincy and destroyed the indigenous systems of government. Furthermore colonial rule established professional armies in Africa. These armies have been retained ever since and have become very important political actors in the modern

African states. Finally, and the most important negative political effect of colonialism, was the loss of African sovereignty, freedom and independence, and with this the loss of the right of Africans to manage or even mismanage their own affairs, and to play a role in international affairs.

No less far-reaching were the effects of colonial rule in the economic field. The first and positive effect here was the provision of an infrastructure of roads, railways, harbours and even in some cases, airports. Not many new railway lines have been built since the colonial period. The introduction of cash crops and the mining industries were also very successful and there is no doubt that many farmers, including Africans, who produced the cash crops certainly benefited from these activities. Thirdly, colonialism led to the rapid spread of the money economy or the use of currency rather than the system of barter, which in turn, as we have seen, led to the commencement of banking activities in West Africa and the integration of the economy of West Africa into that of the world in general.

But there were some serious negative economic effects too. Built as it was to service the colonial economy, the infrastructure that was provided was never adequate and whole parts of some of the colonies especially those without mineral resources or good soil for cash crops, were often left without roads or railways. Colonialism thereby caused uneven economic development in nearly every colony. Secondly, industrialisation, more particularly manufacturing, was completely neglected and West African states became therefore the producers of raw materials and consumers of manufactured goods imported from abroad to the exclusive advantage of the metropolitan countries and the shareholders of their companies who were able to profit from captive markets. Not only was industrialisation neglected but the importation of manufactured products killed the pre-existing African industries that produced these goods. All this, therefore, delayed the technological development of Africa. Moreover, the appearance of many expatriate trading firms and companies led to the elimination of Africans from the import-export business and later from the retail trade as these companies extended their commercial activities inland. Africans were also completely excluded from any control in the mining industries, despite the fact that they had been mining gold, for example, for centuries. The profit of the mining companies furthermore were repatriated to the metropolitan countries. In banking too Africans were discriminated against and it was very difficult for African businessmen to raise capital through loans from the European banks. Finally, no serious attempts were made by the colonial rulers to diversify the agricultural economies of the colonies and so many of these colonies came to have single-crop economies which have not proved easy to change since. On balance, colonial rule did more harm than good in the economic field and resulted in the ruthless exploitation of West Africa.

Finally, in the social field, the impact of colonialism was also mixed. On the positive side, colonial rule certainly caused an increase in the population of West Africa especially from the 1910s onwards. This was partly the result of the economic changes, the establishment of hospitals, the provision of good drinking water, improvement in sanitary conditions and the launching of campaigns against epidemic diseases such as sleeping sickness, bubonic plague and yellow fever. Secondly, colonial rule resulted in the abolition of such backward-looking institutions and customs as domestic slavery and the killing of twins. Thirdly, colonialism caused the emergence of new towns and the rapid development of old ones. Abidjan, Takoradi, Lome and Port Harcourt were examples of the former while Lagos, Accra, Kumasi, Dakar, Wagadugu and Kano represent the latter. The population of Accra, for example, rose from 17 892 in 1901 to 135 926 in 1948; that of Lagos from 74 000 in 1910 to 99 000 in 1936 and 230 000 in 1951 and that of Abidjan from 800 in 1910 to 10 000 in 1914 and 127 000 by 1955, and that of Dakar from 19 800 in 1916 to 32 000 in 1936 and to 132 000 in 1945. Fourthly, there was a great spread of Christianity, Islam and above all western education, especially at the elementary level in West Africa.

Colonial rule also introduced a new social structure into West Africa. In place of the pre-colonial social classes of the traditional ruling aristocracy, the ordinary people, domestic slaves and a small educated elite, by the 1930s and 1940s a new society had emerged, sharply divided into urban and rural dwellers. The urban dwellers had become divided into three main subgroups: the educated elite, which consisted of senior civil servants, doctors, lawyers, architects, professors and university lecturers and managers of expatriate firms and businessmen; the sub-elite which consisted of clerks, teachers, nurses or junior civil servants; the urban workers or proletariat which consisted of wage-earners such as store-assistants, messengers, labourers, tailors, etc. In the rural areas, there emerged for the first time two new classes: a landless proletariat, plus those migrant workers who had left their homes and had become employed as labourers on the cocoa and groundnut farms or plantations; and a class of peasants who had established their own farms and produced cash crops for sale, many of whom became quite wealthy. It should be emphasised that in some ways this new social structure was an improvement on the traditional structure since it was based more on individual effort and attainment rather than on birth.

The final positive colonial impact in the social field was the creation of a *lingua franca* for each colony or set of colonies. In all the colonies, the mother tongue of the colonial power became the official language; in many cases it also became the main means of communication between the different ethnic groups that make up the population of each colony. It is significant that these languages have remained the official languages even to this day.

But if colonialism did have some positive social impact, it did have some serious negative effects too. The first serious negative effect was the creation of a gap between the urban and rural areas which has remained to this day. The second was the uneven social development that was introduced into each colony. While some parts and the main urban centres had the schools, colleges and hospitals, other parts were denied these facilities. Furthermore, not only were the educational facilities grossly inadequate but the curricula introduced were mostly irrelevant to the needs of the countries. Thus a huge problem of illiteracy was created while the type of education provided encouraged respect for white collar jobs and dislike for manual labour and agricultural work. The *lingua franca* also discouraged the development of any African language into a national language. Finally, under colonial rule, not only was African culture condemned but the African himself was looked down upon, humiliated, and discriminated against both secretly and openly, and this created in some Africans a deep sense of inferiority which has not entirely disappeared even after two decades of independence.

18   The rise of nationalism in West Africa

The partition of Africa and the establishment of colonial rule did not mean only the loss of African sovereignty. It also meant, an attempt by the colonial powers with varying degrees of success and for primarily selfish reasons to change the economy, culture and way of life of the African. Contrary to what some colonial historians and defenders of colonial rule in Africa have maintained, the Africans never accepted colonial rule and the destruction of their religions and way of life. Just as an overwhelming majority of them fought in defence of their lands and sovereignty in the early days, they also resorted to all sorts of methods to resist colonialism in Africa later on. Colonialism aroused a new, unifying consciousness among all Africans both rural and urban dwellers, both traditional rulers and their subjects, both the educated and uneducated and both the employed and unemployed – a consciousness of themselves as Africans, of being oppressed, exploited and humiliated. This common consciousness gave rise to anti-colonial, or nationalist feelings and ambitions not only in West Africa but throughout colonial Africa.

What then were the objectives of this national or anti-colonial feeling, and what methods were adopted to achieve them? From the available evidence, it is clear that these objectives and methods varied from period to period, and three periods can be discerned, as we shall see below.

African nationalist activities 1890s–1919

From the 1890s until the end of the World War I in 1918, the main objectives of anti-colonial or nationalist activities were to overthrow the newly-imposed colonial system and regain independence and sovereignty, to protest against certain specific features or measures of the colonial system and have them corrected or abolished, or to seek to play a role in that system. The methods that were adopted in the rural areas consisted mainly of revolts and rebellions, migrations and boycotts, while in the urban areas and among the educated elite, the methods included strikes, looting and the formation of youth movements, clubs and associations and even churches to send petitions and delegations and to campaign in the newspapers.

During this early period the most popular of these methods was the rebellion. Let us look at one or two of these rebellions in a little detail to show their real causes and objectives. An early rebellion was led by Mamadu Lamine in Senegal. He started his rebellion at the head of a large army in 1885 with a view to driving all the French out of Senegal. He attacked the French fort at Bakel which to him symbolised French presence in the area. When this attack failed, he resorted to guerilla tactics. However, assisted by

Ahmadu, the son of al Hajj Umar Tall and head of the Tukulor empire, the French succeeded in defeating him in December 1887 and in suppressing the rebellion.

A further example can be found is the Hut Tax rebellion that broke out in Sierra Leone in 1898. This rebellion was touched off in 1898 by the proclamation of the protectorate in 1896 and the introduction of British district commissioners and courts which annoyed the traditional rulers, by the abolition of the slave trade and slavery and above all the imposition of a tax of five shillings on every house in the Sierra Leone protectorate. The Temne chiefs refused to pay the tax and rose up in rebellion, led by the famous warrior-chief, Kebalai, the *bai bureh*. The Tenewere joined by the Mende and they attacked and looted trading stations and killed any British officials and troops and everybody suspected of working with or helping the colonial administration. Their sole aim was to throw the British out of the protectorate and by May 1898, the rebel armies were less than forty kilometres from Freetown. However, the British were able to suppress this rebellion with the help of two companies of soldiers brought in from Lagos.

A third rebellion was that of the Asante in 1900 led by a woman, Yaa Asantewaa, the Queen of Edweso. This rebellion was also touched off by a number of measures taken by the British with a view to establishing the colonial system and consolidating their position in Asante. The first was the deposition of many chiefs and the appointment of people who were traditionally not qualified to succeed them. The second was the imposition of a tax of four shillings per head in 1897 to pay for the cost of the 1896 invasion. The third was the opening of schools in Kumasi by the Basel missionaries who also began to interfere in the customary matters of thue Asante. The fourth was not only the abolition of slavery but the seizure of land for freed slaves. The fifth was the forced recruitment of people to carry goods and machinery to and from the coast. But the final straw was the demand for the Golden Stool made by the British governor in March 1900. Since the Asante considered the stool, as we have seen already, as the sacred symbol of the soul and unity of the nation, they of course rose up in rebellion in its defence, to throw out the British and restore their exiled king. Again with their superior weapons, the British were able to suppress the rebellion; they arrested Yaa Asantewaa and many other Asante rulers and deported them to join Prempe I in the Seychelles where Yaa Asantewaa died.

The second most common weapon of resistance used by West Africans during this period was migration. This was used particularly by Africans in the French, German and Portuguese colonies, mainly because of forced labour, oppressive direct taxation, the *indigénat* and, finally, corporal punishment of offenders. Large numbers of the population, for instance, migrated from Upper Volta and Ivory Coast to Ghana during the period under review. In 1916 and 1917, more than 12 000 people left the Ivory Coast for Ghana. Large numbers also left Togo for Ghana and in 1910 as many as 14 000 migrated from the Misahohe district alone. In the colonies themselves, whole villages were evacuated when the taxmen or the labour recruiters arrived. In some of the plantations and on the construction sites, some of the workers showed their opposition by refusing to go to work or by pretending to be sick and staying away or by destroying expensive machinery.

In the urban areas and among the educated people and the workers, the objectives were not so much the overthrow of the colonial system, but higher pay, an increase in facilities for education and representation on the legislative and executive councils. The principal method or strategy adopted during this period was the formation of clubs, unions, literary associations, even churches and sects, and a few political parties, which used petitions, delegations, campaigns, the newspapers and strikes to press their demands. Examples of such societies and clubs were the Aborigines Rights Protection Society (ARPS) founded in Ghana in 1897, the Young Senegalese Club founded in 1910, the Peoples' Union and the Anti-Slavery and Aborigines Protection Society formed in Nigeria by the educated elite and the chiefs between 1908 and 1912, and a host of ethnic, literary and old boys' associations founded especially in the British colonies.

Some of these early elite groups were quite successful in their demands for reform. It was largely as a result of the ARPS campaign in 1898 that the British dropped their proposed Land Bill, designed to give them control over all the unoccupied land in the Gold Coast colony. The Young Senegalese Club contributed to the election success of Galandou Diouf to the General Council in 1909; it later formed the nucleus of one of the early Senegalese political parties. Another early Senegalese political party, the Republican Socialist Party, helped to get its founder-member Blaise Diagne elected as the first African deputy to the French Chamber of Deputies in July 1914. Diagne was to remain the most important nationalist in French West Africa until his death in 1934. In Dahomey, a harsh and unpopular governor was recalled to France and his activities investigated thanks to the efforts of an anti-colonial group in Paris, led by Dahomean ex-teacher Louis Hunkanrin.

In protest against the condemnation of African culture and the domination of the churches by white missionaries a number of Nigerian Christians broke away to found the first Ethiopian Church in Nigeria in 1888, the Native Baptist Church. In the Muslim areas of Senegal too, the Muridiyya sect was founded by Amadu Bamba in the late 1880s in protest against the French colonial system that had already uprooted and disorganised so many people. Bamba's movement attracted thousands of such people who settled in newly-created villages devoted to religion and the cultivation of groundnuts. Indeed, the French were so alarmed by his success that they arrested and exiled him first to Gabon and then to Mauretania. He was later repatriated but was kept under house arrest until his death in 1927. His sect, however, continued to thrive in Senegal.

A further religious movement emerged, this time in Ivory Coast, led by William Wade Harris, a Liberian evangelist. He launched his crusade in the Ivory Coast in 1914, and won over 100 000 converts in a matter of only two years, most of whom were people who had also been uprooted and disorganised by the new colonial measures. The young educated men also saw in the movement an opportunity for leadership and resistance to French colonialism and so joined and became leaders of the churches which soon sprang up all over the country. It is not surprising, then, that the French deported him to his country where he died in obscurity. His church, however, continued to exist and even spread into Ghana where it has remained active to this day.

African nationalist activities 1919–1939

During World War I resistance continued and intensified in the rural areas where because of the increased conscription of soldiers and carriers and increased direct taxation, even more revolts and rebellions broke out. In the urban areas, and especially among the educated elite who on the whole remained loyal to the colonial rulers during the war, resistance died down. Immediately after the war, however, nationalist activities were resumed and grew in intensity throughout the inter-war period from 1919 to 1939.

The reasons for this intensification are not hard to find. The first was the impact of World War I itself. As indicated already, conscription of Africans during the war greatly increased and this aroused a great deal of anger especially in the French colonies. The war also proved to the African that the white man was after all not a superman but an ordinary man who could be as easily frightened as any African and who could therefore be challenged. Furthermore, those educated Africans who had remained loyal to the colonial powers and had assisted them expected to be rewarded by means of more privileges and an increased role in the colonial set-up; these expectations were not fulfilled and so they resumed and intensified their anti-colonial activities.

The second reason for an increase in anti-colonial activity lay in the continuing disturbance in the social order within the colonies. By the inter-war period the colonial rulers had consolidated their alliance with the traditional rulers, eliminating any effective role for the elite or the ordinary people in the control of their affairs. Those of the elite who had been educated overseas returned home to even more disappointment and frustration since their expectations were much greater than those trained at home.

Another important factor was economic. The late 1920s and early 1930s were marked by a series of worldwide economic crises which caused the prices of exports to drop and those of imports to rise. These changes coupled with the discrimination that the banks and the shipping lines practised against Africans and the active competition from the expatriate and Syrian trading firms accelerated the downfall of many African businessmen and the dismissal of workers who therefore joined the anti-colonial bandwagon.

Finally, the inter-war period saw the spread from the United States and the West Indies of pan-Africanist ideas that the black peoples throughout the world form a single race and have a personality, culture and soul which should be recognised and respected by the white races, and that all blacks should unite and fight against racial discrimination, oppression and colonial domination. The activities of Marcus Garvey and William DuBois in the United States and the organisation of pan-African congresses in Paris in 1919, London, Brussels and Paris in 1921, Lisbon in 1922 and New York in 1927 greatly assisted the nationalist leaders in Africa.

There are, however, some interesting differences between the nationalist activities of this period and those of the former period. First, the objectives were now not the overthrow of the colonial system but rather its improvement and above all, for an increased and meaningful role of the African in that system. Secondly, whereas in the first period, the leadership of nationalist activities was concentrated in the hands of the traditional rulers in the rural areas and in those of the educated elite and the traditional rulers in the urban areas, in the inter-war period, the traditional rulers were by and large eliminated from the leadership role and most of them in fact became the strongest allies of the colonial rulers. It was the illiterate young men in the rural areas and the educated elite and the urban workers who now organised and led the protest movements. Thirdly, methods such as rebellions, uprisings and revolts were almost completely abandoned in favour of the more peaceful methods of petitions, newspaper campaigns and delegations; the inter-war period also saw the formation of a large number of elitist clubs, societies and religious groups as well as genuine political parties and trade unions to conduct these activities. Fourthly, probably because of the limited nature of the research that has been conducted into nationalist activities in the rural areas, it would appear that these activities were stronger and more determined in the urban than in the rural areas. Fifthly, nationalist activities in West Africa assumed international dimensions and became pan-Africanist in outlook.

Nationalist activities in British West Africa 1919–1939

In a survey of the nationalist activities in British West Africa it is important to note the number and variety of organisations which appeared during this period. In Ghana alone, as many as fifty clubs and literary associations were formed. The Nigerian Youth Movement was formed in 1934, and the West African Youth League was founded by I.T.A. Wallace-Johnson in 1938, with branches in Sierra Leone and Ghana. All these organisations actively campaigned for better representation, improved educational facilities, higher salaries and an end to racial discrimination by means of newspapers, petitions and involvement in local elections and in strike action. But only one of them, the West African Youth League, actually demanded total independence from colonial rule.

Similarly the early political parties such as the National Congress of British West Africa (NCBWA) and the National Democratic Party (NDP) formed in Ghana and Nigeria in 1920 and 1923 respectively, did not have radical aims; they merely demanded a reform of the colonial system and an active African role in it. The NCBWA, however, unlike the clubs and associations, had branches in all the British colonies in West Africa, and its membership, drawn mainly from African professional and business circles, was influenced by the pain-Africanist activities and ideas of DuBois and Marcus Garvey. The NDP, formed by Herbert Macaulay, was a particularly prominent force in Lagos, winning elections in 1923, 1928 and 1933 until its defeat by the Nigerian Youth Movement in 1938.

Although trade unions were not officially allowed by the British until 1932 in the Gambia, 1939 in Sierra Leone and Nigeria, and 1941 in Ghana, a number of unions did emerge during the inter-war years. The first of these was the Railway Workers' Union of Sierra Leone, formed first in 1919 then reorganised in 1925 to include both skilled and unskilled workers. It organised strikes in 1919, 1920 and 1926 over wages and treatment of workers during sickness. Other groups of workers also entered into strikes and boycotts with the aim of improving their working conditions – the workers of the Ashanti goldfields went on strike at Obuasi in Ghana in 1924 and in 1925 the Enugu coalminers struck for higher wages.

In the rural areas African producers came together to form organisations such as the Gold Coast and Ashanti Cocoa Federation and Gold Coast Cocoa Farmers Association formed in the 1930s. They organised the cocoa hold-up and boycott of imported goods in 1930/31 and 1937, which has been described as the last and most significant demonstration of rural discontent in British West Africa before World War II. Again in the rural areas of Ghana there was a revival of the traditional associations of young commoners known as *asafo*. They obtained the destoolment of many divisional chiefs who had abused their traditional powers by selling or renting stool lands to expatriate mining companies, or by enforcing levies or compulsory labour at the request of the colonial administration.

However, it is evident that despite all these efforts, the end of the inter-war period saw a colonial system that was very firmly established in both the urban and rural areas. What, then, were the reasons for the failure of all these activities? Firstly, neither the Congress nor the youth movements, nor the political parties enjoyed the following of the masses. They were therefore rejected by the colonial rulers on the grounds that they were unrepresentative of the people. Secondly, there was no connection between the movements in the rural areas and those in the urban areas and each of them could therefore be dealt with separately and therefore relatively easily by the colonial rulers. Thirdly, neither the Congress nor the youth movements were prepared to use any radical or violent methods to achieve their objectives – obviously owing to the lessons they learnt from the failure of the violent methods of the earlier period. Above all, the leaders of the various clubs and movements often fought among themselves. In all the colonies there were often conflicts between the conservatives and the moderates, between the old and the young professionals and leaders, and between the new educated elite and the traditional rulers, and all these conflicts weakened the nationalist activities. It was certainly the conflict between the new and relatively young leaders of the Congress and the older leaders of the ARPS, and between the traditional rulers led by Nana Ofori Atta, the Omanhene of Akyem Abuakwa, and the members of the Congress led by Casely Hayford, that caused the failure of the nationalist movement in Ghana. The effectiveness of the Lagos branch of the NCBWA was also reduced as a result of internal quarrels, personality conflicts and the opposition of conservative leaders such as Sir Kitoyi Ajasa. In 1930, the death of Casely Hayford who was the main spirit behind the NCBWA gave the final blow to any coordinated anti-colonial activities in British West Africa.

Finally, the British colonial rulers, like the French, were also not ready to make any serious concessions and therefore did not hesitate to use harsh methods to suppress any forms of resistance; for example, they crushed the 1926 strike of the Sierra Leonean railway workers with dismissals and victimisation, and in 1938 they deported both Azikiwe and Wallace-Johnson from Ghana.

Nationalist activities in French West Africa 1919–1939

Anti-colonial or nationalist activities in French West Africa were far less widespread than in the British colonies during the inter-war years. In Senegal, Blaise Diagne and his political party continued their efforts towards equality and African control of the administration and of municipal councils; Diagne also assisted in the organisation of the early pan-African congresses. But under French political and economic pressure he became less and less radical; eventually he lost the support of the Senegalese elite and in the early 1930s he represented the metropolitan government at an international labour conference and defended the use of forced labour in French West Africa. He died in 1934 as a pro-French conservative. His political successors – his arch rival Galandou Diouf and the Socialist Lamine Gueye – followed in a broadly similar pattern until the post-war years.

The only other French colony besides Senegal in which significant nationalist activities took place was Dahomey. There were three distinct groups who allied against the French: the royal lineage led by Sohingbe which had been barred from succession by the French who refused to recognise more than one Porto Novo dynasty; a group of revivalist Muslims, mainly Yoruba, also from Porto Novo; and the political organisation of Louis Hunkanrin, the Dahomean radical leader who had earlier been active in Paris where he had links with communist and anarchist parties and from where he returned to his own country in 1921.

Tension came to a head in 1923 when the French governor, Fourn, raised taxes by five hundred per cent, despite Dahomey's reduced export earnings. The three anti-colonialist groups joined to organise a campaign of passive resistance against the taxes and the high prices of imported goods. Workers, including those from the port of Cotonou, went on strike, people refused to pay taxes and imported goods were boycotted.

This passive resistance lasted from 13 February to early March 1923, and it was repressed with extreme brutality by the French administration. Governor Fourn called in troops from Togo and Ivory Coast and declared a state of emergency which lasted three months. During the period, the army collected taxes, seized firearms, burnt some villages and evacuated others. Finally nearly all the leaders of the resistance movement, including Hunkanrin and Sohingbe were arrested and exiled to Mauritania. Only Hunkanrin survived exile.

This event and its outcome marked the end of any planned anti-colonial activity not only in Dahomey but throughout French West Africa. It also illustrates how the French, even more than the British, refused to tolerate any serious challenge to their rule. So, on the eve of World War II, nationalist activities were at their lowest ebb and colonial rule had become permanent, or so it seemed, throughout West Africa.

19 The independence revolution in West Africa

Contrary to what the colonial rulers and even many of the Africans themselves had expected, colonialism did not last for ever. Indeed, within only a period of two decades after World War II, all the colonies in West Africa, except the Portuguese one of Guinea, won their independence. The British colony of the Gold Coast was the first to do so in March 1957 under the name of Ghana, the name of the famous empire of the Western Sudan. Ghana was followed by the French colony of Guinea in 1958; two years later, Nigeria and the rest of the French colonies in West Africa also regained their independence and sovereignty; the British colony of Sierra Leone followed in 1961 and the Gambia in 1965. Considering the speed with which this was accomplished, there is every justification in calling this change a revolution. The fascinating question is how this incredible political revolution can be accounted for.

The reasons are many and complex. The first key is the very nature of colonialism itself. At its worst, colonialism was tyrannical, exploitative and oppressive and denied the racial equality of black and white; at its most enlightened, it was paternalistic, and deprived colonial subjects of their inalienable right to manage their own affairs. In either form, colonialism was basically foreign domination maintained by force, and sooner or later, like all such dominations, it was bound to be challenged and overthrown; in the words of the famous English clergyman, Trevor Huddleston, 'Foreign domination cannot coexist with freedom.' Even where colonialism provided good government, it could not be saved either, for, as the old saying goes: 'Good government is no substitute for self-government'.

The impact of World War II

The second and very important reason for the independence revolution was the impact of World War II, both on the colonial powers and on their African subjects. In the first place, the war physically and psychologically, weakened all the European powers that took part in it, including the colonial powers of Britain, France and Belgium. This weakness, therefore, made them less anxious and able than before to really resist African demands. Secondly, as a result of the war, the United States of America and the Soviet Union emerged as the two leading world powers. Fortunately for colonial Africa, both powers were in favour of ending colonial rule in Africa, though for very different reasons, and both therefore put a great deal of pressure on the colonial powers both during and immediately after the war, to end their overseas rule.

The war also led to the issue of the Atlantic Charter as well as the foundation of the United Nations Organisation (UNO) and both of these had a favourable impact on the anti-colonial movement. The Charter proclaimed 'the right of all people to choose the form of government under which they live,' and wished to see 'sovereign rights and self-government restored to those who had been deprived of them.' Though Churchill and his Conservative party denied that these principles applied to the African colonies, the Labour party under Attlee, the Americans, and many educated Africans insisted that they did. Azikiwe for instance, prepared a memo entitled 'The Charter and British West Africa' in which he demanded 'immediate reforms and representative government in West Africa'. The General Assembly of the UNO also provided a useful forum for attacks and pressure on colonial governments by the African, Asiatic, American and the Communist delegations as well as by anti-colonial pressure groups operating in Europe, the Soviet Union and the United States. Thus, the war and the birth of the United Nations Organisation greatly assisted in converting the colonial powers to the idea of internal self-government or representative government, if not of total independence. It should, nevertheless, be added that even Britain which was the most sympathetic of the colonial powers in this respect, thought a minimum period of about fifty years would be necessary before this could be achieved.

Even more important and decisive, however, was the effect of the war on Africa itself. First, the war brought about such economic and social developments in the colonies in Africa and at such a rate as had never been known before – in agriculture, mining, provision of harbours and airports, and even some manufacturing. As a result, Africans were made to expect more after the war, but their expectations were never fulfilled, which further strengthened anti-colonial feeling. Secondly, the setting up of marketing boards to market raw materials produced in the colonies and the discrimination practised by these boards against African businessmen intensified nationalist feelings. But the most important impact of the war was on the African soldiers themselves. As the very perceptive British information officer in Kampala quite rightly observed: 'The man [African] at the war is being thrown in contact with Europeans in a way as never before. The returning African cannot be quite the same. They will have fought and lived side by side with foreigners, black and white. They received at any rate in the Middle East, the same food, the same clothing, they drank side by side in the canteens the same beer, they were fighting the same battle . . . they will have seen the world sufficiently to realise that they can have improved homes, better food, better conditions and better pay for work undertaken . . . How are we going to keep them down on the farm after the war?' This was true not only of the Ugandan ex-servicemen but of all African ex-servicemen. Furthermore, after all the suffering and the struggles, the African soldiers were expecting adequate pensions and employment on their return home, but these hopes were not fulfilled. It is for all these reasons that the ex-servicemen became so active in the anti-colonial activities after the war.

The Pan-African Congress of 1945

It should be obvious then that World War II created an atmosphere in which colonialism could not continue to exist in its old form, while it made the revival of the attack on it in the colonies more or less inevitable. One of the factors in this renewed attack was the Pan-African Congress held in Britain in Manchester in 1945. Though this congress was the sixth in the series of congresses held since 1900, it differed from all the others in a number of significant ways. In the first place, African students in London played a far more active role in the organisation and running of this congress than in any of the others. Indeed, one of the two joint secretaries was no other than Kwame Nkrumah of Ghana, the other being the West Indian radical pan-Africanist George Padmore. Secondly, far more Africans attended this congress than at any other time, among whom were Obafemi Awolowo, H. O. Davies and Jaja Wachuku from Nigeria; J. E. Taylor, Ako Adjei and Dr Armattoe from Ghana; Jomo Kenyatta from Kenya and Hastings Banda from Malawi.

More important still were the demands that were made by this Congress. For the first time, the delegates did not demand just a reform of the colonial system, but rather complete independence. 'If the western world is still determined to rule mankind by force,' stated one of the resolutions, 'then Africans, as a last resort, may have to appeal to force in the effort to achieve freedom even if force destroys them and the world.' Another resolution entitled significantly 'Declaration to the colonial workers, farmers and intellectuals' called on all of them to unite and form an effective organisation to fight against imperialist exploitation and for independence. This resolution also recommended the use of such methods as strikes and boycotts, positive action and other non-violent strategies. It is clear then that this congress not only called for independence but also drew up the methods that were to be used, namely an effective organisation of the masses and all classes through trade unions and political parties and the use of non-violent means and of force if necessary. The third and final aspect of this Congress was that most of the Africans who attended soon returned to their respective countries and there applied, as we shall see below, the methods formulated at the Congress, thereby adding extra radical spirit to the nationalist activities which were already in motion.

Nationalist activities and parties

As was the case in World War I, Africans on the whole remained loyal to the colonial powers during the war years and contributed everything they could either voluntarily or under covert or overt pressure to the war effort. However, as soon as the war ended, nationalist activities were revived and intensified for a number of reasons. First, the period immediately after the war saw an acute shortage of consumer goods, leading to an astronomical increase in prices for which the colonial powers and their expatriate firms were held responsible. Moreover, though the British increased the Colonial Development and Welfare Fund (CDWF) set up in 1940 to £5 million sterling a year for development projects, and £50 000 for research in 1944, and though the French also set up *Fonds pour l'Investissement pour le Développement Economique et Social* (FIDES) in 1944, in recognition of French Africa's services to Free France, the funds made available were too small to make any real impact while there was no increase in industrialisation and economic development. All this caused a great deal of anger, disappointment and frustration in the economic field after the war, which led to the Nigerian national strike of 1945, the Dakar railway strike of 1947/8, the boycott and looting of European goods in Ghana in 1948, and the demonstration by the miners of the Enugu mines in 1949.

Secondly, though immediately after the war both the British and the French introduced some constitutional reforms, these fell far short of the expectations of both the educated elite and the masses. The British Burns constitution of 1946 gave Africans a majority of eighteen seats out of the thirty-one on Ghana's legislative council – however, only five of these were to be filled by direct election; the remainder were to be nominated by councils of chiefs, thus strengthening their powers to the disadvantage of the educated elite, the ex-servicemen and the ordinary people in general. Such was the opposition to this constitution that it lasted only two years instead of the ten years' expected minimum. The Richards constitution of Nigeria (1947) aroused similar opposition – forty-one out of the forty-five-member legislative assembly were to be either nominated by the colonial administration or indirectly elected by the chief-dominated regional councils.

The new French constitution (1946) on the other hand, abolished the much hated *indigenat* and turned all the inhabitants of French Africa into citizens. Each territory was given its own elected assembly, and twenty-seven African deputies were directly elected as representatives in the National Assembly in Paris. Though this constitution went much further than the British ones in meeting the political aspirations of the educated African elite, it did not entirely satisfy them. They objected to the powers given to the territorial assemblies which were merely advisory and to the two-college electoral system introduced, and so they continued to press for changes.

Finally, the continuation of the colour bar in all the colonies, the refusal to provide increased facilities for higher education, and, in Ghana in particular, the refusal of the British to establish a university college for that colony alone, further intensified the disgust for the colonial system.

For the above reasons, there is no doubt that nationalist and anti-colonial activities were resumed with increased intensity after the war. But what made these activities different from most of the previous ones were their objectives and methods. In all the colonies except those of the French, the objectives now were no more the reform or improvement of the colonial system, but rather its total abolition and the regaining of independence and sovereignty. In French West Africa, on the other hand, the objectives were the abolition of racial discrimination and full equality of rights and privileges for both black and white, and above all the maintenance of French West Africa as a single federation rather than having it broken up into individual states.

Not only were the objectives different but so also were the political parties that were formed and the methods and strategies that were used. The parties that were formed by the nationalists in British West Africa after the war were the United Gold Coast Convention (UGCC), the Convention Peoples' Party (CPP) and the Northern Peoples' Party (NPP) in Ghana in 1947, 1948 and 1954 respectively; the National Council for Nigerian Citizens (NCNC), the Action Group (AG) and the Northern Peoples' Congress

(NPC) in Nigeria in 1944, 1950 and 1951 respectively; the National Council of Sierra Leone (NCSL) and the Sierra Leone Peoples' Party (SLPP) both in 1950, and the United Party and the Peoples' Progressive Party (PPP) in the Gambia. In French West Africa the *Rassemblement Démocratique Africain* (RDA) and the *Bloc Africain* were formed in 1946 and the *Bloc Démocratique Sénégalais* (BDS) in 1948. The formation of political parties was not allowed in Portuguese Africa until after 1954, when the African Party for the Independence of Guinea (PAIGC) was formed.

Not only did all the parties except those formed in French West Africa ask for total independence but they were organised in such a way that they could no more be ignored or easily suppressed by the colonial powers. First of all, unlike the earlier associations and clubs, these parties were not elitist parties but were, by and large, made up of a mixture of the elites, many of the traditional rulers and to varying degrees, the masses in the rural areas. Kwame Nkrumah's CPP in Ghana was the most broadly-based of all the West African parties of this period, both in terms of its leadership – dominated by teachers, junior civil servants, trade union leaders and ex-servicemen, rather than the traditional professional aristocracy of chiefs, lawyers and big businessmen – and its support, which commanded a much larger mass following in the towns and the rural areas than the UGCC. Most of the parties in West Africa, however, were more traditional in their choice of leadership; indeed the NPL of Nigeria and the SLPP of Sierra Leone were dominated by the traditional rulers.

Secondly, unlike the earlier clubs and associations, these parties had full-time officers, party offices, flags, symbols, propaganda vans and slogans – in short, all the paraphernalia of modern political parties the world over. Some of course were much more effectively organised than others.

Thirdly, all of them used practically the same methods or tactics to press their demand for independence. They organised rallies and meetings throughout the length and breadth of their countries; they sent petitions and delegations to the local administrations and imperial governments and the United Nations, to express their grievances and demands; they organised strikes and boycotts to draw attention to their activities internally and externally; and they actively took part in the various elections that were organised under the various constitutions. Thus for example, there were elections in Ghana in 1951, 1954 and 1956, all of which were won by the CPP, and in Sierra Leone in 1951 and 1957, which were won by the SLPP.

There were, however, some significant differences, which go a long way to explain why nationalist activities gathered momentum earlier in British than in French West Africa, secondly why some countries gained independence before others, and thirdly why particular political parties emerged as winners in particular countries. The first of these differences was that while the parties that emerged in French West Africa were inter-territorial parties with branches in the whole of the federation, the parties that now emerged in British West Africa were confined to specific colonies. Secondly, whereas the parties that emerged in French West Africa were either branches of parties existing in France or were very closely identified with them, those that emerged in British West Africa had no links whatsoever with any of the parties in Britain. Thus the RDA formed in 1946 was at least in the early years very closely linked with the French Communist

Party, while the *Bloc Africain* had strong ties with the French Socialist Party, the SFIO. The parties in British West Africa, therefore, could speak for each colony and could also demand a complete break with the metropolitan country while those of French West Africa could not.

Even in British West Africa, there were differences in the parties that emerged. In Ghana, whereas the first two parties to emerge, the UGCC and the CPP, were truly national parties, that is, they had branches throughout the different regions of the country and had members among all the ethnic groups of the country, the parties that emerged in Nigeria, Sierra Leone and even the Gambia, were not. In Nigeria, the NCNC was essentially a party of the Igbo and was confined to the eastern region of the country, the AG was that of the Yoruba and was dominant in the western region, while the NPC was the party of the Fulani and the Hausa and controlled the northern region of the country. In Sierra Leone, the NCSL formed in 1950 was the party of the Krio of the south while the SLPP, led by Dr Milton Margai, was the party of the people of the protectorate. Finally, in the Gambia, the United Party led by Pierre Njie was, like the NCSL, a party of the Krio while the PPP led by David Jawara was the party of the people of the protectorate. Thus, while the British had no way of playing one party against the other in Ghana, they could do so in the other three colonies, and they did.

Moreover, whereas there was no serious disagreement between the two main parties in Ghana about the date for the attainment of independence, there were very sharp differences of opinion on this issue between the parties of the northern regions and those of the southern regions in the other three British colonies. There is absolutely no doubt that it was these major differences between the parties of Ghana and those of the other colonies that explain why Ghana was the first to win its battle for independence, not only in British West Africa, but in the whole of West Africa.

There is yet another reason which explains more particularly why Ghana won independence under the banner of the CPP led by Kwame Nkrumah, rather than that of the UGCC as the first party to emerge under the leadership of J. B. Danquah and Pa Grant. Nearly all the parties in both British and French West Africa used only constitutional and non-violent methods in the fight for independence; only the CPP in Ghana, were prepared to use non-constitutional and even violent means, such as strikes and violent demonstrations, boycotts and the looting of goods, and what Nkrumah called 'positive action' to achieve their ends. Thus, whereas Nkrumah and many of his closest supporters like Gbedemah and Kofi Baako and Krobo Edusei were gaoled and became 'prison graduates' which further endeared them to the masses, none of the other great party political leaders followed the same radical course. It was largely his radical approach, coupled with his own particular charisma and political ability which turned Kwame Nkrumah into the most popular nationalist leader, and his party into the party with the largest mass following in the whole of West Africa. It is not surprising then that it won the elections of 1951 and 1954 and the last independence elections of 1956.

However, radical methods alone did not necessarily result in victory; in French West Africa, the RDA had also become a popular mass party in the late 1940s, but it failed at this time on account of other factors which we will now examine.

The reactions and responses of the colonial powers

Colonial reactions provide the last of the answers as to why and when the independence revolution in West Africa took place when it did why British West Africa on the whole and Ghana in particular took the lead and, finally, why Portuguese Guinea did not win its independence until 1974.

As we have seen already, there is no doubt that right from the beginning the British regarded each of their African colonies as a separate entity not connected with Britain. Moreover, during and after World War II, the British adopted the policy of granting independence to each of the colonies as soon as they became convinced that that colony was ready for it. Indeed, Arthur Creech-Jones, the then Colonial Secretary of the Labour government declared in 1948: 'The central purpose of British colonial policy is simple. It is to guide the colonial territories to responsible government within the Commonwealth in conditions that ensure to the people concerned both a fair standard of living and freedom of oppression from any quarter'. In fact, what the British looked for was not so much a fair standard of living and freedom of oppression from any quarter, but rather that the nationalist leaders were not communist-inspired and that there was agreement among the rival political parties on independence, on a constitution and on a date for independence.

Thus, except in those areas where there was a sizeable British settler community, the British did not show much hostility to nationalist activities nor did they suppress them with any brutality. For example, as soon as they seemed convinced that Nkrumah and his CPP were the most popular force in Ghana by their victory at the 1951 elections, they readily released him from prison and asked him to form the government, and from then on co-operated with him until independence was achieved in March 1957. With the Ghanaian victory, that of the other British colonies came to depend very much on when the parties involved could agree on a date and a constitution, and this was achieved in Nigeria in 1960, in Sierra Leone in 1961, and in the Gambia in 1965.

The reactions and responses of the French and the Portuguese were the very opposite to those of the British. As we have seen, both of them right from the beginning regarded their colonies as mere overseas provinces of the mother country; the French constitution of 1946 talked of an indivisible union and even increased the representation of the colonies in the French assembly. Though as a result of their humiliating military defeat by Vietnamese nationalists at Dien Bien Phu in the French Colony of Indo-China (and Vietnam) the French became more amenable to moderate constitutional changes in Africa. The constitution of 1956 and the accompanying laws still retained the concept of the French Union and only broke up the federal structure of French West Africa into its component colonies and granted each colony internal autonomy within the French Union. Even when de Gaulle came to power in May 1958, his battle-cry was 'The Republic, one and indivisible', and his policy was the creation of a Franco-African 'Community', not that of independence.

Right from the beginning until 1958, therefore, the French repressed all demands for any radical reforms with extreme brutality – as they did in Madagascar in 1946 at a cost of 11 000 dead according to official figures, and 80 000 according to those of the Malagasy nationalists. Between 1948 and

1950, they also persecuted the RDA in French West Africa and especially in Ivory Coast, not so much because of its radical demands but because of its association with the French communists. They arrested the RDA leaders, dismissed chiefs and civil servants who were sympathetic towards that party, gave every assistance to the rival political parties, used force to break up strikes called by the RDA and brutally banned all meetings of the RDA after thirteen Africans had been shot by French troops at Dimbokro in Ivory Coast.

As a result of all these measures, while the CPP won the elections in Ghana in 1951, the RDA lost the French assembly election of the same year, beaten by the anti-RDA parties supported by the French. Indeed, in order to survive, the RDA under Houphouët-Boigny had to break its links completely with the French Communist Party and abandon all its radical programmes, which had not even included a demand for independence. As soon as this was done, the RDA once again gained the support of the French government, and therefore won the elections of 1956.

Indeed, although some of the young French Africans and trade union leaders, such as Sekou Touré, began to demand independence from 1956 onwards, it was not until 1958 that de Gaulle himself made this an issue during the referendum which he organised in French Africa in September 1958 in which African were invited to vote 'Yes' or 'No' to staying under French rule within the newly created 'French Union'. Only Guinea under Sekou Touré voted to secede from the Union. Even this came as a shock to de Gaulle and his government, and Guinea was given the necessary punishment; though it was granted independence in 1958, the French withdrew all their personnel, together with even the office equipment and telephones. It was only the timely loan of £10 million sterling by Nkrumah to Sekou Touré that saved Guinea from total collapse. But once Guinea became independent and survived, and inspired also by the independence of Ghana in 1957 and Togo in 1960, all the French colonies in Africa also ultimately demanded and were granted independence by November 1960.

It should be obvious, then, that the French colonies in West Africa did not become independent till between 1958 and 1960 primarily because of the reactions of the French government to nationalist activities and demands – reactions that were a direct consequence of their union policy. It is important to note that the Portuguese also stuck to the same stupid policy of 'overseas Portugal' and therefore repressed all demands for independence until they were forcibly thrown out of Africa by the African liberation forces of Guinea, Angola and Mozambique after wars which raged throughout the 1960s and the first half of the 1970s.

It is clear, then, that the fall of colonial rule in West Africa was caused by a whole complex of factors – the nature of colonialism itself, the impact of World War II, and in particular the pressure exerted on the colonial power by the two great powers of the USA and the Soviet Union and by the UNO itself, the impact of the 1945 Pan-African Congress, the nature and activities of the political parties that emerged during and after the war, and finally the responses of the colonial powers to these activities. The question then is, what have these African states made of their independence? We shall examine this in the final section of this book.

20 Political and constitutional developments

The broad political development and changes that have taken place in the first two decades of West African independence follow a general pattern. First of all, most states entered independence with Westminster-style or Paris-style constitutions, with democratically elected assemblies, and multi-party systems consisting of a ruling party opposed by one or more opposition party. Secondly, after a few years most states had become, in practice if not in name, one-party states. Thirdly, Republican constitutions replaced monarchical ones in the former British colonies. Fourthly, a number of attempts were made to create political unions out of two or more states, with mixed success. Fifthly, by 1970 half of West Africa's states had experienced military coups which overthrew corrupt civilian regimes and replaced them with military governments. In the 1970s there were fewer coups in West Africa (eight, in contrast to fifteen before 1970) and in the late 1970s there was a noticeable trend back towards civilian rule and multi-party democracy. However, in the early 1980s there was a new wave of military coups.

Multi-party politics

At independence Nigeria's federal constitution reflected the former British system of administration and the party political rule we observed in earlier chapters. The country was divided into three regions, each dominated by a political party based on the support of the majority ethnic community in the region. Thus, there was a Yoruba-dominated Action Group (AG) government in the West, an Igbo-dominated National Council of Nigeria and the Cameroons (NCNC) government in the east and a Hausa-Fulani-dominated Northern Peoples Congress (NPC) government in the North. From 1954 to the coup of 1966 there was rivalry among the two southern parties (AG and NCNC) to win a political alliance with the NPC and thus share in the federal government. At independence, Nigeria was governed by an NPC-NCNC alliance with Dr Azikiwe (NCNC) as Governor-General and Sir Abubakar Tafawa Balewa (NPC) as Federal Prime Minister. The real ruler of the country, however, was the leader of the NPC and Premier of the Northern Region, Sir Ahmadu Bello, the Sardauna of Sokoto. The leader of the federal opposition was Obafemi Awolowo, the AG leader.

In the 1959 federal elections Awolowo had sought support for the AG from the ethnic minorities in the East and North by championing the cause of creating more states. The federal government responded in 1961 by proposing to create a Mid-West state around Benin out of the non-Yoruba minorities of the West and in 1962 by imprisoning Awolowo and many of his leading followers on charges of treasonable felony. A group of Yoruba politicians under Chief Samuel Akintola broke away from the AG to form a new party, the Nigerian National Democratic Party (NNDP). Akintola's aim was to ally with the NPC in the federal government; he was supported by the Sardauna who planned to drop his ally the NCNC. In this intra-party contest, Akintola became Premier of a minority regional government of the Western Region.

The announcement of the results of the 1962 federal census in February 1964 further heightened ethnic tension. The results showed that over half of Nigeria's population of 55 million lived in the North, which dashed the NCNC's hopes that the south would 'win the census' and take over the federal government after reorganisation of constituencies. The census led to a new alliance between the NCNC, the AG and the small opposition parties of the North who together formed the United Progressive Grand Alliance (UPGA). They were opposed in the 1964–65 federal election by the Nigerian National Alliance (NNA), composed of the NPC and the NNDP. Although there was widespread violence and vote rigging, the elections were not cancelled, and the NNA claimed to have won. After a few days of crisis Azikiwe and Balewa patched up a federal government of NNA and UPGA (but not AG) members.

Ethnic conflict in Nigerian politics exploded in violence on three occasions between independence and the first coup in 1966. The Tiv-supported United Middle Belt Congress (UMBC) won the Tiv constituencies in the North in the 1959 election in alliance with the AG. The NPC government of the North retaliated by bringing false charges against UMBC leaders. The Tiv reacted in 1960 by carrying out mass arson attacks on NPC offices and homes, and the Nigerian army had to be used to restore law and order. Serious anti-NPC rioting broke out again among the Tiv in 1964. The most spectacular violence, however, occurred during the Western Region election of 1965. The election became a physical battle between NNDP and UPGA mobs. The NNDP feared an UPGA victory in a democratic ballot and rigged the elections. Officially, UPGA won only 15 out of 88 seats but Akintola was unable to govern because of widespread disorder. The federal government sent army units into the West in order to instal Akintola's regional government in Ibadan. This attempt to use the army for partisan political ends was to contribute to the military coup of January 1966.

Another multi-party system where the parties were broadly split along ethnic lines was in Sierra Leone. From independence in April 1961 to the military coup of March 1967, Sierra Leone was plagued by the ethnic rivalries of the ruling Sierra Leone People's Party (SLPP) led by Prime Minister Sir Milton Margai (1961–4) and his brother Albert Margai (1964–7) and the opposition All People's Congress (APC) led by Siaka Stevens. The SLPP gained most of its support in the south particularly among the Mende chiefs. The APC got the support of the Temne and other ethnic groups opposed to the increasing Mende domination of the government, and from professionals, clerks, teachers and students in the towns concerned about the economic chaos and open corruption, bribery and nepotism displayed by the ruling party. In the 1962 elections the SLPP won 29 seats and the APC 20. Milton Margai remained in power by combining with independents and twelve chiefs in the legislature to control 54 of the 74 seats. In 1964, the conciliatory Sir Milton died and he was replaced as Prime Minister by his brother Albert, a man of autocratic tendencies. Albert aroused intense opposition by appointing three nominated members to the Freetown City Council to deprive the APC of its elected majority, thereby antagonising non-Mende ministers and replacing them by Mendes when they resigned, appointing his own strong supporter as Chief Justice, proposing a one-party state and living in an openly luxurious style. In the March 1967 elections the SLPP won 28 seats, the APC 32 and independents six. Albert Margai refused to concede defeat and the army had to step in to prevent ethnic civil war.

The Gambia has been a rare example of a state where multi-party politics have survived for at least two decades after independence. In the pre-independence elections in 1962 Dawda Jawara's People's Progressive Party (PPP), with its base of support in the hinterland won 19 seats against 13 for the United Party (UP) of Pierre N'Jie. Jawara became Chief Minister, then Prime Minister at internal self-government in October 1963 and led the country into full independence in February 1965. In the 1966 elections the PPP got 24 of the 32 seats. This pattern of multi-party democracy has continued. In 1975 Sheriff Dibba, the first Vice-President, was dismissed but he was allowed to form a new party, the National Convention Party (NCP). In the 1977 elections the PPP won 28 seats, the NCP five and the UP two. In 1982 the PPP won 27 seats, the NCP three and independents five. In the presidential election Jawara defeated his opponent Sheriff Dibba, winning 137 000 votes against Dibba's 52 000. The elections were reportedly free of violence and contested on issues not on personalities or ethnic rivalries. The Gambia was nearly shattered by the abortive coup of 1981, when sections of the Banjul working class tried to take over the government.

Single-party states

While some states retained a multi-party system after independence others soon turned to a single party system. Ghana, Guinea, Sierra Leone and Senegal were good examples.

In Ghana, Nkrumah's Convention People's Party (CPP) government was faced at independence in 1957 by a number of regionally-based opposition parties. The CPP's first major step against the opposition was the 1957 Avoidance of Discrimination Act, which banned various ethnic organisations. This Act inspired opposition parties to unite to form the United Party which began to spread throughout the country. Nkrumah then brought in the Preventive Detention Bill (July 1958) which gave the government powers 'to imprison, without trial, any person suspected of activities prejudicial to the state's security'. Regional assemblies were abolished and leading opposition MPs were arrested. The news media came under the complete control of the CPP. The new republican constitution of July 1960 gave Ghana's president the power to rule by decree. Finally, in the January 1964 plebiscite, voters had to decide whether Ghana should become a one-party state. The result was 2 773 920 in favour and only 2 452 against but these figures were the result of open and widespread rigging. Nkrumah had confused one-partyism with a ruthless form of dictatorship. His one-party state reduced ethnically-based opposition but only to the extent of uniting vast numbers of Ghanaians from all regions against his political dictatorship and the failure of his economic policies. Nkrumah's one-party experiment was thus an important factor in the military coup that overthrew him in 1966, as we shall see later. He failed to realise that even in a one-party state the government can only rule effectively with the co-operation of various groups in society and that compromise is a necessary art of any government that claims to rule by popular consent.

Senegal also moved away from multi-party to one-party politics. The ruling party at independence in 1960 was the *Union Progressiste Sénégalaise* (UPS). Authority was shared between President Senghor and Prime Minister Mamadou Dia. In December 1962 Senghor accused Dia of attempting to carry out a coup and had him imprisoned. In 1963 a referendum approved a new constitution which strengthened presidential powers. In the National Assembly elections later in that year the ruling UPS won nearly all the seats. This decisive victory was followed by riots in Dakar by supporters of opposition parties claiming electoral fraud. The police fired on the rioters and about a hundred people were killed. After 1963 opposition declined as some parties were banned. In 1966 the last legal opposition party joined the UPS, and Senegal had become a one-party state.

One-party government in Guinea had its origin in the pre-independence elections in 1957 when Sekou Touré's *Parti Démocratique de Guinée* won 57 out of 60 seats. The independence constitution of 1958 declared the ruling PDG to be the country's sole political party. Sekou Touré was not only President of the Republic but also Secretary General of the PDG and as a result he closely controlled all aspects of politics and the economy by exercising highly centralised control over both the government and the party. Sekou Touré's orders in the central National Political Bureau of the PDG were passed down to local party committees which had a major share in implementing government and party policies. Sekou Touré believed that only a single party leading the mass of the people could achieve the socialist economic objectives he aimed at. Every adult was a member of the PDG by paying party dues as part of government tax. He also hoped to use the PDG as an instrument to eliminate ethnicism. He had some success in achieving this aim up to about 1970. In parliament, members had to represent constituencies outside their ethnic areas and senior party officials and civil sservants were posted to areas away from their areas of ethnic origin. Sekou Touré formed a government of national unity including representatives of all ethnic groups. However, his collectivisation of agriculture after 1970 aroused much opposition among the Fula who became the focus for growing discontent with the PDG dictatorship.

As in Guinea, the Ivory Coast emerged into independence with a single nationalist political party, the ruling *Parti Démocratique de la Côte d'Ivoire* (PDCI), whose leader, Felix Houphouet-Boigny, became the country's President. The PDCI, like Guinea's PDG, was used for the twin purpose of uniting various ethnic communities and ensuring general support for government policies. The PDCI advocates free-enterprise capitalism not socialism; it has allowed expression of some different opinions but no discussion of alternative policies such as socialism. In spite of this, in the early 1960s a radical wing of the party made up mainly of young graduates returned home from France and attacked the party's and government's economic policy as being too conservative. Houphouet-Boigny reacted by having some of the radicals imprisoned. In 1963 hundreds of alleged anti-government plotters, including ministers, MPs, party officials and civil servants were imprisoned and many other officials were dismissed. The victims of this purge were accused or suspected of having socialist views. In 1968 the PDCI government dealt firmly with violent student protests against the domination of the Ivorian economy by French business interests. Since 1970 Houphouet-Boigny and the PDCI have continued to rule with a firm hand against critics of Ivorian capitalism.

In Sierra Leone a one-party system emerged gradually. The return to civilian rule in 1968 and the coming to power of Siaka Stevens whose APC had been elected a year earlier, was marked by a return to multi-party democracy. However, for ten years the ruling APC steadily undermined the opposition SLPP, getting some SLPP MPs unseated on election petitions, dismissing SLPP chiefs, detaining SLPP leaders at various times, and in 1973 bullying the SLPP into not contesting the parliamentary elections. In May 1978 Sierra Leone was officially declared a one-party state after a landslide 'yes' vote in a referendum. Remaining SLPP MPs joined the APC.

How can the trend towards one-party rule in independent Africa be explained? Several reasons have been suggested. Some people have argued that the one party system was more traditional and more African than the multi-party system and should, therefore, be adopted. This reason has been advanced by many African leaders themselves and by many political scientists. However, it is not very convincing as traditional African political systems were not so much one-party as no-party. In other words there were no political parties as we know them today. This argument is more of an excuse than a reason for one-party rule. Others argue that given the large number of different ethnic groups in African states one-party systems are more effective in bringing these groups together into one nation as multi-party systems would tend to encourage ethnic divisions. There is some logic in this view but, on the other hand, there is no reason why legislation should not be used to make sure that all parties were national multi-ethnic parties. Such legislation has in fact been used in several West African countries. The third reason for one-party systems that is often put forward is that only single parties are capable of mobilising the mass of the people for economic and social development. African leaders, such as Nkrumah, Sekou Toure and Nyerere, have themselves made use of this argument. However, again there is no reason why different parties organised on a nationwide basis could not also work towards national goals, as is the case say in Britain or the USA.

In reality, the most important reason for the one-party system, however, has been the tendency of elected African leaders to try and destroy the opposition in order to perpetuate their own power. In our opinion, a multi-party system made up of true national parties would serve African states better than the one-party system. A multi-party system encourages constructive criticism of the government, real accountability by those in power, moderation in action and, above all, constitutional change of government through the ballot box.

Republican government

At independence the constitutions of the ex-French colonies provided for a republic, as in France, with a strong executive president similar to that of the French Fifth Republic under de Gaulle. The British, on the other hand, left monarchical constitutions in Ghana, Nigeria, Sierra Leone and the Gambia. In each of these states the British monarch remained the constitutional head of state, and was represented in each country by a governor-general. Real political authority, as in Britain, was in the hands of the elected Prime Minister, who was the leader of the majority or largest party in the national assembly. It was not long before these four states abandoned the British monarch as head of state, and replaced her with a popularly elected president under a republican form of government.

Ghana became independent in 1957 with Kwame Nkrumah as Prime Minister and Lord Listowel as Governor-General. In 1960 Ghana became a republic, the governor-generalship was abolished and Nkrumah became head of state as President. Likewise in Nigeria at independence in 1960 Dr Nnamdi Azikiwe succeeded Sir James Robertson as Governor-General, a post he held until 1963 when Nigeria became a republic and Azikiwe became President. However, the President of the First Republic in Nigeria was not a strong executive president. Power was shared, or divided, among the president, the federal prime minister and the leader of the largest party who was also the northern regional premier. When the Second Republic was established in Nigeria in 1979 the president was given strong executive authority in an attempt to provide more stability and direction in central government than had been possible under the First Republic (1963–66). In Sierra Leone the first Governor-General at independence in 1961 was Sir Henry Lightfoot-Boston, a Sierra Leonean: his successor, Sir Banja Tejan-Sie, was hostile to the projected republican constitution and was suspended from office. In 1971 Prime Minister Siaka Stevens became Sierra Leone's first executive president. When the Gambia became independent in 1965 Dawda Jawara was Prime Minister but he became President when a Republic was declared in 1970.

Attempts at political union

An important theme in the history of West Africa in the early years of political independence was the attempts to create political unity on a regional scale, as part of a wider theme of pan-Africanism. There were short-lived political unions like the Ghana-Guinea Union and the Mali Federation. More recently, the Senegambian Confederation has been set up.

The Ghana-Guinea Union

Kwame Nkrumah was a strong pan-Africanist and consistently advocated a union of African states. When Guinea became independent in 1958 and France cut off all aid to Guinea, Nkrumah offered Guinea a loan of £10 million for ten years and proposed a Ghana-Guinea Union to Guinea's President Sekou Touré. Nkrumah hoped the Union would be the beginning of a united Africa. However, Sekou Touré was content to agree to the Union in principle but to allow it to develop no further than an alliance of general agreement in matters of foreign policy. No common institutions, either political or economic, were set up. Occasionally cabinet ministers of one country attended cabinet meetings of the other, in spite of the lack of a common language. Geographically the Union was not viable because Ghana and Guinea lacked a common border, and for this reason Sekou refused to agree to merge Guinea's banks and currency with Ghana's. In 1960 Mali joined. The three member states shared a common stance in foreign policy of radical pan-Africanism and Third World neutralism. This foreign policy alliance broke up when Nkrumah and Keita of Mali were overthrown by the military in 1966 and 1968.

The Mali Federation

On the eve of independence the nationalist leaders of Senegal, Soudan (later Mali), Upper Volta and Dahomey (later Benin) drew up plans to federate as an answer to French plans to dismember the former federation of AOF. However, Upper Volta withdrew from the scheme under pressure from the Ivory Coast with which it was linked economically by railway to Abidjan, and Dahomey's assembly rejected the federal constitution because it had no common border with either Senegal or Soudan. Therefore only Senegal and Soudan (Mali) joined the Mali Federation. These two states were geographically contiguous and formed a natural economic unit with a railway and the Senegal river linking the two countries. This union was inaugurated early in 1959 but it broke up after only a year and a half. Why did it fail? First of all, the politicians of the two countries failed to work together and form a single ruling party. There was little in common between multi-party Senegal with its long tradition of free debate and the Soudanese (Malian) branch of the RDA which ran a one-party state and discouraged discussion and dissent. Secondly, Senegal's ruling party, the UPS, advocated moderate socialism whereas the Malian RDA was fervently Marxist. Thirdly, Senghor of Senegal favoured a loose federal structure whereas Keita of Soudan supported a strong unitary government. Fourthly, the more conservative Senghor opposed Keita's plans to Africanise the civil service rapidly, expel all French troops and nationalise foreign firms. Senegal and Soudan (Mali) became independent in June 1960, with Senghor as President and Keita as Prime Minister of the Federation. Growing tension between the two leaders led to a final crisis in August when Senghor deported Keita and other Soudanese ministers in Dakar to the Soudan, which renamed itself Mali.

The failure of the Ghana-Guinea Union and the Mali Federation discouraged further attempts at political union in West Africa for over twenty years. In the 1970s, economic unions were set up with some success, as we shall see in the next chapter. However, in the early 1980s another experiment was made in political union: the Senegambian Confederation.

The Senegambian Confederation

The roots of the Senegambian Confederation go back nearly twenty years before it was founded in 1981. On Gambian independence day in 1963 the Gambia and Senegal signed three agreements on defence, common foreign representation and co-operation in the development of the Gambia River. Later an office was set up in Banjul as the secretariat of the Senegal-Gambian International Committee to handle all matters regarding association between the two countries. But in practice little was done to co-ordinate economic or political activities between Senegal and the Gambia. Then the abortive coup in Banjul in July 1981 changed the situation rapidly. The coup was suppressed by Senegalese troops sent into Banjul by Senegal's President Abdou Diouf at the request of President Jawara of the Gambia who had been attending Prince Charles's wedding in London. On his return to power, President Jawara embarked on·negotiations with Senegal to effect a political union. By the end of 1981 the Confederation of Senegambia was set up. Diouf became Chairman and Jawara Deputy Chairman of the Confederation. In November 1982 a joint cabinet of nine ministers of whom four are Gambians was appointed to deal with confederal affairs. In May 1982 the union was approved by a massive vote of support for Jawara and his government in presidential and general elections. Plans are underway to integrate the administrations, military and police force, currencies and economies of the two countries, and to co-ordinate their foreign policies and communications. There will be a confederal assembly of 60 deputies, a third of them from the Gambia. At the time of writing, work has already begun on a combined dam and bridge across the Gambia river to provide irrigation downstream and a direct route between Dakar and Casamance region in southern Senegal.

Military intervention in West African politics

At the time of independence for most of Africa, around the year 1960, very few people could have forecast the future powerful role of the military in African political affairs. From the first military coup d'état in West Africa – in Togo in 1963 – to the coup in Guinea in 1984 – there have been thirty successful coups in twelve of the sixteen ECOWAS states, apart from a number of abortive coups. Some countries have had more than one coup: Togo and Sierra Leone have each had two, Nigeria has had five, Ghana and Upper Volta have both had five and Benin six.

Causes of military coups

There are a number of different causes of the military coups that have taken place in West Africa. In the first place most coups have been in response to the inefficiency, corruption and repression of the previous regime – whether civilian or military. In such instances coups can be regarded as reform coups. Some coups take place because law and order has broken down and the army is needed to restore it. Coups are sometimes ideological in that soldiers seize power in order to introduce a new political and economic system into the country. There is also evidence that some coups have been engineered by foreign intelligence agencies – though because all such action is necessarily covert it is not easy to prove this. A final important cause of coups is to be found in the ambition and self-interest of the military – or at least of certain sections of it. In practice, as we shall see, most coups involve a mixture of these factors. It is also important to remember that coups can take place when there is already a military government in power.

West Africa's first coup, Togo 1963

The first military coup in independent West Africa took place in Togo in January 1963 when President Sylvanus Olympio was assassinated by a band of ex-French colonial army veterans led by Sergeants Eyadema and Bodjolle. The veterans, aided by elements in Togo's army, set up a military junta but quickly installed a civilian regime led by Olympio's political rival Nicholas Grunitzky. What motivated this coup? There was dislike of Olympio's political tyranny, but this was not a reform coup. The main motivating factors were personal self-interest, and regionalist or ethnic self-interest, because the veterans were mainly Kabre from the north and Olympio preferred to recruit from unemployed school leavers in the south. Personal rivalry and regionalism, were also factors in Togo's second coup in January 1967, when Grunitzky was overthrown by Eyadema, who was alarmed at the collapse of Grunitzky's alliance with a northern vice-president and the threat of another takeover following civilian demonstrations. Eyadema's ruling council contained a majority of northerners. Therefore, the Togo coups were coups of personal ambition rather than coups aiming at reform.

Ghana's coups, 1966–1981

Ghana's first coup on 24 February 1966 was to some extent a reform coup and to some extent a coup to defend the interests of the military. When Colonels Kotoka and Ocran and Major Afrifa overthrew Nkrumah while he was on a tour of the Far East, they overthrew a corrupt, tyrannical and incompetent government. To that extent the soldiers were acting not solely for their own benefit but for all the peoples of Ghana. On the other hand, the soldiers were also strongly influenced by military and professional grievances against Nkrumah. The presidential guard was being steadily expanded and equipped and trained by the Russians whereas the rest of the army – British-trained and pro-western – suffered from a lack of basic equipment. Nkrumah had also forced the retirement of professionally competent commanders such as Major-General Otu and Lieutenant-General Ankrah. Therefore, the Ghanaian coup-makers were acting to protect their efficiency and professionalism from political interference.

The second Ghanaian coup took place in January 1972, when Colonel Ignatius Acheampong overthrew the elected Progress Party government of Dr Kofi Busia and set up the National Redemption Council. In some ways it resembled a reform coup. Busia's government in power since the elections of 1969 had had some success in implementing schemes of rural development and reviving the economy but it also made itself unpopular. There was general dismay at the corruption of some of Busia's ministers, at the Prime

Minister's increasingly dictatorial methods, at his policy of 'dialogue' with South Africa; and not least at his harsh though realistic and necessary financial policies in response to the collapse of cocoa prices on the world market. However, Acheampong's personal ambition and the self-interest of the soldiers were the decisive factors for Busia had cut the army budget by 10 per cent. Acheampong restored officers' privileges and although he carried out some reforms such as launching 'Operation Feed Yourself' which brought down the cost of food, he soon began to indulge in corruption. Acheampong was also anxious to forestall a move by more radical junior officers.

Acheampong was himself overthrown in Ghana's third coup in 1978. Acheampong's government fell victim partly to the economic crisis that followed the quadrupling of the price of oil by OPEC countries in 1973 and 1974 and led to acute shortages of imported goods and galloping inflation. But it was Acheampong's favouritism, corruption and incompetence and above all his proposal for a 'Union Government' composed of army, police and civilians that led to a civilian revolt that encouraged his own army to overthrow him. The civilian revolt was non-violent and led by professional groups and university students. A referendum on the Union proposal produced a highly suspect 'yes' majority. At the same time three hundred civilian opponents were detained. On 15 July 1978 a group of officers overthrew Acheampong in a palace coup and Lieutenant-General Akuffo became head of state. This coup was a reform coup to the extent that it paved the way for elections and a return to democracy, but it failed to deal with corruption and economic mismanagement. Ghana's fourth coup on 4 June 1979 conducted by junior officers and NCOs made Flight-Lieutenant Jerry Rawlings Chairman of the Armed Forces Revolutionary Council and was a much clearer example of a reform coup. Rawlings was determined to root out corruption in the military as well as the civilian elite before the handover to civilians. He carried out a 'housecleaning' exercise, enforcing price controls and allowing the execution of three former heads of state – Afrifa, Acheampong and Akuffo – and five other senior army officers, for enriching themselves while in office. Meanwhile elections were held and Dr Hilla Limann formed a civilian government in October 1979. Widespread corruption and economic mismanagement under Limann led to Ghana's fifth coup, on 31 December 1981, when Rawlings again took over. The coup that brought Rawlings back to power was an ideological coup undoubtedly inspired by a desire to restructure Ghanaian society and transfer power 'to the people' and to end corruption and social injustice.

Coups in Nigeria, 1966–1983

The first Nigerian coup in January 1966 was to some extent a reform coup. The leader of the junior officers who carried out the coup, Major Chukwuma Nzeogwu, was a puritanical idealist eager to clean up public life. Ethnic rivalries in Nigerian politics before 1966 had led to a breakdown of order, and the soldiers had been used to restore law and order in Tiv country and the Western region. With their own professional codes of conduct and disciplined life-style, the soldiers were shocked by that other major evil in

Nigerian politics – massive financial corruption. Therefore, Nzeogwu and his colleagues wanted to get rid of ethnicism and corruption. In the coup on 15 January Nzeogwu set up a Revolutionary Council in Kaduna and declared its aim was 'to establish a strong, united and prosperous nation free from corruption and political strife'. Although the coup officers took over Kaduna, Ibadan and most of Lagos they were unable to consolidate the coup because the army commander Major-General Aguiyi-Ironsi rallied loyal troops and police and all the coup-makers were captured. Ironsi set up a military council to rule the country because President Azikiwe was on convalescent leave in Britain and other senior politicians had been killed.

The first Nigerian coup was not, however, simply or even mainly a reform coup. Self-interest and power rivalry were at least as important factors as the desire to reform Nigeria. Most of the coup-makers were Igbo, a few were Yoruba and none were northerners. Many of them were UPGA supporters anxious to overthrow the northern-dominated federal government which had used questionable methods to defeat the UPGA alliance in the recent federal and Western regional elections. In the coup the leaders of the ruling NPC-NNDP alliance were killed. Tafawa Balewa, the federal prime minister, Okotie-Eboh, the federal finance minister, the Sardauna of Sokoto, the Northern regional premier and Chief Akintola, the Western regional premier were all killed along with a number of senior officers, most of them northerners, who resisted the coup. Therefore, the January coup in Nigeria would seem to have been an attempt by southern officers not only to eliminate corruption but also to overthrow northern political domination and advance southern political interests.

The second Nigerian coup, in July 1966, was a clear example of a coup motivated by factors of self-interest and regional power rivalry. It was partly a revenge coup, directed against Igbo officers, because northern soldiers came to regard the January coup, rightly or wrongly, as an Igbo coup, and wanted to avenge the killing of northern officers and politicians in January. The July coup was also an attempt by northern junior officers and NCOs to resist threatened southern domination of the army and politics. The north was alarmed by the military government's Decree No. 34, issued in May, which abolished the regions, unified the federal and regional public services and planned to divide Nigeria into thirty-five provinces. Northerners feared the end of federalism would lead to northern civil servants being replaced by more educated southerners. In late July there was an outbreak of mob killings of Igbos in northern towns and cities. On 29 July the northern soldiers rose, in the north and west. Ironsi and forty-two other Igbo officers were killed. A northern Christian, Lieutenant-Colonel Yakubu Gowon, who Ironsi had made chief of staff and who took no part in the July coup, was made commander-in-chief and head of state by the predominantly Middle Belt sergeants and corporals. The second Nigerian coup was essentially the product of an internal dispute within the military over issues of promotion and recruitment, but this dispute also ran along regional lines.

The third, fourth and fifth Nigerian coups were all reform coups. Brigadier-General Murtala Muhammad overthrew General Gowon in a bloodless coup in July 1975 to provide the decisive leadership, in which Gowon was lacking, to tackle financial corruption and economic and administrative mismanagement, as well as to set a clear timetable for the

159

return to civilian rule. On 31 December 1983 Major-General Buhari took over from the civilian President Shagari with what appeared to be the same aim of tackling severe problems arising from corruption and mismanagement, this time not only in administration and the economy but also in the form of massive electoral fraud in the federal elections in August that year. However, continuing economic mismanagement and decline in the standard of living led to Nigeria's fifth coup in August 1985 when Major-General Babangida took over from Buhari.

Other coups

There have been coups in most West African countries and there is not enough space here to go into them all in detail. As with the coups in Nigeria and Ghana there have been many different reasons for the coups. Lt-Col Kountche's coup in Niger in 1974 replacing the government of Hamani Diori, for example, was a reform coup in response to the corruption and inefficiency of the Diori regime at a time of widespread poverty and suffering due to the drought in the Sahel. The coup in Guinea in April 1984 that ook place immediately after the death of the former President Sekou Touré was a popularly-backed protest against the corrupt, nepotist and fiercely repressive government that had been created by twenty-five years of Sekou Touré rule. The most recent of the coups in Upper Volta (now renamed Burkina Faso) led by Capt Thomas Sankara was clearly modelled on the example of Jerry Rawlings in Ghana. In Burkina, Sankara's young and populist leadership is committed to a revolutionary programme of social, economic and political reforms as the only solution to the desperate poverty of the country. However, other coups have been less idealistic. For example, the coup led by Master Sergeant Doe in Liberia in 1980 was motivated more by the selfish ambitions of the military than by the urge to 'clean up' the corrupt regime of the 'True Whig' party led by President Tolbert.

Effects of military rule

What have been the results of military rule in West Africa? Has military rule helped to accelerate economic development, to curb corruption and ethnicism and to promote political stability?

Examples of West African states undergoing rapid economic transformation under military regimes are unknown outside Nigeria, whose mineral oil resources generated considerable economic expansion in the early and mid 1970s. However, these resources would probably have been developed just as rapidly under a civilian regime. In any case, General Gowon who presided over Nigeria's 'oil boom' was overthrown in 1975 for, among other reasons, economic mismanagement and his failure to control financial corruption. A modest degree of economic success has been achieved in Eyadema's Togo but only owing to special favourable conditions such as regularly high-priced phosphate exports and the opportunity to smuggle (or as it is euphemistically called 're-export') imported goods to neighbouring

Ghana. Apart from Nigeria, most economic growth has taken place in Ivory Coast which has maintained civilian rule.

What about financial corruption? Most military regimes have not only failed to stop it but have even indulged in it. In Ghana under the Ankrah regime (1966–69) army budget allocations increased annually by 22 per cent while funds for social services were cut severely. In 1969 General Ankrah was forced to resign after admitting he solicited funds to start a new political party. General Afrifa took over from Ankrah but before the soldiers handed over to Dr Busia they arranged large gratuities for themselves. Acheampong restored special officers allowances. In Doe's Liberia military expenditure has increased disproportionately. Socialist ideology is no automatic remedy against corruption as the example of Benin shows clearly. On the other hand, General Murtala Mohammed in Nigeria (1975–76) took strong action to deal with corrupt and inefficient civil servants and army officers by dismissing them. Rawlings in Ghana and Sankara in Burkina Faso have likewise taken drastic action against corruption in public life and the economy. These few examples, however, are an exception to the general rule.

To sum up, overall the military has failed to speed up economic development and has failed to combat corruption effectively. The trend towards a return to civilian rule in the late 1970s was assisted by the discovery by the soldiers that they were no better equipped than civilians for coping with severe economic and social problems.

What success has the military had in combating ethnicism and political instability? Some military rulers, like some civilian presidents, have governed by favouring one ethnic group or combination of groups. In Togo, Eyadema has favoured the northern Kabre and Moba peoples. In Nigeria, the establishment of military rule so inflamed ethnic tensions that the disastrous Civil War (1967–70) broke out. The ethnic nature of the two coups in 1966 stirred up fears and jealousies among the country's different communities and led to the terrible killings of Igbos living in Northern Nigeria and of northerners living in Eastern Nigeria in September 1966. The behaviour of soldiers in killing ethnic 'enemies' in January and July 1966 encouraged mobs of civilians to commit terrible deeds in September. Soldiers did little to stop the September killings and several units joined in the massacres. The massacres caused Lieutenant-Colonel Odumegwu Ojukwu, military governor of the East, to consider secession of the East from Nigeria in order to save Igbo lives. In May 1967 federal head of state Gowon decreed the division of Nigeria into twelve states. Ojukwu interpreted the measure as an attempt to deprive his region of a large proportion of its oil revenues. He also believed that the oil would make the East economically secure if it seceded. Ojukwu proclaimed the Eastern Region as the independent republic of Biafra on 30 May 1967. Therefore, between January 1966 and June 1967 Nigeria's soldiers were responsible for ethnic massacres and the break-up of the country. Up to that point, the military governments of Nigeria, far from managing to reduce ethnicism and maintain political stability, had made the situation worse than ever and brought Nigeria to a condition of total chaos.

The Civil War was disastrous as tens of thousands of soldiers died on both sides and hundreds of thousands of Igbos died in the famine caused by the federal blockade and extended 'Biafran' resistance. Fortunately, at the end of the war a far-sighted policy of reconciliation was put into practice. The victorious federal forces carried out a massive food relief programme. Many Igbos were reinstated in the federal civil service and armed forces, and many returned to their homes and businesses in the North and West.

Military rulers have reduced ethnicism in some ways. In Sierra Leone the National Reformation Council (1967–68) banned the use of a citizen's ethnic affiliation on government documents or in the press. The Council itself was composed of two representatives from each of the four administrative divisions of the country and, as in the Gowon government in Nigeria, the minor ethnic groups were given strong representation. When Gowon increased the number of states in Nigeria from four to twelve in 1967 he helped to provoke the outbreak of the Civil War but, in the long run, this breaking up of the former big regions helped to weaken ethnic regionalism and reduce old fears of northern or southern domination. His successor Murtala Mohammed increased the number of states to nineteen. General Obasanjo (1976–79) presided over the creation of a new constitution designed to force ethnic groups to co-operate with each other in the national interest.

West Africa's soldiers have a very mixed record as regards bringing about political stability. First of all, a coup may sometimes be justified as the only way of removing a dictatorial one-party regime but it cannot be justified for removing an elected government in advance of the next round of elections, except under very special circumstances. Military rulers have often governed badly and added to political instability by provoking coups against themselves by junior officers, as in Sierra Leone in 1968 or Ghana in 1978 and 1979. On the other hand, in some cases coups have contributed to stability. In Benin the soldiers took power to prevent ethnic violence in 1963, 1965 and 1969. The two coups in Sierra Leone in 1967 and 1968 had as their objects the setting up of a more stable civilian democracy.

Return to democracy

Following the wave of military coups in the 1960s there was a trend towards a return to civilian rule and multi-party politics. In Sierra Leone in 1968, in Ghana in 1969 and again in 1979, and in Nigeria in 1979, the soldiers handed power back to the civilians. In some states, such as Togo and Mali, a soldier has remained head of state whilst the government has effectively become civilian. In Upper Volta General Lamizana's government was made civilian in 1978 when he won the election standing as a civilian president.

In Ghana the soldiers who overthrew Nkrumah were eager to return to the barracks at an early date, especially after the return from exile of Dr Busia, who was widely regarded as a potential Prime Minister. Ghana's second return to civilian rule, in 1979, was largely a result of strong civilian pressure on the military regimes of Acheampong and Akuffo. In 1979 Dr Hilla Limann's People's National Party won a clear majority and Limann was elected President in July and took office in October.

In Nigeria the Obasanjo government approved a new constitution drafted by a committee of civilians and amended by a constituent assembly of professionals and representatives of other special interests. The president was to have strong executive power on the United States model. There were two ingenious devices in the constitution designed to discourage ethnic divisions. Firstly, before parties could be allowed to register they had to prove that they had active branches in at least thirteen (two-thirds) of the nineteen states. Secondly, the president could only be declared elected if he won 25 per cent of the votes in two-thirds of the states. These measures would force presidential candidates to seek nationwide instead of regional support. Five parties were given approval to contest the 1979 elections. The National Party of Nigeria won more votes than its rivals and its leader Shehu Shagari was elected President ahead of his defeated rivals Awolowo of the United Party of Nigeria and Azikiwe of the Nigeria People's Party. Shagari was accordingly inaugurated as President of the Second Republic in October 1979. Unfortunately, the new Nigerian constitution failed to work effectively because of human failings. By 1983 corruption was far worse than it had been before 1966 and electoral malpractice was rife. The best designed constitution cannot work if politicians disregard its spirit and purpose.

Senegal has not had a coup but the elections of February 1978 marked the first example of a one-party state turning itself into a multi-party democracy, with the aim of eliminating ethnic tensions. The elections were to be fought by parties representing issues and policies not ethnic groups or personalities. The ruling *Union Progressiste Sénégalais* (UPS) was renamed *Parti Socialiste* (PS) and propounded moderate socialism. Its opponents were the liberal democratic *Parti Démocratique Sénégalais* (PDS) led by the lawyer Abdoulaye Wade, who also stood against Senghor in the presidential election, and Mahmout Diop's Marxist *Parti Africain d'Indépendance* (PAI). The ruling PS gained 82 per cent of the vote and 83 out of 100 seats in the national assembly on the basis of proportional representation. The PDS got 17 per cent of the vote and 17 seats. In the presidential election Senghor gained 82 per cent of the votes against 17 per cent for Wade.

Senghor established a further landmark in the development of constitutional government in independent Africa by retiring as President in 1980 and observing the election of his Prime Minister Abdou Diouf as the new President.

Return to military rule

The early 1980s has seen a general return to military rule in West Africa, with coups in Liberia, Upper Volta (three times), Guinea-Bissau, Ghana, Nigeria and Guinea. An attempted coup in the Gambia was suppressed only after heavy fighting and military intervention from Senegal. The continuing and deepening economic crisis in West Africa, which is part of a world recession, has made it more than usually difficult for civilian governments to govern effectively, a task that has not been helped by persistent corruption, economic mismanagement and, in Nigeria, electoral fraud. This new swing of the pendulum back towards military rule has happened in spite of the fact that, as we have seen, military governments have had no more success on the whole, than civilian administrations in tackling West Africa's economic and social problems.

21 Economic developments

What economic policies have been pursued by West African governments? Much attention has been devoted to improving transport, especially motor roads. In agriculture, the emphasis has been upon cash crop production for export, which has more than doubled since independence, although from the late 1970s more attention has been paid to food production. In industry, the emphasis has been on encouraging the growth of manufacturing and mining. A number of governments have pushed through Africanisation in various branches of business. Some governments (such as Ivory Coast, Senegal and Nigeria) have followed a capitalist or free enterprise path towards economic development while others (such as Nkrumah's Ghana, Guinea, Benin and Guinea-Bissau) have attempted to carry out socialist policies in trade, agriculture and industry. The following paragraphs offer a basic review of the major aspects of West African national economies since independence.

Communications

Some new railway lines have been built since independence, principally to improve communications from mining areas in Liberia and Guinea to export centres on the coast. Also, lines have been extended to Maiduguri in Nigeria and Ngaoundere in Cameroun. Far more work has been done on building new motor roads and upgrading old ones, especially in Nigeria and the Ivory Coast where funds generated from oil wealth or agricultural production have made it possible to finance a nationwide network of tarred highways. Maritime transport has progressed with the building of new ports, such as Tema near Accra and San Pedro in the Ivory Coast and the modernisation of older ones. Several West African states have formed their own national shipping lines, such as Ghana's Black Star Line and the Nigerian National Shipping Line (NNSL). These lines have linked up with the British-owned Elder Dempster Lines and Palm Line to form the UK/West Africa Lines (UKWAL), which in 1964 introduced container shipping to West Africa and revolutionised freight-handling methods. In West Africa air travel has replaced sea travel for long-distance international passengers, and most West African countries now run national airlines for external and internal services.

In the 1950s a telephone call from Kano to Niamey had to be routed via London, Paris and Dakar. In the late 1970s and early 1980s much work was done on linking West African national telecommunications networks directly by microwave, telephone, telegraph, telex and data transmission. In the 1970s Nigeria set up a system of domestic satellite communications including radio and television broadcasting. The rapid expansion of broadcasting is indicated by Nigeria having five million radios and 85 000 television sets in 1975.

Agriculture

In agriculture, the emphasis on cash crop production for export led to the neglect of food production until the late 1970s. Most West African states have experienced less of self-sufficiency in food supplies, while rapid population growth has increased the gap between food demand and food supplies. An increasing amount of scarce foreign exchange has been spent on food imports, such as millet, rice, dairy produce and sugar in Senegal, and wheat and rice in Ivory Coast and Nigeria as the urban middle classes adopt a western diet.

Other factors besides population growth have also hampered local food production: heavy increases in the cost of fertilisers and agricultural machinery; lack of government extension services and storage facilities; poorly developed marketing systems, low price incentives to peasant producers, especially when governments have deliberately kept prices of agricultural products low in order to prevent urban discontent; and migration to the cities of young educated people capable of modernising the rural economy. In addition, although many co-operatives were set up in the 1960s to handle producer, marketing and credit functions, nearly half of them have collapsed because they could not raise sufficient profits to expand their membership. Some measures were taken to encourage production, like Ghana's Operation Feed Yourself when the Acheampong government encouraged individual, small-scale farming and Nigeria's 1977 Operation Feed the Nation. Such measures were well-intentioned but often mismanaged and under-funded. In Nigeria's fiscal year 1977/78 only one per cent of recurrent expenditure was devoted to agriculture and rural development. Lack of government support made it unprofitable for farmers to grow rice, cassava, millet, maize and sweet potatoes. Only in Ivory Coast and Senegal has official encouragement led to significant progress in market gardening and fruit farming.

Even cash crop production has suffered from severe problems. The fall in world cocoa prices in the 1950s and 1960s undermined Ghana's economic progress. When cocoa prices rose again under Acheampong in the 1970s Ghana was unable to take advantage of the situation because crops were small, trees were ageing and above all, because Ghana's currency was officially overvalued. As a result, enormous quantities of cocoa were smuggled to neighbouring Ivory Coast and Togo, where it fetched higher prices in a more valuable currency, the CFA franc. Neglect of all types of farming led to Nigeria having to import groundnuts and palm oil from the late 1970s, whereas these crops had been principal exports in the 1960s. President Shagari (1979–83) tried to carry out a 'Green Revolution' to boost agricultural production in Nigeria. However, the scheme failed mainly because the fall in oil prices reduced federal and state expenditure on subsidised fertilisers for farmers, severe drought affected at least nine northern states and too much was spent on grandiose river basin projects which take many years to yield good returns. In fact, food imports and prices soared in those four years.

In some West African states the development of agriculture has been hindered by inappropriate socialist economic policies. Nkrumah spent enormous sums on setting up state farms in Ghana using tractors imported from Communist countries but the farms were inefficient and output was low.

165

Co-operatives failed to make much progress because Nkrumah's central parastatal control body stifled local initiative. In Sekou Touré's Guinea, collectivisation of farms and state control of marketing of agricultural produce since 1973 did not led to the expected increase in production. Much agricultural machinery was imported and motorised production brigades, equipped with tractors, were set up. However, food production declined as farmers were obliged to sell their produce at low, fixed prices to co-operative stores run by party officials, many of whom proved to be corrupt. Only a combination of American food aid and large-scale emigration of Guineans prevented an outbreak of mass starvation in Guinea and there was widespread resistance to the government's agricultural policies.

In Guinea-Bissau, a more appropriate form of agricultural socialism has proved to be more successful. From independence onwards priority was given to food, and by 1980 the country was almost self-sufficient in rice. Diversification has also ensured that large crops of maize, potatoes and soya beans have been produced. Some state collective farms and regional agricultural teams were set up to demonstrate to smallholders the advantages of new crops, crop rotation, fertilisers and collective work. Village life was made more attractive by a village electrification programme that has now reached much of the country.

Expansion of agriculture has played a major part in the 'Ivorian miracle' in which the Ivory Coast experienced an annual growth rate from 1950 to 1975 of over 7 per cent, largely as a result of greatly increased production of cocoa, coffee and timber for export. As a result the per capita income of the country rose from 145 dollars in 1960 to 450 dollars in 1975. President Houphouet-Boigny's government has deliberately encouraged the export sector and the use of foreign capital, know-how and labour as the keys to economic growth. French managerial and skilled labour together with unskilled plantation and construction workers from neighbouring countries have been encouraged in the Ivory Coast. Other factors which have helped economic growth have been heavy public investment in infrastructure; good producer prices for the main agricultural products; diversification away from the three main export commodities and the introduction and development of other crops; political stability and the avoidance of large military expenditures; a low population density (only 21 inhabitants per square mile in 1975) which means fertile land is available to all Ivorians; and finally the geographical advantage that no part of the country extends into the drought-prone Sahel zone. Ivorian agriculture has some problems: in spite of diversification, the country remains over dependent on exports of coffee, cocoa and timber, whose world market prices are highly unstable. However, the government has played a major role in negotiations for international coffee and cocoa pricing and quota agreements. Impressive steps have been taken to improve living conditions in rural areas by providing education, health and transport amenities; and food processing industries are being set up in the interior.

Timber production has accelerated since independence particularly in the Ivory Coast and Liberia. However, forests are being cut down faster than they can be replanted. In the Ivory Coast the total disappearance of the original rain forest, with resulting ecological imbalance and less rain is forecast for the year 2000. The French and Lebanese-owned timber companies which cut about 500 000 hectares a year are now co-operating with a World Bank re-afforestation programme but can replace only 25 000 hectares a year. All over West Africa peasant families are reducing tree cover in an unsystematic manner in the search for firewood. Government controls over tree-cutting are everywhere inadequate.

Manufacturing industries

The newly independent states devoted a lot of attention to industrialization. In all states a number of industries producing substitutes for important imports such as cotton, textiles, beer, soft drinks, paints, footwear, printing, soap, cigarettes and cement were set up. These new industries were often developed as a partnership between foreign private companies and the national government, which usually only had a minority (less than 50 per cent) shareholding. Tariff protection was provided for the new industries, even if this meant consumers had to pay high prices. To attract investors, industrial estates were built, for example at Tema near Accra, at Trans-Amadi, Port Harcourt, and on the seaward side of Abidjan, and in or near other cities. Investors were guaranteed against nationalisation, given tax concessions, and allowed to repatriate a high proportion of their profits. An alternative path to industrial development has been the creation of state-run industries. Guinea, Mali and Ghana have all followed this path.

However, only Nigeria and the Ivory Coast have succeeded in attracting significant investments in manufacturing. In Nigeria, the Second and Third National Development Plans (1970–74 and 1975–80) used the revenue resulting from higher oil prices to give priority to the establishment of a whole range of manufacturing enterprises. The light consumer industries established in the 1960s have been further developed and a start has been made in industries such as industrial chemicals, fertilisers, pesticides, vehicle assembly and the vast steel plant being built at Ajaokuta. Industrial development in Nigeria has, however, slowed down as a result of the world economic depression and the fall in oil prices from the late 1970s.

In the Ivory Coast, production from manufacturing industries grew at the astonishingly high average annual rate of 18 per cent between 1960 and 1970. Much of this early industrial growth was, as usual, in import substitution industries. Since 1970 industrial areas have been developed outside Abidjan in towns such as Bouake, Dimbokro, Agboville and Yapougon. Dams have been built to provide hydro-electric power for industry and since 1970 the emphasis has been on the growth of export-oriented agricultural processing industries, such as coffee-powdering, chocolate manufacturing, palm-oil extraction and pineapple and citrus-fruit canning. Vehicle assembly plants have also been set up. However, unlike Nigeria with its vastly greater supplies of mineral oil and natural gas, the Ivory Coast's industrialisation depends heavily on foreign capital, mainly French. The Ivory Coast has made no attempt to develop heavy industry as Nigeria has done.

However, despite all the effort and money that has been invested in manufacturing, output has been extremely low and today many of the factories are at a complete standstill. There are several reasons for the failure of manufacturing industries in West Africa. In the first place many of the industries were inappropriate for West Africa since they had to depend on imported raw materials and expatriate technical manpower. Immediately after independence when West African exports commanded good prices on the world market and foreign exchange was readily available this was not a great problem. However, in the 1970s the prices of West African exports such as cocoa and groundnuts fell and foreign exchange was in short supply so that industry could not afford to import the raw material, spare parts and labour it required. This problem was particularly acute for countries which did not have any oil reserves. A second factor in the failure of West Africa's manufacturing industry has been that in cases where there have been partnerships between local West African firms and multi-national companies the terms of the agreement generally favour the multi-nationals. Under such partnerships it is difficult, for example, for West African firms to retain profits generated in West Africa and so West African industry is still dependent on international capital. A third problem relates to the poor quality, inexperience and widespread corruption amongst the African managerial class. A fourth problem has been that many of the factories were created and sited in particular locations for political rather than for economic reasons, and so it is very difficult to make such factories profitable. Another major problem has been quite simply that, however generous the terms offered by African governments to private investors, it is very difficult to attract private foreign investment to West Africa. For all these sorts of reasons the industrial record of independent West African states has been very poor, and it is clear that if any progress is to be made in the 1980s there will have to be a great deal more thought about new approaches.

Minerals

The mining industry in West Africa has expanded since 1960 in a number of states. In Mauritania and Liberia, considerable foreign investment in the mining of iron ore has led to near exhaustion of the original supplies, but several other states contain vast quantities of certain minerals which are already in profitable production: Guinea with a third of the world's high quality bauxite reserves, Senegal and Togo with phosphates, Niger with uranium and Nigeria with oil and natural gas. Guinea's bauxite and iron ore deposits have been developed since 1958 by western mining groups with some involvement by the USSR and Japan. A Canadian firm began to mine bauxite near Boke in 1958 and two years later an American-European company began to process and export aluminium. In 1973 Boke was expanded when a US-led consortium built a connecting railway to a new port at the coast. In 1974 the Kindia mine was begun, with Soviet assistance. Iron ore mining is centred in the Nimba and Simandou mountains. The success of Guinea's mining sector is in sharp contrast to the failure of its agricultural sector.

Like oil, phosphate mining benefited from a three fold increase in the world market price in 1974. Senegal uses much of its revenue from phosphates to guarantee high producer prices to groundnut growers. Togo's phosphate revenues have helped to develop port infrastructure and agricultural diversification schemes. Niger's uranium mine in the remote Ahir region was opened in 1971, and uranium has now become the country's principal export. Nigeria's oil and natural gas supplies, in the south-east of the country, were first exploited in the 1960s but have been fully developed since the civil war.

Nigeria's government, anxious to use oil revenue to develop the country, had already begun to take control over the oil companies in 1972, when the companies agreed to give the government 55 per cent of their profits. In June 1973 the government took a 35 per cent share of the ownership of Shell/BP, increasing this to 55 per cent in 1974 when a similar percentage share was taken in other companies. These shares were held by the Nigerian National Petroleum Corporation. The NNPC's stake in the oil producing companies was raised from 55 to 60 per cent in 1979 and BP's remaining 20 per cent in Shell-BP was nationalised by the Nigerian government in response to BP's involvement in the supplying of oil to South Africa. Oil refineries were opened at Port Harcourt in 1965, at Warri in 1978 and at Kaduna in 1980. Natural gas exists in enormous quantities in the Niger delta but little of it has been exploited, although gas manufacturing plants have been set up at Port Harcourt, Aba, Ughelli and Warri. Ivory Coast has also been producing some 400 000 tons of oil per annum since 1980.

Africanisation

Africanisation of economies has proceeded faster in some West African states than in others. The Nigerian Enterprises Promotion Degree of 1972 specified twenty-two categories of business to be reserved exclusively for Nigerians, of which some were required to have 100 per cent Nigerian participation, others 60 per cent. An amendment to the decree in 1977 provided for 60 per cent local ownership of all banks and, nationalisation of some large companies. The measures encouraged the growth of an indigenous, capitalist middle class. In Guinea-Bissau the indigenisation decree of 1976 enabled the state to acquire major shareholdings in all Portuguese firms and thereby broke the Portuguese monopoly of exclusive trading companies. In the Ivory Coast, attempts have been made to encourage Africanisation in industry by the government buying shares in French companies and selling them off to interested individuals; however this scheme has failed to meet with much response so far. In Senegal much lip service has been paid to Africanisation but little has been done, and French managers continue to direct operations in industry, banking and other businesses. In the Ivory Coast, since independence the European population has grown from 15 000 to 50 000. In Senegal, there has been a similar increase in the number of expatriates. Lebanese entrepreneurs, owners of wholesale and retail cloth businesses and grocery chains, have continued to flourish, especially in the Ivory Coast and Senegal.

The history of banking systems in West Africa is a pointer to the respective degree of Africanisation in English-speaking and French-speaking states. The four former British territories have established four separate central banks, each with a reserve system allowing it to have its own currency and make its own clearing arrangements. In contrast, nearly all the former French colonies have remained in the franc zone and share a common Central Bank, the *Banque Centrale des Etats de l'Afrique de l'Ouest*. They have as currency the CFA franc. Most of *Banque Centrale's* foreign exchange reserves are held at the French treasury in Paris.

Urbanisation and migration

The growth of the towns has accelerated at an uncontrollable rate in independent West Africa as people migrate from the countryside in search of employment, improved amenities and a more attractive life. Urban population in Africa as a whole rose from 11.3 per cent in 1960 to nearly 20 per cent in 1978. The growth of some cities has been explosive. Abidjan's population has rocketed from 157 000 in 1964 to 400 000 in 1970 and nearly a million in 1980, Accra's population rose from 388 000 in 1960 to 546 000 in 1970 and a million in 1980. Lagos had 450 000 people in 1962, about a million in 1970 and about 2 million in 1980. Many of the migrants to the cities have found not work but a squalid existence as squatters in shanty towns. Alienation, poverty and crime have grown apace in West Africa's cities, largely as a result of the imbalance between the population growth and the rate of provision of low cost housing and public services.

Migratory labour does not always go to the cities. Since independence the colonial pattern of labour migration continues, with Ghana, Ivory Coast and Nigeria continuing to provide seasonal employment in their coffee, cocoa and groundnut plantations for migrants from Benin, Togo, Upper Volta and Niger, and Senegal's groundnut farms receiving a large number of labourers from Mali. However, since independence many migrants have married in their place of work and become permanent residents there. In the course of time, economic recession and growing unemployment have caused several West African governments to expel these African settlers. Ghana's Aliens Compliance Order in 1969 led to the expulsion of 80 000 Togo nationals and several tens of thousand Nigerians without work permits. Early in 1983 Nigeria expelled two million aliens – most of them Ghanaians. Yet it would appear that mass migration across national borders has benefitted the country employing foreign labour such as Ivory Coast more than the country receiving remittances sent home by workers in other lands like Burkina Faso/Upper Volta.

Industrial relations

West Africa's trade unions played significant roles in the struggles for political independence but have been far less influential and important after independence. With the exception of Guinea and some regimes in Ghana where trade unions have been close to the ruling party (Sekou Toure was Secretary-General of the party and head of the union confederation in Guinea), rulers from professional classes and the military have allowed little scope for trade union activity. Since independence, government controls over trade unions have become firmer and their leaders have often exhorted workers to help develop the country by working harder and longer, and looking unfavourably on trade union leaders who have campaigned for workers' rights like higher wages, shorter working hours and better working conditions. As the leading employer in each state, governments also tend to be suspicious of trade unions.

However, some important examples of industrial action have taken place. The Nigerian general strike which lasted for two weeks in June 1964 started among junior staff in the public sector in protest at their low salaries in contrast to those of senior civil servants, MPs and ministers. The strike was non-violent and was not ethnically based. The unity of the trade unions involved won modest wage increases for the workers. The military government was less ready to accomodate the demands of the unions and in 1969 it decreed an end to all lockouts and strikes. The Udogi Commission, whose award was paid in January 1975, doubled the wages of the lowest paid workers. Private sector and professional workers then went on strike to secure extension of the awards to them. Eventually the Gowon government agreed on a general 30 per cent minimum pay rise. The result was a massive consumer spending boom, and accelerating inflation which soon wiped out the value of the awards. This in turn led to more strikes and the detention of trade union leaders. In 1977 a government decree limited wage increases to 7 per cent in the coming year, when inflation was running at over 60 per cent.

Perhaps the most effective worker organisation in West Africa is the Mouride brotherhood or Muridiyya in Senegal, to which more than half of the peasant producers are affiliated. Abdou Lahatte Mbacke, their leader or khalifa-general since 1968, recommended withdrawal from groundnut production in order to reduce his followers' indebtedness to the state marketing agency. President Senghor's reaction in 1973 was to annul the co-operative's debts and in 1974 virtually to double the producer price.

Economic co-operation and ECOWAS

What has been achieved in the way of economic co-operation between West African states? If Africa is ever to be truly united, it is probably most sensible to start with economic unity on a regional basis, then move on to political unity much later. Modest steps along these lines were the creation of international authorities to develop the resources of major rivers and lakes in West Africa, between 1964 and 1972. Later, more fully-fledged economic unions were set up, such as the Mano River Union and ECOWAS. In 1964 nine West African states from Nigeria to Guinea set up the newly created Niger River Commission, for the purpose of joint development of water supply, navigation, hydro-electricity, irrigation and fishing. A few joint projects have been carried out. In the Chad Convention of the same year, Nigeria, Niger, Chad and Cameroun agreed to a joint study of the lake region and joint use of its resources. In 1972 Senegal, Mali and Mauritania set up the Organisation for the Development of the Senegal River. Work has begun on the construction of two dams, one of which (Manatali), will generate hydro-electric power for the working of iron ore deposits in both Senegal and Mauritania. Work is going on to make the river navigable up to the Malian border.

The Mano River forms the border between Liberia and Sierra Leone. In October 1973 Presidents Tolbert and Stevens established the Mano River Union to work for the joint economic development of their two countries. The union's activities have covered the development of infrastructure, the setting up of a free trade area and the drawing up of plans for a joint industrial enterprise. In 1975 the Mano river bridge, linking the two countries and reducing the 700 mile long road journey from Freetown to Monrovia to 300 miles, was formally opened. The bridge is a vital link in the planned trans-African highway (from Dakar to Mombasa) and its early effect has been a rapid improvement in inter-state transport and trade. In 1976 it was agreed that goods manufactured in either member state would qualify for freedom of movement in the other, free of customs duties or quota restrictions. Guidelines were worked out to harmonise external tariffs, customs law and regulations, excise laws and trade statistics. In 1978 a common market with full free trade and common standardised external tariffs against outside imports, was set up. Work on a hydro-electric power plant on the Mano river and on upgrading the Freetown-Monrovia road to international standards was begun. Training institutions have been set up to produce skilled manpower for joint projects in forestry, telecommunications, customs and excise and commercial shipping. A United Nations team has identified ten industries that could be undertaken on a union basis, and there have been plans for a postal union and joint earth satellite stations for advanced telephone and telex services.

The year 1980 saw the expansion and the decline of the Mano River Union. It expanded when Guinea joined and the population doubled from 5 to 10 million. Guinea's accession should create opportunities for more viable industrial programmes. However, the Liberian coup has led to political disputes between Sierra Leone and Liberia. President Stevens, shocked at the killing of President Tolbert, was unprepared for a long time to recognise Doe as head of government in Liberia. The coup in Monrovia has slowed down the early impetus towards economic union. Mutual trade between Sierra Leone and Liberia is, at the time of writing, only 7 per cent of the total trade of the two countries. Hopefully, the impetus of the Mano River Union will be restored as its member states co-operate as fellow members of ECOWAS.

The main hope for West Africa's economic and eventual political union may well lie in a successful future of the Economic Community of West African States (ECOWAS). Set up under the Treaty of Lome in May 1976 ECOWAS has sixteen member states covering all of West Africa's two million square miles and 150 million people. Its broad aims are: to set up a customs union over fifteen years by progressive reduction of import duties, so that the whole of West Africa would then become a free trade area, with free movement of people, services and capital; and to co-ordinate industrial development. ECOWAS is administered by an executive secretary with the headquarters in Lagos. There are commissions dealing with transportation, monetary problems, customs and so on. Major decisions are taken by the council of heads of states or by the ministerial conference. One of the first decisions was to set up an ECOWAS fund under the control of a managing director to finance community projects, especially in the poorer states, and to pay compensation to members who suffered as a result of liberalisation of trade policies.

What has ECOWAS achieved in its early years? In 1979 the fourth heads of states summit, at Dakar, imposed a freeze on all customs and tariffs in all member states on goods originating within West Africa. This meeting also issued the protocol on free movement of peoples which has been implemented. In 1981 tariffs on raw materials and processed goods originating within the Community were removed, and compensation was paid to some countries. Decisions were made to devote the ECOWAS fund to a development strategy that gives priority to agriculture and related industries and to transport and communications. Loans were raised from international financial institutions in Western Europe and North America. The 1982 summit announced the beginning of various programmes: a ten-year reafforestation project to check the southward spread of the Sahara desert in the Sahel region; an agricultural plan designed to raise food production; a social and cultural programme including student exchanges between member states and the award of scholarships; and a telecommunications programme to link all states with direct telephone and telex services. Among the joint economic ventures undertaken so far are Nigerian and Liberian investment in Guinea's national iron mining company; and co-operation between Nigeria and Niger in food production, transport and telecommunications. ECOWAS has played a role in normalising relations between a number of different West African states in dispute.

ECOWAS has not achieved as much as was hoped, partly as a resort of the problems of getting co-operation and commitment from sixteen different countries but partly also as a result of external factors in the world market outside the control of ECOWAS or its member states. Periodic sharp falls in world commodity prices, which cause poor export earnings and balance of trade difficulties for African countries, are likely to be a feature of the international economy for many years to come.

22 Social developments

African nationalist political parties campaigned for political independence in the 1940s and 1950s not only for the inherent right of Africans to rule themselves, but also with the aim of accelerating progress in crucial areas of social development like health and education.

Health and basic amenities

At independence, West African states inherited very inadequate public health services from the colonial rulers. Minute government sums were spent on health services and the very few doctors in West Africa concentrated on the welfare of the European community. Missions provided a number of hospitals, dispensaries and doctors to supplement government medical services but the total even as late as 1960 was woefully inadequate. What have African governments done to improve medical services? In Nigeria, for example, the number of hospitals and clinics doubled to over 7 000 between 1960 and 1980 and the number of doctors trebled to over 7 500 in the same period. All over West Africa there has been a steady expansion in numbers of doctors, nurses, pharmacists, hospitals and dispensaries. Much has been done, in co-operation with international agencies, to control epidemics and reduce the incidence of communicable diseases. In the 1960s and 1970s a massive vaccination programme against smallpox, directed by the World Health Organisation (WHO) and the US Agency for International Development, was completed and smallpox was eradicated from West Africa. WHO has also helped to reduce the number of people suffering from leprosy and sleeping sickness (trypanosomiasis). By the earlier 1970s river blindness had crippled more than a million people in an area spanning seven countries, mainly in the fertile Volta river basin, but since 1974 the whole area is being reclaimed by WHO in a twenty-year programme. So far the programme has been so successful that it is to be copied in the Senegal river basin. Volunteer re-settlers have rebuilt villages in the area to meet the needs of modern agriculture, such as producing cotton in Burkina Faso/Upper Volta.

In spite of these achievements, the fact remains that after two decades relatively little overall progress has been made in improving West Africa's medical services. One of the major obstacles has been the rapid growth of population and the general failure to organise effective family planning services. Consequently the provision of more medical services and personnel has barely kept pace with the increase in the number of people. Another problem is that the average protein intake is low and as a result many people in West Africa suffer from malnutrition which weakens their resistance to various diseases. The available evidence for the last twenty years shows a rise in the incidence of gastro-intestinal illnesses, partly because of the rapidly rising population and the strain on inadequate water and sewer systems in the cities. Bilharzia has increased as a result of irrigation and hydro-electric power schemes. Malaria remains the most widespread and serious public health problem in West Africa.

Although the number of hospitals has risen, they remain very unevenly distributed. Rural areas have four fifths of the population but very few hospitals. Millions have no ready access to a rural clinic, still less to a doctor. Even provision of hospital services in the cities has been outstripped by the growth in population. Nigeria in the 1970s built many fine new hospitals, but they have functioned inefficiently because of inadequate equipment, or insufficient maintenance because of irregular water and electricity supplies. Some recently built hospitals had no maintenance departments when they opened.

In the developed world there is, on average, one doctor for every 600 people. In 1977 most West African countries had around 15 000 people per doctor according to UN figures. Nigeria has 14 814 per doctor. Guinea-Bissau was best provided with about 7 000 people per doctor, but six states had more than 20 000 people per doctor and Upper Volta, Mali and Niger all had around 50 000 people per doctor. To make matters worse, the growth of private health institutions has taken many qualified doctors out of the government health services. Governments have spent little on improving health services, often only one or two dollars per head per annum. The Obasanjo government in its review of Nigeria's Third National Development Plan cut back on prestige projects and placed greater emphasis on health and housing; there was a fivefold increase in allocations to health from the original figures of 314 million to 1 700 million naira. However, to date no Nigerian city has a central sewerage system, while refuse collection and storm-water drainage systems are very inadequate. In the rural areas, only one in six Nigerians has access to piped water. West African governments have been slow to realise or to act upon the realisation that health would be better promoted by determined preventive measures such as better nutrition, access to clean water, good housing and improved sanitation. Little has been done to train more paramedical workers who, although not doctors, are qualified to carry out simpler medical tasks, treating common diseases such as parasitic infections, tuberculosis and malnutrition.

The provision of good housing for the people has been low on the list of priorities of West African governments. There is a severe shortage of low-rented houses in the towns and middle-income households benefit most. Thus the shanty towns proliferate. Under the Obasanjo government Nigeria raised its production of low-cost housing from 60 000 units to 200 000 – still an excessively small figure for a population of over 80 million.

Education

Independent West African governments have expanded education at all levels – primary, secondary and higher. An oil-rich nation like Nigeria has been able to introduce universal primary education, increasing the number of primary school pupils from 3.5 million in 1976 to 11.5 million in 1980, and opened twelve universities with 50 000 students in 1980 as well as over 200 teacher training colleges with over 250 000 students. The statistics for education in Ghana in the first fifteen years of independence typify the enormous quantitative gains in education in independent Africa, with primary and middle school enrolment leaping from 571 580 to 1 365 203, that of secondary schools from 9 860 to 71 860 and that of training colleges from 3 873 to 18 814. University expansion was equally rapid. In 1961 the University College of Ghana, Legon, became the University of Ghana. In the same year the Kwame Nkrumah University of Science and Technology was founded in Kumasi. In 1962, the University College of Cape Coast was set up, to train graduate teachers, and it became a university in its own right ten years later. The Institute of African Studies was established at Legon in 1961 to enable post-graduates to study for higher degrees in that field.

A similar process of quantitative educational expansion can be observed all over independent Africa, as, for example, in Burkina Faso/Upper Volta and Niger where primary education enrolment between 1960 and 1970 increased respectively from 60 000 to 120 000 and from 30 000 to over 100 000. An important factor in such rapid increases, at primary level, has been more free enrolment.

Government spending on education has risen enormously since independence. In the Ivory Coast for example, it has doubled every four or five years since 1960. Between 1960 and 1973 the share of education and training in the total recurrent budget grew from 22 to 33 per cent, a larger proportion than any other country in the world, except possibly Kenya. In Nigeria, especially since the introduction of universal primary education, expenditure has risen rapidly, at both federal and state levels, and may well be close to a third of recurrent budgets.

Apart from expansion in numbers and of facilities there has been some progress in Africanising teaching personnel, curricula and syllabuses, although the results vary considerably from one country to another. An important factor in Africanising teachers has been the rapid decline of missionary control over primary and secondary education, secularisation of staff and a corresponding increase in state control of the educational system. In the 1960s secularisation did not immediately lead to full-scale Africanisation, because of shortages of qualified African teachers. Schools in former French Africa were, except for Guinea, heavily staffed by former colonial educational personnel. In former British colonies large numbers of contract teachers were provided by the British government aid programme and volunteers from the US Peace Corps. In the late 1970s most of the expatriate staff were phased out of English-speaking Africa and replaced by graduates from the new African universities. In French-speaking Africa, however, expatriates have stayed much longer, especially in the Ivory Coast and Senegal where Africanisation of secondary education has in effect been a low priority.

Curricula and syllabuses have been Africanised to varying extents. By 1970, for example, most secondary school students south of the Sahara were studying predominantly African history and literature for 'O' level courses, even though their teachers might, at first, be mainly Europeans. The West African Examination Council (WAEC) has played key roles in syllabus revision. WAEC was set up in 1952, to organise and administer exams more suited to the needs of West Africa. In 1955 the first West African School Certificate exam was conducted. In subsequent years much has been done to revise existing British overseas syllabuses and devise new syllabuses suitable for West African requirements.

In some areas of education little progress has been made and a number of new problems have arisen. Quantitative gains have in some countries led to qualitative losses. For example educational expansion in Nigeria has led to a marked decline in standards especially in the primary schools, largely because of the temporary shortage of trained and/or experienced teachers. The performance of the WAEC in recent years has been marked by inefficiency, exam leakages, frequent cancellation of exams and the growing unwillingness of universities abroad to accept students with WAEC exam passes.

Another serious problem arises from the comparative neglect of technical education, caused largely by the lack of adequate or suitable teachers of technical subjects, even from abroad. For example, in 1961 Nigeria had just over 4 000 full and part-time trainees in government technical institutes and trade centres, and another 2 700 being trained in private industry. The federal government set an annual target of 5 000 new technicians and 50 000 artisans and craftsmen; however, such a programme required the raising of the number of technical teachers from 91 to over a thousand and they were simply not forthcoming. Ghana managed to increase enrolment in technical schools from 4 956 in 1965 to 8 345 in 1971, and the Busia government provided substantial funding for technical schools. However, enrolment has been hindered by the attitude of many pupils who prefer academic work.

In spite of the widespread expansion of primary education, literacy levels in West Africa remain very low. In few West African countries does literacy exceed 30 per cent, and on average for every three or four literate men there is only one literate woman. This particular imbalance has serious implications, for most girls become mothers, and their influence on their children is invariably much more important than the father's.

Another serious problem which affects all West African countries without exception is the rising number of unemployed among primary school leavers since the 1960s and secondary school leavers since the 1970s. In a number of countries the problem of unemployed university graduates had appeared by 1980. Educational expansion has everywhere far outstripped the pace of economic development. At the same time very few of the educated unemployed have received any kind of suitable training for working in agriculture, nor are their attitudes and expectations directed towards participation in rural development. Radical states like Guinea and Guinea-Bissau have changed the curricula of primary and secondary schools to prepare pupils for careers in agriculture and rural trades. In the Ivory Coast the number of technical training centres for rural areas is being increased. However, a very great deal remains to be done in this field in nearly all West African countries.

Religion

What changes have occurred on the religious scene in West Africa? What have been the fortunes of, respectively, the historic Christian churches brought originally by European missionaries, the independent African churches, Islam, and African traditional religion? Religious scepticism, agnosticism and even atheism appear to have grown: nevertheless, religion in various forms has proved remarkably resilient. Mosques are still packed on Fridays and, unlike in much of the Western world, churches in West Africa are crowded on Sundays. All over West Africa thousands of new mosques and churches have been, and are being, built. Traditional religion also remains strong. West Africans continue to be religious people.

In the historic churches (Catholic, Anglican, Methodist, Presbyterian and Lutheran) Africanisation has taken place, particularly in the Roman Catholic church in which the clergy were overwhelmingly European before 1960. Togo had a black majority of Catholic bishops by 1965 and in other states the episcopate was mainly African by 1972. Rome was quick to appoint African archbishops to head the church in each state, e.g. Yago in Ivory Coast, Zoungrana in Upper Volta, Gantin in Benin and Amissah in Ghana in 1960, Zoa in Cameroun in 1961, and Dosseh in Togo and Thiandoum in Senegal in 1962. Ordinations of African Catholic priests increased steadily and by 1975, there were over 3 000 African Catholic priests in West Africa. However, since the number of Catholics has been growing proportionately more rapidly than the number of priests, the church has given more responsibility to African catechists and local parish councils in rural areas who will manage a parish in the absence of a priest for long periods.

The historic Protestant churches (the Anglicans, Methodists and Presbyterians) were more Africanised than the Catholic Church before independence. Since then the national synods and conferences have reflected the effective independence of local Protestant churches from the parent churches in Britain. As early as 1961 the Methodist Church of Ghana became fully autonomous with its own conference, having previously been subject to the British Methodist Conference. The Presbyterian churches of West Africa also become autonomous from the parent church in Scotland. The Anglicans neither became autonomous nor shed their colonialist-sounding name, but more Africans were placed in responsible administrative posts and attempts were made to integrate aspects of African culture into the liturgy.

The African-run historic churches have shown a far greater interest in ecumenism or church unity. In Nigeria the Church Union Movement in the early 1960s proposed an initial union between Presbyterians, Methodists and even Anglican dioceses in southern Nigeria. The union never took place as scheduled in 1965 because of fears of Anglican domination, divisions over the ministry and the failure of leaders to consult properly the bulk of the congregations. In spite of this failure, the Christian Council of Nigeria, an association of historic Protestant churches, has done good joint work in religious education, pastoral training and the medical and urban ministries. The Catholics, however, have done far more in the field of education, expanding the number of their schools at all levels while the older Protestant churches have pulled out of some of theirs.

West Africa's historic Protestant Churches have played an important part in the work of the All-African Conference of Churches (AACC) established in 1959, and now with its headquarters in Nairobi. The AACC deals with the ecumenical co-operation, education, refugees, famine relief and human rights. The first general secretary was Sam Amissah of Ghana and the most controversial was the radical Canon Burgess Carr of Liberia, who resigned in 1978. In 1961 the World Council of Churches (WCC), an ecumenical Protestant organisation, elected Sir Francis Ibiam of Nigeria one of its six presidents. Both the AACC and the WCC have announced support for liberation movements in southern Africa.

Although white missionary effort in the 'historic' churches has declined since independence, there has been a great increase in the activities of missionaries of North American fundamentalist churches such as the Seventh Day Adventist Church, Mennonites, Christian Church, Universal Christian Church, Church of God, Church of Christ, Watchtower Church, United Pentecostal Church, etc. These new style Baptist and pentecostal churches have been very active in Ghana and in the Nigerian Middle Belt. There were over 7 000 North American Protestant missionaries in Africa by the early 1970s, most of them in West Africa. In some cases these fundamentalist churches have more followers than the old 'colonialist' churches. They could represent a very powerful lever for the spread of a certain type of American culture in West Africa.

The fastest growing Christian churches in West Africa since independence have, however, been the African independent churches. Such churches flourished in the colonial period partly in reaction to white domination of the historic churches. They Africanise religious practice by emphasising the importance of not only prayer and bible reading but also faith-healing, music and dance in worship, and thus fulfil the social and psychological as well as the spiritual needs of many African people. There is some evidence that the independent churches have grown more rapidly as a popular response to the disillusionment with the failures of the new African rulers. For example, in southern Ghana from about 1960 there was a sudden outbreak of new, small, independent healing churches.

Aladura is the fastest growing Christian group in Nigeria. 'Aladura' means 'prayer people', and is not a church but a type of movement. It emerged in 1930 but has spread from its western Nigerian home to other areas of Nigeria, along the West African Coast to Sierra Leone and abroad to London (in 1964). The Aladura movement has three groups: the Christ Apostolic Church (CAC) and other Apostolic Churches; the Cherubim and Seraphim, which has many factions; and the Church of the Lord. The CAC is the largest and most powerful group, and survived without disruption the deaths of its major prophet Babalola in 1959 and its first president Sir Isacc Akinyele in 1964. The CAC runs a large number of schools, a teacher training college and pastoral college to train clergy. In addition to the emphasis on prayer the CAC stresses certain doctrines, such as the ban on the use of doctors and hospitals. The Seraphim and the Church of the Lord are less clearcut on doctrine, have developed special spiritual techniques for successful prayer, and have an abundance of prophets and far fewer full-time pastors than the CAC. In all the Aladura churches, lay activity is intensive and the democratic spirit is very strong.

In Ghana, the arrival of American pentecostal missionaries in the 1960s gave a spurt to the growth of independent churches. Yoruba migrant workers also set up Ghanaian Aladura churches. One of the most successful Ghanaian independent or Spiritual churches has been the Eden Revival church founded by Charles Yeboa-Korie after a vision in 1963. This charismatic young man in his twenties developed a church out of a praying and healing circle, with long night services, new hymns, hand-clapping and dancing and faith healing prayers over patients. Very soon, Yeboa-Korie developed a poultry farm, schools and a brass-band and launched a full-scale evangelisation mission. His church was the first independent church to be addmitted to the Ghana Christian Council.

Aladura has made Christianity the religion not just of small groups of western-educated people but also of large numbers of poorly-educated and illiterate folk in the city slums and on the farms.

In independent West Africa relations between Christians and Muslims have been generally good. In countries like Burkina Faso/Upper Volta, Sierra Leone and Nigeria a large Muslim population had readily accepted the political leadership of a largely Christian elite, although in Nigeria Muslims have made rapid strides in the professions and politics. In Senegal, Senghor was for twenty years the Christian president of an overwhelmingly Muslim country. Foreign journalists who portrayed the Nigerian civil war as a struggle between the Islamic north and Catholic 'Biafra' were ready to ignore the basic facts that many Christians including Catholics fought on the federal side and that several of the federal leaders including the head of state, were Christians.

The growth of Islam has accelerated since independence. It would appear that for every Christian convert there are several converts to Islam. By 1970 probably half of West Africa's population was Muslim compared to 35 per cent being Christians. Nigeria's Muslims constitute the largest Islamic community in Africa south of the Sahara. To help spread Islam and to strengthen converts national organisations were set up, such as the Jama'atu Nasril Islam in 1961 and the Islamic Council of Nigeria in 1973. Muslim missionaries, teachers and doctors from Pakistan, Egypt, Saudi Arabia and Libya have come into Nigeria in large numbers. Graduates from Cairo's Al-Azhar University now teach in several Nigerian universities. Increasing numbers of Muslims are obtaining university degrees and moving up the ranks in the armed forces. In Ibadan, the largest Muslim city south of the Sahara, electronically amplified *muezzin* call believers to prayer from the university campus beds. Chartered planes from Kano fly thousands on the *hajj* to Saudi Arabia. Nigeria's figure of 106 000 pilgrims to Mecca in 1977 was second only to that of Indonesia.

The rapid flow of religious ideas from other parts of the Islamic world with the return home of pilgrims, students and traders has led to a proliferation of sects and brotherhoods in Nigeria. The traditional powerful brotherhoods like the conservative Qadiriyya and the more democratic Tijaniyya have had vast followings throughout Muslim West Africa since pre-colonial times. In the 1970s and 1980s their domination of Muslim life in Nigeria has come under sharp challenge. The modernising Ahmadiyya brotherhood, originating in Pakistan, emphasises adaptation to a technological age, sponsors secondary education and flourishes among Yoruba-speakers. The Ahmadiyya was branded as heretical in 1974 and condemned by the Sultan of Sokoto, spiritual heir to the caliphate. However, the Ahmadiyya is a positive and constructive movement compared with some of the millenarian sects that have arisen recently among the rural and urban poor of some northern Nigerian states. In December 1980 a rising of the followers of the Camerounian sect led by a self-proclaimed prophet, Mohammed Umarua Maitatsine, in Kano old city led to a massacre in which several thousand people were killed. Umarua's sect was an extreme fundamentalist one and rejected the bicycle, radio, television and even money. Umarua was killed in the fighting sparked off after when his followers murdered an orthodox Muslim at afternoon prayers. Further riots by Umarua's followers in Maiduguri and Kaduna in October 1982 and Yola in 1984 led to several hundred deaths, including those of a hundred policemen.

In Senegal, rivalry between the three major Muslim brotherhoods, the Qadiriyya, the Tijaniyya and the Muridiyya, has sometimes led to rioting, but fundamentalist sects have had little or no impact. The fragmented 800-year old Qadiriyya is estimated to have the allegiance of 13 per cent of the population. The serious rivalry is between the Tijaniyya, which possibly still has the largest number of adherents and the Muridiyya, which is gaining fast and may by now outnumber the Tijaniyya. The Tijani *marabouts* dominate the state-sponsored 'official' Islamic reform programmes and stress their doctrinal purity and commitment to devotional rigour in contrast to the liberal Muridiyya. The Tijaniyya is divided into three lodges which recognise no overall leadership, whereas the Muridiyya are united in obedience to their khalifa at Touba. The Muridiyya has well over a million disciples (*talibes*) and is rapidly growing. Apart from its traditional support from the peasants in the groundnut belt, where it acts as a welfare society, the Muridiyya has spread into the towns, establishing missions among the poor and settling rural migrants in businesses large and small. Mouride traders can be found not only in Dakar but in EEC capitals like Paris and Brussels. In the late 1970s the Muridiyya made converts for the first time among the French-educated students in the high schools and the university. An association of Mouride students has been active since 1977, studying the poetry of the brotherhood's founder Amadu Bamba and a Muslim university is under construction in Touba.

The progress or decline of traditional African religion in West Africa since independence is difficult to assess, because of lack of reliable statistics of traditional believers. Censuses indicate that adherents of traditional religion compose between 15 and 20 per cent of West Africa's population at the present time. Traditional religion has survived and has influenced both Christianity (especially the independent churches) and Islam (some of the new sects). There is a strong respect for traditional religion, which was described in Idowu's classic study *Olodumare* (1962) as basically monotheistic and moral. Asare Opoku in his book *West African Traditional Religions* shows that religion is at the root of African culture. It seems certain that many Christians and Muslims continue to be influenced by many traditional beliefs and values, and some even practise a number of traditional religious customs. As Idowu says, it is well known that even Africans who are 'practising Christians' and go to hospitals, insure themselves by also taking medicine prepared in the traditional way. Similarly, many West African Christians and Muslims accept the spiritual and moral values of African traditional religion and do not see so much the differences as the similarities between the old religion and their new one, the one religion reinforcing the other.

23   Cultural developments

Under colonial rule African culture was scorned and the African himself was looked down upon. What steps have been taken, since independence, to assert and revive African culture?

Governments of independent states in some ways played an important part in this revival. Apart from their massive contributions in the field of education they have also financed international festivals, such as the First Festival of Negro Arts in Dakar in 1966 and the Second World Black and African Festival of Arts and Culture (FESTAC) in Lagos in 1977. These festivals have helped to increase public awareness of the work being done by writers and artists. Folk and modern dance companies have been set up with government aid. For instance, in 1959 Guinea created a national ballet company and in the early 1960s the Ghana dance Ensemble was founded as a result of the combined efforts of the government and the Institute of African Studies at the University of Ghana, Legon. The expansion of publishing in West Africa has received some help from governments – the Gaskiya Corporation of northern Nigeria has published much Hausa literature and the Ghana Publishing Corporation has published some poetry of quality – although a greater role in fostering the work of West African writers has been played by major overseas commercial publishing houses.

In the 1970s a number of new indigenous publishing houses emerged as viable businesses in Nigeria, and university presses in Nigeria and Ghana have published a range of academic and literary works.

Literature and drama

A number of factors have encouraged the growth of written literature in independent West Africa. The first is the spread of literacy following the expansion of education by the state. The second factor is the growth of a body of educated people who have developed the habit of reading literature as a special discipline in schools and at university. The third factor is cultural nationalism which has inspired many West Africans to write. A fourth factor has been the continuing tradition of oral literature which has influenced the themes and styles of much recent written literature.

What themes run through West African literature of the independence period? A major theme of the late 1950s and 1960s was cultural nationalism: depiction of heroic events in African history; a sympathetic portrayal of pre-colonial society; exposure of the effects of colonialism and assertion of African self-identity. Chinua Achebe described his first novel *Things Fall Apart* (1958) as 'an act of atonement for my past, the ritual return and homage of a prodigal son'. Cultural nationalism was part of the anti-colonial campaign. Sembene Ousmane of Senegal immortalised the railway workers' strike against French rule in his novel *God's Bits of Wood* (1960). The same theme was repeated in Achebe's *No Longer At Ease* (1960) and *Arrow of God* (1964). Achebe's novels are nationalist not only in theme but also in style and expression because he has enriched English with African similes, metaphors and proverbs. In much the same way Francis Bebey of Cameroun in his novel *Agatha Moudio's Son* (1968) has Africanised the French language by making it express African patterns of thought and humour.

Soon after independence West African writing took up a new theme: criticism and condemnation of the faults of the new society under African leadership. Prominent among the novels in English of post-colonial protest are, from Nigeria, Wole Soyinka's *The Interpreters* (1965) and *Season of Anomy* (1973), Achebe's *A Man of the People* (1966), and, from Ghana, Ayi Kwei Armah's *The Beautiful Ones Are not Yet Born* (1968) and Kofi Awoonor's *This Earth, My Brother* (1971). In French, one should mention, from Guinea, Camara Laye's *A Dream of Africa* (1966), with its stark vision of tyranny; from Ivory Coast, Ahmadou Kourouma's *The Suns of Independence* (1968) and from Senegal, Malick Fall's *The Wound* (1967) and the works of Sembene Ousmane: *The Money Order* (1965), *Xala* (1974) and *The Last of the Empire* (1981).

Writing in African languages has increased since independence, especially in Nigeria. The most widely read Nigerian writer, the Yoruba language novelist D. O. Fagunwa, died in 1963, but his five novels have continued to be immensely popular. Amos Tutuola has translated his *The Palm Wine Drinkard* into Yoruba. In recent years Achebe has produced poetry in Igbo, his first language. Work of quality has come from the poet Alhaji Abubakar Iman, writing in Hausa. The most striking example of literature in a West African language has perhaps been the professional Yoruba theatre, begun in the 1950s by Hubert Ogunde and others. Ogunde's company, Folk Opera Troupe, has performed Yoruba culture plays with traditional dance music, and topical plays on political issues. E. K. Ogunmola has developed Yoruba opera, using more purely Yoruba music. In 1962 Duro Ladipo founded Mbari Mbaya Club in Oshogbo partly as a theatre workshop; his tragedy *Obo Koso* triumphed at the Berlin Festival in 1964. One of Ladipo's actors, Obatunde Ijimere, has written plays in Yoruba which have also been successful when translated into English, *Everyman* and *The Imprisonment of Obatala* (1966).

Wole Soyinka's plays are written in English but he has Africanised the language and dramatic form by his use of Yoruba themes and of mime and dance. From *A Dance of the Forests* (1960) to *Opera Wonyusi* (1981), Soyinka has explored various themes from traditional Africa to an attack on the evils of the present. J. P. Clark's most successful play is *Ozidi* (1966), based on the corpus of traditional Ijo literature which he collected, translated and published in Ijo and English and which is performed in the style of traditional Yoruba theatre, every scene being alive with song and dance.

In Ghana, Efua Sutherland founded the Ghana Drama Studios in Accra, developed drama at the University of Ghana's Institute of African Studies, and has written several major plays, notably the tragedy *Edufa* (1967). Ama Ata Aidoo's *The Dilemma of a Ghost* (1965) and Joe de Graft's *Muntu* (1975) are, in their different ways, concerned with the conflict between African and western culture.

Leopold Sedar Senghor, the poet-president of Senegal, wrote much of his poetry on the themes of *negritude* (recognition of Africa's own cultural identity) in the 1930s and 1940s, but *Nocturnes* appeared in 1961. Like Senghor, Ghanaian poets have been heavily influenced by the tradition of oral poetry. The influence of Ewe oral tradition is seen in the verse of Kofi Awoonor, Kofi Anyidoho and Adali Mortey. Kwesi Brew and Ama Ata Aidoo draw upon Akan traditions in their poems. The Nigerians, Chris Okigbo, who was killed in the Civil War, Gabriel Okara, Clark and Soyinka have also produced poetry of great merit. From the middle of the 1960s 'protest' poetry has been prominent. Okigbo and Soyinka attacked the empty promises of the independence politicians. The same theme inspired Gambian Lenrie Peters in his collections *Satellites* (1967) and *Katchikali* (1971).

The cinema

West African film production has been dominated by the work of Sembene Ousmane, who has adapted some of his own literature to the cinema screen. Sembene has made films in the French, Wolof and Jola languages. His full-length feature films include *La Noire* (Black Girl) made in 1966, *Mandabi* (The Money Order), *Emitai* (Thunder Gods), *Xala* (Impotence) and *Ceddo* (The Resisters) in 1977. In his films as in his literature Sembene concentrates on the struggles of ordinary people against colonialism and corruption in the independence period and defends African culture. Senegalese cinema has also been responsible for Safi Faye's remarkable *Man Say Yay* (I, Your Mother). The West African film industry has been encouraged by Upper Volta's sponsoring of the First African Film Festival in 1970; by the Ghana Film Industry Corporation's production of feature films like *Genesis Chapter X* and *Contact*, by Kwaw Ansah's *Love Brewed in an African Pot* with its theme of class conflict, by Francis Oladele's establishment of Culpenny-Nigeria Films Ltd which has begun to produce films based on Achebe's novels. Other notable productions have been Olusegun Oyekunle's *The Broken Cells*, with its Pidgin English screenplay, Ola Balogun's *Money Power*, Kramo Lacien Fadika of Ivory Coast's *Djelli* and Souleman Cisse of Mali's *The Wind* with its themes of political autocracy, African versus western values and the aspirations of youth.

Music

West Africa still has outstanding performers of traditional music in the villages and some highly accomplished traditional artists like the Ghanaian drummer Mustapha Tette Addy, the Malian singer Fanta Sacko and Guinea's balafon, kora and balon player Kouyate Sory Kandia, who have used western technology to record and distribute their music in the cities and abroad. However, transistor radios have helped to turn successive generations of

West African youth away from traditional music. Also changing tastes have caused highlife music, in its heyday in the 1940s and 1950s to give way to newer styles of popular music.

In the late 1960s Afro-American soul music in the form of James Brown, Chubby Checker and Ray Charles records and the rock music of Jim Hendrix became more popular than highlife. In this way, American popular music with its roots in West Africa began in its turn, to inspire West African music. West African musicians quickly developed their own distinctive styles of Afro-American-influenced music. The Heartbeats of Sierra Leone, the first major soul band in West Africa, toured Ghana and Nigeria in 1966 and had a great impact. Afro beat, a mixture of highlife, jazz, traditional music and rock, dominated the 1970s. Afrobeat's most spectacular performer has been Fela Anikulapu Kuti of Nigeria.

The visual arts

West African visual arts such as sculpture and painting have taken new directions since independence. The number of traditional sculptors has declined rapidly and much of their production is, in any case, of poor quality, for sale to European tourists and expatriate workers. On the other hand, a number of West African sculptors have been producing work of outstanding quality, blending modern and traditional styles. Among them are the Nigerians Ben Enwonwu, perhaps the world's leading wood carver, Abayomi Barber, Felix Idubor, Francis Osague and Emmanuel Jegede.

West Africans are in the forefront of the new generation of modern African painters. In 1961 the German-born Ulli Beier and Suzanne Wenger set up art workshops in Oshogbo from which emerged the folk art of Twins Seven Seven (Taiwo Olaniyi), Jimoh Buraimoh and others. Work of high quality has come from Uzo Egonu, Bruce Onobrakpeya, Chuks Anyanwu and Ben Enwonwu of Nigeria, Kofi Antobam, Ablade Glover and Kobina Bucknor of Ghana and Iba N'diaye of Senegal. All these artists have turned to African culture for inspiration. Egonu, Glover and N'diaye have achieved international reputations in Europe and North America.

The major problems African artists must face are lack of encouragement from their own people, including those in government, and the fact that foreign tourists, who usually know nothing about art, remain the principal buyers. Successive Ghanaian governments from Nkrumah onwards have given help to sculptors and painters through the Arts Council and its regional cultural centres. Greater provision for art education in schools would do much to encourage widespread interest and support in the visual arts generally.

Broadcasting

At independence, West African governments inherited state-owned broadcasting systems and they have expanded them considerably since. For example, the Nigerian Broadcasting Corporation by 1975 had domestic and international services in four languages and could boast of five million radios and 85 000 television sets. This expansion has, in some ways, had undesirable effects, especially as far as advancing African culture is concerned. West African television networks buy many programmes from Europe and America, and relatively little has been invested in the production of original well-produced programmes locally. As a result, imported TV shows have imposed foreign cultural values far more widely than colonial education managed to do. Although local programmes have helped to encourage the establishment of national, trans-ethnic consciousness and an awareness of the richness and quality of African culture, much remains to be done.

Sport

In sport, West Africans have begun to make their mark on the international scene. West African athletes – like the sprinters Alice Anum and Ernest Obeng of Ghana, Kone of the Ivory Coast and Nigeria's 4 × 100 metres relay team which won the gold medal in the 1982 Commonwealth Games – take part in athletics meetings throughout the world. Daley Thompson, perhaps the world's greatest athlete and world record holder in the Decathlon has a Nigerian father. In tennis, Yannick Noah, a Camerounian who has now taken French nationality, is ranked amongst the top ten tennis players in the world. Nigeria's Nduka Odizor defeated several top players at the 1982 Wimbledon tennis championships and won many fans with his exciting play and sportsmanship. West Africa has a long tradition of producing first-class boxers and this tradition has been maintained since independence by boxers such as Ghana's amateur team which won the 1962 Commonwealth Games in Perth, Australia, and by the professional world title fighters Dick Tiger of Nigeria and Roy Ankrah and Floyd Robertson of Ghana. Azumah Nelson of Ghana became world featherweight boxing champion in 1985. In football most international impact has been made by Cameroun's goalkeeper Thomas Nkono, star forward Roger Milla and their colleagues who performed so well in the 1982 World Cup in Spain. The Cameroun team was unbeaten, it drew with Peru, Poland and Italy, the eventual champions. It failed to go through to the next round only on goal difference; and it proved to the world the new world-class quality of African football. Nigeria's Junior under-16 team, the 'Baby Eagles', won the world cup for their age-group in China in 1985.

Thus, in the first two decades of political independence, much progress has been made in the revival of African culture in West Africa, in literature, the cinema, music and the visual arts, and West African sportsmen and sportswomen have shown the ability to compete successfully in international competitions.

24 West Africa and the wider world

Nkrumah and pan-Africanism

Kwame Nkrumah, the leader of Ghana, was the main driving force in West Africa's relations with the wider world in the early post-independence period – partly because Ghana became independent several years earlier than most of its neighbours, and also because Nkrumah's foreign policy was radical and dynamic. Nkrumah aimed at achieving the total liberation of the African states. He launched these policies by hosting the two Accra Conferences of 1958, the Conference of Independent African states in April, attended by eight states (most of them North African) and the All-African People's Conference in December, attended by delegates from 62 nationalist organisations in 28 countries. These were followed by the all-Africa Trades Union Federation Conference in 1959, also in Accra. Nkrumah followed up the conference by giving grants to freedom fighters and political parties in many colonial countries, and by his efforts to set up the Ghana-Guinea Unions. However, in the end Nkrumah became a divisive rather than a unifying factor among the new independent states of Africa. Not only did he give support to political exiles from other independent states; he openly accused many of the new French-speaking states of being still subordinate to France, of being 'client states, independent in name'.

Initial groupings and the formation of the OAU

The early 1960s saw the division of African states into two opposing groups, the Monrovia group and the Casablanca bloc. Nkrumah dominated the Casablanca bloc which consisted of radical states such as Ghana, Guinea, Mali, Algeria and Egypt. All these states favoured diplomatic and economic ties with the eastern socialist countries as well as with the West, as part of a neutralist or non-aligned foreign policy; they were prepared to experiment with socialism at home; they supported the radical Patrice Lumumba and, after his murder, backed his followers against their rivals in the Congo (Zaire). The members of the Monrovia group were Liberia, nearly all the French-speaking states and Nigeria. It was a group of conservative states which followed a pro-western rather than a non-aligned foreign policy, which favoured capitalism and western aid and investment and rejected socialism and aid from the East, and preferred to be neutral between the competing factions in the Congo. (It should be pointed out, however, that Nigeria, in spite of its links with the Monrovia group, adopted radical policies towards French nuclear tests and South Africa.) At the Second Conference of

Independent African States, held in Addis Ababa in June 1960 the Monrovia group opposed Nkrumah's proposed union of African states, fearing his ambition to be president of Africa.

The Casablanca bloc was not under the control of Nkrumah. Indeed, the other members of the group turned against the African union proposals. President Tubman of Liberia invited Nkrumah and President Sekou Toure of Guinea to a conference in Saniquelli in the Liberian interior and won Sekou Toure over to his idea of a loose association of states in preference to Nkrumah's proposed closer union. Nigerian diplomacy also played a role in detaching members of the Casablanca bloc. As a result, a conference of independent African states was held in Addis Ababa in May 1963 and the Organisation of African Unity (OAU) was born.

The aim of the OAU was stated in Article II of the 1963 Charter: to promote unity and solidarity of African states; to defend their sovereignty, territorial integrity and independence; and to eradicate colonialism in Africa. Signatories to the Charter, who included all independent African states, agreed to harmonise and co-ordinate their policies in diplomacy, defence, economic co-operation, education, and cultural, scientific and technical co-operation. Among the organs set up were the assembly of heads of states and government, to meet at least once a year; the council of ministers to meet twice a year; the secretariat with an administrative secretary-general, and a commission of mediation, conciliation and arbitration. The assembly later set up further commissions which dealt with a variety of social, economic and political issues. The OAU's budget was to be provided by contributions from member states. The absolute independence of each member state was recognised and Nkrumah's hopes for a close union were dashed.

The OAU: successes and problems

West Africans have played a prominent role in the administration of the OAU. The first Secretary General (1964–72) was the dynamic Diallo Telli of Guinea, who unfortunately died after he left office as a political prisoner in his own country. His successors Nzo Ekangaki (1972–4), William Etekti-Mboumoua (1974–8) (both from Cameroun), Edem Kodjo of Togo (1978–83) and Peter Onu of Nigeria (1983–85) have been less effective partly because Africa's heads of states and foreign ministers have restricted the Secretary-General's executive role and partly because new problems have arisen for the OAU.

West African states, like the rest of Africa, have witnessed both the successes and failures of the OAU in its first twenty years of existence. The OAU has done useful work to assist refugees in co-operation with the United Nations High Commission for Refugees (UNHCR). However, civil wars in Africa, wars between African states and the continuation of colonialism in the white-ruled south have kept the number of Africa's refugees above the one million mark ever since the formation of the OAU. The OAU has been unable to prevent civil wars in Ethiopia, Chad, Zaire, Nigeria and Angola, although it did play a key role in ending the Sudanese civil war in 1972. The

OAU peacekeeping operation in Chad in 1981–82 was a failure largely because of the financial problems in the upkeep of the force. The OAU was helpless to stop the Ivory Coast, Gabon, Tanzania and Zambia recognising 'Biafra' in the Nigerian civil war. It was unable to prevent or stop wars between member states in the late 1970s between Ethiopia and Somalia in 1977–78, Uganda and Tanzania in 1978–79, and Morocco and Mauritania against the Sahrawi independence forces, over the disputed territory of the Western Sahara (formerly Spanish Sahara).

The war in the former Spanish Sahara since 1976 has presented the OAU with one if its gravest problems and is also of direct concern to West Africa because of the involvement of Mauritania. When Spain decolonised in 1976 Mauritania refused to recognise the independence and made an agreement with Morocco to partition the phosphate-rich desert territory between the two African states, the larger section in the north going to Morocco. Moroccan and Mauritanian forces occupied the few coastal towns of the Western Sahara while POLISARIO declared the independence of the Sahrawi Arab Democratic Republic (SADR). For eight years, until the time of writing, POLISARIO has waged a guerilla war in an effort to gain control of the territory, operating largely from bases and refugee camps inside Algeria. POLISARIO has received much military and financial aid from radical states like Algeria and Libya. POLISARIO concentrated at first on trying to knock weaker Mauritania out of the war and even made a long-distance raid on Nouakchott, Mauritania's capital. By 1978 Mauritanian forces had been defeated, the country was bankrupt and Mauritania was in fact being defended from POLISARIO by Moroccan troops and the French air force. In July 1978 a military coup in Nouakchott overthrew President Ould Daddah. The new Mauritanian government soon signed a ceasefire with POLISARIO, which has continued the war against Morocco alone. In July 1980 the OAU Freetown summit came close to collapse when it appeared that a majority, including some West African states, might vote for the SADR to be seated and Morocco and other conservative states, including some in West Africa, threatened to walk out. In February 1982 a majority did vote for the SADR's admission, and as a result more than a third of the OAU's member states boycotted the 19th OAU Summit in Tripoli in August of that year.

Therefore, West African states have been in different camps in disputes between OAU members. These divisions are further reflected in policy towards South Africa. A number of African states, (Malawi, Zaire, Gabon, Ivory Coast and, for a time, Ghana and Liberia) have at times supported a policy of dialogue with South Africa in an attempt to bring about change there by discussions with its white leaders. Most states have supported the opposite policy, of backing diplomatic, sporting and economic sanctions against South Africa and encouraging liberation groups like the African National Congress (ANC). These conflicting policies are further evidence of the fact that the OAU has no authority over the policies of member states. Nigeria has followed a consistently firm policy against white racism in southern Africa. At the 1961 Commonwealth Heads of States Conference in London, Nigeria's Prime Minister Tafawa Balewa, although conservative in many aspects of foreign policy, was as determined and influential as Nkrumah or Nyerere of Tanzania in forcing South Africa's withdrawal from the Conference and the Commonwealth. In 1979, on the eve of the

Commonwealth Heads of State Conference in Lusaka, the Nigerian government of General Obasanjo took over British Petroleum's operations in Nigeria, at a time when it seemed the British Government was not prepared to take a strong line with Zimbabwe's white settler-dominated government. The takeover of BP may have helped to encourage Britain to speed up the arrangements for Zimbabwean independence under a properly elected black majority government early in 1980.

Relations with the 'great powers'

In their relations with the 'great powers', West African states have shown the same divisions that are reflected in their differing policies towards African problems. These divisions can be observed in a study of West Africa's relations with France, which has the most direct involvement in West Africa. France conceded independence to its remaining West African colonies in 1960 (having accepted Guinea's independence in 1958) but ever since has sought to play a directing role in the affairs of the new states, through defence agreements, economic organisations and its control of financial aid. For example, although Nigeria in 1962 rescinded its earlier defence agreement with Britain, countries like the Ivory Coast and Senegal have maintained sizeable French garrisons. French forces were withdrawn at the request of the host states from Mali in 1961, Benin in 1965 and Niger in 1974, but Mauritania welcomed French military assistance in the Saharan War. France has tried to maintain its economic control over the French-speaking states through organisations such as the *Union Africaine et Malgache* (UAM), *Organisation Africaine et Malgache de Coopération Economique* (OAMCE) renamed *Organisation Commune Africaine et Malagache* (OCAM) in 1965 and finally the CEAO. The CEAO, an economic community of Francophone West African states, was set up in 1974 to prevent Nigeria dominating the projected ECOWAS. Most of French-speaking Africa continue to use the CFA franc, a currency tied to that of France.

France's influence in West Africa has been challenged at various times by its former colony Guinea and by the major English-speaking states. The bad relations between France and Guinea from 1958 to 1963 were a result of French policies rather than Guinean radicalism. As we have seen Guinea accepted Ghanaian aid at independence but it also turned to the USSR and the USA for assistance. However, disillusionment with the Russians caused President Sekou Toure to turn again to France in 1983 when several technical assistance agreements were signed, arranging to train Guineans in France and to send French experts to Guinea. French assets seized by Guinea in 1958 were released and France resumed paying pensions due to Guinea ex-soldiers and civil servants, including arrears. France's nuclear tests in the Algerian Sahara in 1960 were strongly condemned by Ghana and Nigeria who both broke off diplomatic relations with Paris. Nigeria was at loggerheads on this issue with its Monrovia group partner Ivory Coast which approved of the French tests and of French military action against the FLN, the Algerian nationalists. Nigerian relations with France were at rock bottom when France gave indirect support to the Biafrans in the civil war and encouraged Ivory Coast and Gabon to recognise the Biafran regime.

Nigeria's relations with Britain were soured during the civil war when Harold Wilson's government delayed giving military assistance to the federal forces. Britain's economic decline has reduced her influence in West Africa but she continues to play a major role in the cultural field, by providing many personnel in Nigeria's educational expansion.

The USSR, in spite of assistance at crucial times to Guinea and Nigeria, has not had much influence in independent West Africa. At Guinea's independence the USSR provided the new state with a loan of £12 million. From 1958 to 1961 Sekou Touré maintained close ties with the USSR. He brought in 1 500 Soviet technical advisers who helped to develop Guinea's rich mineral resources, especially bauxite. However, Sekou Touré was an African socialist and a devout Muslim, not a Communist, and he expelled the Russians in 1961 as a result of the 'teachers' plot' against him; he believed the teachers were imbibing revolutionary marxist ideas from the Soviet aid personnel. In his socialist period (1960–66) Nkrumah brought in Soviet advisers in industry and state agriculture and built up a Soviet-trained personal guard company. His trade and aid agreements with the USSR and other Communist countries was worth £100 million by 1962. However, Nkrumah believed he was balancing Communist aid against Western influence and he continued his commitment to non-alignment in foreign policy. In any case, Soviet influence in Ghana ended when Nkrumah was overthrown. Strongly capitalist Nigeria purchased considerable military hardware from the USSR from the beginning of the civil war and has used Soviet assistance in the construction of the Ajaokuta steel complex, but the USSR has had no influence on Nigerian foreign or economic policies.

Nigerian foreign policy has shown an equal independence of the dictates of the USA. This was shown clearly during the Angolan civil war. General Gowon had provided financial support for all three Angolan liberation movements – FLNA, UNITA and MPLA. When South African troops invaded Angola in 1975 to assist the conservative FLNA and UNITA against the radical socialist MPLA, Nigeria's new leader General Murtala Mohammed ignored the express wishes of the USA and recognised the MPLA as the sole legitimate government of Angola. This Nigerian initiative persuaded the rest of Africa to follow suit.

On the whole, West African states have managed to accept what little American economic aid has been available (for example, assistance in Guinean mining and in Ghana's Volta River Project) without abandoning non-alignment in foreign policy. An exception was Tubman's Liberia, which historically has been the USA's main bridgehead in Africa; it is not only a recipient of investment and loans but also it is a centre of American public relations in West Africa. Monrovia became the site of the Voice of America transmissions to Africa. Tubman was so strongly pro-American and anti-Communist that he refused to allow the USSR to have an embassy in Monrovia and he did not recognise Communist China. However, Tubman's successor Tolbert made Liberia's foreign policy more non-aligned when he allowed the USSR to open an embassy in 1972. He recognised Communist China in 1977 and made a state visit to Peking in the following year.

West African roles in international organisations

West African states are linked economically to the European Economic Community (EEC) by a series of trade conventions. What does West Africa, or Africa generally, gain from these agreements? The Treaty of Rome (1957) that set up the EEC preserved the special treatment of French colonies through trade preferences and aid. The EEC set up the European Development Fund. The Yaounde Convention was signed between the EEC and nineteen independent African states in 1963. Nigeria joined the convention by a special trade agreement in 1966. Under the convention nearly all the agricultural exports of the African associates entered the EEC without paying duty; in return the African states reduced customs duties on imports from the EEC, but they retained the right to protect their infant industries against EEC competition. The 1975 Lome Agreement between the EEC and 46 African, Caribbean and Pacific (ACP) countries allowed the majority of ACP manufactured goods and processed agricultural products to enter the EEC free of duty or quota restrictions. It also set up STABEX, a loan scheme intended to compensate commodity producers for losses in export earnings following a fall in prices in the world market or a natural disaster. Lome II in 1979 extended the list of commodities covered by STABEX and allowed STABEX repayments to be spread over a longer period. Lome I and II provides some assistance to African states but the financial benefits are of marginal value. Because of frequent sharp declines in commodity prices the fund has never been adequate. The Lome agreements do nothing to alter the general situation of African countries as producers of cheap raw materials and foodstuffs for the rich industrialised western world.

Has new-found oil wealth helped West Africa's economic development? Most of the OPEC (Organisation of Petroleum Exporting Countries) members are Third World states and two of them, Nigeria and Gabon, are from West Africa. From 1973 to 1975 OPEC quadrupled the world price of oil. Clearly this helped OPEC countries' development programmes – especially Nigeria's industrialisation and educational expansion – in spite of temporary problems during occasional periods of a glut of oil on the world market. However, most sub-Saharan African states have run up heavy debts in order to pay for their oil imports. The oil price rise also contributed to economic recession in the industrialised nations and as a result there was a sharp fall in demand for African goods. Non-oil producing African nations have failed to persuade OPEC to sell them oil at preferential prices, although some assistance to African nations with balance of payments problems have been provided by the Arab-African Oil Assistance Fund, the Arab Loan Fund for Africa and similar institutions. Nigeria originally intended to sell oil to its West African neighbours at reduced prices, but this was found to be contrary to OPEC rules, so instead Nigeria placed funds in the African Development Bank, to give loans on easy terms to the poorer African countries. But in practice little assistance has been received from the Arabs or Nigeria and many African countries have had to seek loans from the IMF.

What role has West Africa played in the United Nations? Nigeria, Ghana, Liberia, Guinea and Mali (as well as a number of North African states) sent contingents to the UN peacekeeping forces in the Congo (Zaire) in 1960–63, helping to restore law and order and crush the Belgian-backed Katangan secessionist movement. Ghanaian, Nigerian and Senegalese contingents also played a useful peacekeeping role in Lebanon from 1978 to 1982. West African states have been active in the recent campaign by Third World countries to use the UN as a platform to secure a 'new international economic order'. The United Nations Conference on Trade and Development (UNCTAD) has brought the Third World together behind a broadly agreed set of proposals for economic reforms, particularly in world commodity markets and international loan facilities. However, to date there has been little sign of serious interest by the industrialised countries in any worldwide economic development plan to assist the less developed countries. In the meantime, a number of West African states, with balance of payments difficulties, like many other Third World countries, have been forced to seek life-saving loans from the International Monetary Fund (IMF).

The IMF, although it is a UN-agency, is funded mainly by American financial institutions which have a controlling interest, and it imposes austere economic policies (such as cuts in public expenditure) as a condition for loans. One effect of the IMF on Africa has been to ensure the domination of the dollar in currency and foreign trade transactions. Similar to the IMF is the US-controlled World Bank, but it makes development loans on more liberal terms than the IMF. Some observers describe the IMF and the World Bank as instruments of American neocolonialism; others see them as necessary institutions to help keep poorer countries afloat in the world economy. It is an open question whether Africa gains or loses through dependence on US-financed UN lending institutions.

The United Nations Economic Commission for Africa (ECA) was set up in 1958 and has its headquarters in Addis Ababa. Its first Executive Secretary Robert Gardiner of Ghana (1962–76) and his successor Adebayo Adedeji of Nigeria have directed extensive research programmes and the publication of detailed surveys of economic and social conditions in Africa in general and in individual countries. Several institutions have been set up as a result of ECA initiative, such as the African Development Bank (in 1964) and the African Institute of Economic Development and Planning. Since 1974 the ECA has co-operated much more closely with the OAU especially in holding economic conferences and drawing up plans for action to tackle Africa's economic and social problems.

Amadou-Mahtar M'Bow of Senegal, a former Minister of Education in his country, has since 1974 been Secretary-General of the United Nations Educational, Scientific and Cultural Organisation (UNESCO) and has drawn up plans for a New World Information Order to challenge the monopoly of western news agencies and communications systems. In January, 1986 Kenneth Dadzie of Ghana took office as Secretary-General of the UN Conference for Trade and Development (UNCTAD).

It is, therefore, clear that West African states have been participating fully in world affairs. If they are able to solve their serious social and economic problems and reducing their dependence upon loans and aid they will be able to play a more meaningful and useful role still, particularly as mediators between the power blocs of East and West in the interest of world peace and security.

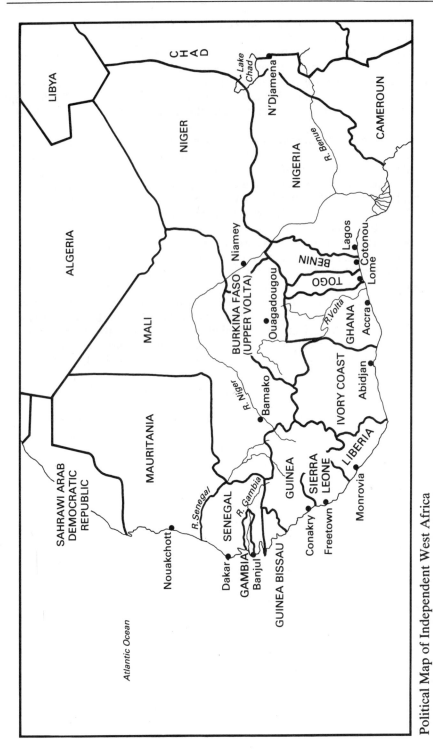

Political Map of Independent West Africa

Independent States of West Africa: Political facts

Country	Date of Independence	Former Name	Leader at Independence	Coup d'état dates	Population (in millions)*	Capital
Benin	1960	Dahomey	Hubert Maga	1963, 1965 1965, 1967 1969, 1972	3.9	Porto Novo (officially) Cotonou (effectively)
Cape Verde	1975	Cape Verde Islands	Aristides Pereira	NONE	0.375	Praia
The Gambia	1965	Gambia	Dawda Jawara	NONE	0.65	Banjul
Ghana	1957	Gold Coast	Kwame Nkrumah	1966, 1972 1978, 1979, 1981	12.6	Accra
Guinea	1958	French Guinea	Ahmed Sekou Touré	1984	5.5	Conakry
Guinea-Bissau	1973/4	Portuguese Guinea	Luis Cabral	1980	1.1	Bissau
Ivory Coast	1960	Ivory Coast	Felix Houphouet-Boigny	NONE	8.3	Abidjan
Liberia	1847	Liberia	Joseph J. Roberts	1980	2.1	Monrovia
Mali	1960	Soudan	Modibo Keita	1968	7.4	Bamako
Mauritania	1960	Mauritania	Moktar Ould Daddah	1978	1.6	Nouakchott
Niger	1960	Niger	Hamani Diori	1974	5.7	Niamey

Independent States of West Africa: Political facts (cont'd)

Country	Date of Independence	Former Name	Leader at Independence	Coup d'état dates	Population (in millions)*	Capital
Nigeria	1960	Nigeria	Nnamdi Azikiwe (Pres.) Sir Abubakar Tafawa Balewa (PM)	1960, 1966, 1975, 1983, 1985	93.0	Lagos
Sao Tome and Principe	1975	Sao Tomé and Principe	Manuel Pinto da Costa	NONE	0.1	
Senegal	1960	Senegal	Leopold Senghor	NONE	6.0	Dakar
Sierra Leone	1961	Sierra Leone	Sir Milton Margai	1967, 1967, 1968.	3.75	Freetown
Togo	1960	Togoland	Sylvanus Olympio	1963, 1967.	2.7	Lome
Upper Volta	1960	Upper Volta	Maurice Yameogo	1966, 1974, 1980, 1982	6.9	Ouagadougou

* The population figures are based on World Bank Atlases and are estimates of the 1983 population on the basis of an average rate of increase of 3 per cent per annum.

Suggestions for further reading

Section one

Adam, H. *The Hausa Factor in West African History,* Ahmadu Bello University Press and OUP, Zaria and Ibadan, 1978.
Ajayi J. F. Ade and Crowder, M. (eds.) *History of West Africa,* Vol 1, 3rd edition, Longman, London, 1985.
Boahen, A. Adu, *Britain, the Sahara and the Western Sudan, 1788–1861,* Clarendon Press, Oxford, 1964.
Cambridge History of Africa, Vols I, II, III, IV, V, Cambridge, 1980.
Clarke, P. J. *Islam in West Africa,* Edward Arnold, 1983.
Hiskett, M. *The Development of Islam in West Africa,* Longman, London, 1984.
Hopkins, J. F. P. and Levtzion, N. *Corpus of Early Arabic Sources for West African History,* Cambridge University Press, Cambridge, 1981.
Levtzion, N. *Ancient Ghana and Mali,* Methuen, London, 1973.
UNESCO *General History of Africa,* UNESCO Heinemann, Vols I, II, IV, Paris London, 1981-.

Section two

Ajayi, J. F. Ade and Crowder, M. (eds) *History of West Africa,* Vol I, 3rd edition, Longman, London, 1985.
Akinjogbin, I. *Dahomey and its neighbours,* Cambridge University Press, Cambridge, 1967.
Daaku, K. Y. *Trade and Politics on the Gold Coast, 1600–1720,* Clarendon Press, Oxford, 1970.
Fyfe, C. *A Short History of Sierra Leone* Longman, London, 1979.
Fynn, J. K. *The Asante and its neighbours, 1700–1807,* London 1971.
Ikime, O., (ed.), *Groundwork of Nigerian History* Heinemann, Lagos, 1980.
Law, R., *The Oyo Empire c. 1600–1836,* Clarendon Press, Oxford, 1977.
Magbaily Fyle, C. *The History of Sierra Leone* Evans Brothers, London, 1981.
Wilks, I. G., *Asante in the Nineteenth Century,* Cambridge University Press, Cambridge, 1975.

Section three

Ajayi, J. F., Ade, and Crowder M. (eds) *History of West Africa,* Vol II, Longman, London, 1974.
Boahen, A. Adu, *Ghana: Evolution and Change in the 19th and 20th Centuries,* Longman, London, 1975.
Crowder, M. *West Africa under Colonial Rule,* Hutchinson, London, 1968.
Crowder, M. (ed.), *West African Resistance,* Hutchinson, London, 1971.

Gann, L., and Duignan, P., (eds.), *Colonialism in Africa*, 5 vols, Cambridge University Press, Cambridge, 1965–75.

Hargreaves, J. D., *Prelude to the Partition of Africa*, Macmillan, London, 1963.

Hargreaves, J. D., *West Africa Partitioned: The Loaded Pause*, University of Wisconsin Press, Madison, 1974.

Hopkins, A. G., *An Economic History of West Africa*, Longman, London, 1973.

Ikime, O. (ed.), *Groundwork of Nigerian History* Heinemann, Lagos, 1980.

Inikori, J. E., *Forced Migration: the Impact of the Export Slave Trade on African Societies*, London, 1982.

Suret-Canale, J., *French Colonialism in Africa, 1900–1945*, Christopher Hurst, London, 1961.

Section four

Akintoye, S. A., *Emergent African States*, Longman, London, 1976.

Arnold, G., *Modern Nigeria*, Longman, London, 1977.

Boahen, A. Adu, *Ghana Evolution and Change in the 19th and 20th Centuries*, Longman, London, 1975.

Decalo, S., *Coups and Army Rule in Africa*, Yale University Press, New Haven and London, 1976.

Dunn, J., (ed.), *West African States: Failure and Promise*, Cambridge University Press, Cambridge, 1978.

First, R., *The Barrel of the Gun*, Penguin, Harmondsworth, 1970.

Gutteridge W. F., *Military Regimes in Africa*, Methuen, London, 1975.

Hastings, A., *A History of African Christianity 1950–1975*, Cambridge University Press, Cambridge, 1979.

Hull, R. W., *Modern Africa, Change and Continuity*, Prentice-Hall Inc., Englewood Cliffs, N. J., 1980.

Jones, T., *Ghana's First Republic 1960–1966*, Methuen, London, 1976.

Kirk-Greene and Rimmer, D., *Nigeria since 1970*, Hodder & Stoughton, London, 1981.

Mazrui A. and Tidy M., *Nationalism and New States in Africa*, Heinemann, Nairobi and London, 1984.

Pedler, F., *Main currents of West African History*, Macmillan, London, 1979.

Webster, J. B. and Boahen, A. Adu with Tidy, M., *The Revolutionary Years, West Africa since 1800*, Longman, London, 1980.

Index